NAPOLEON SURRENDERS

NAPOLEON SURRENDERS

++

Gilbert Martineau

*Translated from the French
by Frances Partridge*

READERS UNION
Newton Abbot 1973

© 1971 John Murray (Publishers) Ltd

First published by John Murray

This edition was produced in 1973 for sale to its members
only by the Proprietors, Readers Union Limited, PO Box 6
Newton Abbot, Devon TW12 2DW. Full details of
membership will gladly be sent on request

Reproduced and printed in Great Britain
for Readers Union by Redwood Press Limited
Trowbridge, Wiltshire

*To the Marquis of Lansdowne
in memory of his family's connection
with these events, with gratitude*

This great man grown old stood alone amid the treachery of men and of fate, on a tottering world, beneath a hostile sky, facing his accomplished destiny and God's judgement.

CHATEAUBRIAND

Adversity will find that I am out of its reach.

NAPOLEON

It is very difficult for history to get at the real facts. Luckily they are more often objects of curiosity than truly important. There are so many facts!

NAPOLEON

CONTENTS

ILLUSTRATIONS

I

THE FALL OF THE EMPIRE

++

The evening after Waterloo – Paris after the battle – the
Emperor re-enters his capital – Cabinet meeting:
Regnault de Saint-Jean-d'Angély speaks of abdication.

++

On June 18, 1815, in the grey light bathing the battlefield, Napoleon
saw his armies defeated. 'The man of battles listened to the last
cannon-shot he was to hear in his life.'[1]

The hoped-for and promised victory, which was to consolidate the
Liberal reign of the Hundred Days, had become a catastrophe. The
cries of 'Long Live the Emperor!', the acclamations that had been
heard all over Europe for the last ten years, striking terror into the
hearts of the enemy, were now expiring in chests riddled by English
and Prussian bullets. The disabled Imperial army was crumbling in
tumult and confusion. The enemy loomed up on every road and
blocked every pass.

Then Wellington raised his plumed cocked hat aloft as a signal for
the final attack, and it was all over with the last god of war. Tortured
by illness, crushed by fatigue, but still clinging to the hope of some
sudden change in his fortunes, Napoleon was to spend this last
evening on the battlefield witnessing the disorderly retreat of his
armies. After the cavalry had been sacrificed by Ney and hacked to
pieces by the English, the Old Guard braved the enemy's bullets,
and withdrew, step by step and shoulder to shoulder, in good order,
thus safeguarding their Emperor's retreat. Napoleon put spurs to
his horse, intending to plunge into the heart of Cambronne's corps
and expose himself to enemy fire, but Soult drew him into the stream
of retreat, imploring: 'Oh! Sire, the enemy has already been fortunate
enough.' He obeyed mechanically and in silence, and was seen riding

[1] Chateaubriand: *Mémoires d'outre-tombe.*

slowly towards Charleroi, his face drawn with pain and exhaustion and tears running down his cheeks. Soult, Jerome, Bertrand, Drouot, Flahaut, La Bédoyère and Gourgaud silently followed their general, as he unwillingly left the battlefield where his career and his reign had just come to an end.

At one o'clock that morning he reached Genappe, and, shaking himself out of his lethargy, attempted without success to rally his fleeing troops; the confusion and noise were indescribable; next he tried to assemble what was left of Grouchy's army and organise a defence against the enemy forces that were now threatening Paris. 'The position of France after Waterloo was critical but not desperate,' he was to explain later. 'Everything had been planned on the assumption that the attack on Belgium would fail. . . . The situation could have been saved, had character, energy and firmness been shown by officers, the Government, the Chambers, and the whole nation. France would have needed to be inspired by feelings for honour, glory and national independence, and to model herself on Rome after the battle of Cannae, rather than Carthage after Zama.'[2]

Had he been Commander-in-Chief alone, Napoleon would probably have devoted the days after Waterloo to regrouping his armies; for by adding to the forty thousand survivors of the great battle Grouchy's thirty thousand, and the 140,000 soldiers posted on the French frontiers, he could still try to stem the invasion. 'My true place is here,' he reasoned. 'From here I could control events in Paris, and my brothers would do the rest.'[3]

Paris . . . it was there, according to those around him, that the outcome would be settled. Remembering the collapse of 1814 and the final blow delivered by Talleyrand, the Liberal sovereign of the Hundred Days now had to put political considerations first, and frustrate the activities of Fouché and his allies, the Republican party and the Royalists, who would certainly take advantage of the disaster to renew their intrigues of 1814 and clamour loudly for abdication. To forestall the reactions of his ministers, as soon as he arrived at Philippeville at two in the morning he dictated two letters to Prince Joseph: one, destined for the Council, left the issue of the battle in doubt, the other gave a faithful account of the defeat.

[2] Las Cases: *Mémorial*, August 26, 1816.
[3] Fleury de Chaboulon: *Mémoires*.

'All is not lost. I believe that when I have assembled my forces I shall still have 150,000 men. The Federates and the National Guard will provide me with 100,000, and the regimental depots another 50,000. I shall thus have 300,000 men ready to confront the enemy at once. I will equip the artillery with carriage-horses. I will conscript 100,000 men, and arm them with muskets taken from Royalists, and from National Guards unfit for service. I will organise a mass levy in the Dauphiné, Lyonnais, Burgundy, Lorraine and Champagne. I will overwhelm the enemy. But I must have help, not hindrance. I shall go to Laon. I am sure to find support there. I have heard no news of Grouchy. If he has not been taken prisoner, as I fear, I can have another 50,000 men within three days; with them I can keep the enemy occupied and give Paris and France time to do their duty. The English are making slow headway. The Prussians are afraid of the peasantry and dare not advance too far. The situation may still be saved; write and tell me what effect this horrible affair has produced in the Chamber. I believe deputies will realise that at this critical moment it is their duty to rally to my side and save France. Prepare their minds to support me worthily.' He signed this dispatch and added in his own hand: 'Courage and Firmness.'[4]

These hopes could only be realised if he himself remained at the head of the army; moreover the letters to Joseph, and the military measures he took in sending orders to Grouchy to assemble his troops, clearly prove that at this critical hour his resolution remained firm: he would march on Rocroi and Laon and reopen the campaign. Soult and his staff now arrived, and after a few moments rest on a wretched bed, Napoleon got into one of the Marshal's carriages, and drove off at full speed towards Laon, escorted by a handful of horsemen and followed by Bertrand, Maret and his aides-de-camp.

During the Hundred Days, the work of governing France had been shared between the members of the Assemblies and ministers acting under the sovereign's direct control. 'A taste for constitutions, debates and oratory seemed to have returned.'[5] To ensure that legislative and executive groups could not combine together disastrously against him, Napoleon had forbidden access to the Chamber to ministers with portfolio, reserving for ministers of State the task of expressing the views of the Cabinet.

But he was reckoning without the astuteness of Fouché, Minister

4 Fleury de Chaboulon: *Mémoires.*
5 Benjamin Constant: *Mémoires.*

of Police, who, from the seclusion of his office and his own drawing-rooms, was busy attacking the Emperor's political plans with the effective weapons of treason, fear and duplicity. He had kindled the blaze by submitting a report on the state of the Empire to the Chamber of Representatives on June 17 – with Regnault de Saint-Jean-d'Angély, Minister of State, as spokesman – declaring to the hesitant and ill-informed deputies that 'he would rather take over all ministerial responsibilities than jeopardise the safety of the State'.

The news of the victory at Ligny, reaching Paris on June 18, disarmed the waverers and encouraged the faithful, especially those in the Chamber, who made haste to assure the sovereign, through Lanjuinais their president, that the Assembly was exclusively made up of passionate admirers and intrepid supporters, 'whose devotion could not be shaken by the most serious reverses'. And that same evening the thunder of the cannon of Paris announced the Emperor's latest triumph to the people of the capital.

By next day, however, Fouché had got wind of the approach of disturbing events: 'Two days without news,' he said to Thibaudeau. 'It is impossible we shall not be beaten.'[6] During the afternoon of June 20, Joseph received the dispatch from Philippeville containing an account of the disaster and the retreat; it was read to the hastily assembled ministers. They kept the secret all that day, but in the evening Carnot was overcome by grief, and, being unable to speak openly of the magnitude of the defeat, allowed his tears to flow in front of his guests. Fouché, on the other hand, set the machinery of his party in motion with the object of sowing panic in all camps: some of his emissaries reported that Napoleon was returning in a rage to seize dictatorial powers, and others that the Chamber was seething with excitement, and about to announce the defeat, and that the Allies would be favourably disposed towards the accession of Napoleon II. 'During the night of June 19 an unknown person left a little pencilled note announcing the destruction of the army with the Duc de Vicence's porter. He rushed round to Carnot, who had received the same news; together they went to see Fouché, who assured them with his usual cadaverous impassivity that he knew nothing of the matter, whereas he really knew everything.'[7]

[6] Thibaudeau: *Mémoires.*
[7] Montholon: *Recits de la captivité.*

For months Fouché had been rehearsing the decisive role that was now offered him by the defeat at Waterloo; hardly had he been appointed Minister of Police, a post that no-one was ready to take on after the return from Elba, when he began to work for the opposition.[8] Passing on the time-absorbing functions of chief of the imperial police to two chief inspectors, he concentrated all his amazing energy and his coldly lucid imagination upon complicated manoeuvres known to no-one but himself, and designed to ensure him recognition, reputation and reward when the regime should fall. As early as March 25, when the Emperor's return was being discussed, he had been heard to murmur in Pasquier's ear: 'He'll be done for within three or four months.' It amounted to an admission that there was not a moment to lose before gaining goodwill for the future: he therefore put a check on the prosecutions against Royalists ordered by Napoleon, and organised the elections, checking the lists of Republicans and Liberals of all descriptions. 'He'll have a little of everything in the next Chamber of Representatives, by God! I won't even let him off Barère and Cambon, nor La Fayette, as you shall see. That'll give it character. The time for exclusions is over, and men of this sort will provide a guarantee for the rest of us – the advanced revolutionaries.'[9]

Confident of the support of these members when the time came, all he had to do to secure his own future was to establish relations with the Royalists and the Allies; when he heard that Louis XVIII had said quite loudly 'that he would be ready to recognise any services the Duc d'Otrante might render him,' Fouché tasted the sweets of the prophecy he had made to Pasquier: 'Napoleon will be obliged to go and join the army before the end of May. Once he has gone, we shall remain in command. I would like him to win one or two battles; he will lose the third, and then it will be our turn to play a part. . . . We shall bring things to a successful conclusion, I assure you.'

[8] The Emperor had been advised to 'haul Fouché over the coals.' 'Oh, I can do better than that!' he exclaimed. 'If a minister is only waiting for a defeat to betray his sovereign, perhaps the latter is only waiting for a victory to have him hanged.' (Lamothe-Langon: *Les Après-Midi de M. de Cambacérès.*)

[9] Villemain: *Souvenirs.* Cambon (1756–1820), former member of the Committee of Public Safety, had lived in retirement since the amnesty of the year IV. Barère (1755–1841) had also belonged to the Committee, and was famous for his eloquence, which had earned him the nickname of 'the Anacreon of the guillotine'. Both were members of the Chamber of Representatives during the Hundred Days.

However, to safeguard his retreat, he made sure of a refuge for himself in England, with Wellington as intermediary.

This devious man, whom Napoleon believed to be a 'scoundrel of the deepest dye', this minister so disturbingly ready to change sides, had suddenly made the dangers menacing the capital appear greater, if less obvious, to the Emperor than the ambushes of the battlefield, and it took very little to persuade him to leave the army and make all speed towards Paris.[10]

✢   ✢   ✢

He called a halt for hasty refreshment near Rocroi, while the party of generals and aides-de-camp excitedly discussed what should be done: only the most faithful were present – Bertrand, Maret, Drouot, Dejean, Canisy, Fleury de Chaboulon, Gourgaud, Flahaut, La Bédoyère and Bussy.

The young, impetuous and devoted La Bédoyère[11] was confident that the threat of invasion would win over the waverers and galvanise the Chambers.

'The Emperor must not stop anywhere on the way', he said, 'but go straight to the heart of national representation; let him frankly confess his misfortunes, and like Philippe Auguste offer to die a soldier's death and hand over the crown to the worthiest man. Both Chambers will reject any idea of abandoning Napoleon and will join his side to save France.'

'Don't rely on that,' put in Fleury de Chaboulon,[12] 'far from being sorry for Napoleon and coming generously to his help, the Chamber will accuse him of having ruined France and wanting to save himself by sacrificing her.'

---

[10] 'Intrigue was as necessary to Fouché as food,' Napoleon used to say; 'he intrigued all the time, everywhere, in every possible way and with everyone. If there were revelations, one could be sure he was mixed up in them. He had a finger in every pie.'

[11] La Bédoyère, Charles, Comte de (1786–1815). Aide-de-camp to Lannes, promoted colonel in 1812, he kept his rank under the first Restoration, but rallied to Napoleon along with his regiment at the time of the return from Elba. General during the Hundred Days, he was condemned to death and shot on August 19, 1815.

[12] Fleury de Chaboulon, Pierre (1779–1835). Auditor to the Council of State, prefect at Rheims at the time of the French campaign, he was a noted patriot, and Napoleon's private secretary during the Hundred Days. After Waterloo he took refuge in England for several years, and it was there he published in 1819 his *Mémoires pour servir à l'histoire de la vie priveé du retour et du règne de Napoléon en 1815*.

'The Emperor is lost if he sets foot in Paris,' cried Flahaut;[13] 'the Chambers will think they can save themselves by sacrificing him; there is only one way of saving him and France: that is to negotiate with the Allies and hand over the crown to his son.'[14]

Someone came to say that the English were less that twenty kilometres away, and Napoleon had to break off his conversation with Maret[15] and take to the road again. Rumours of the defeat had reached Laon, but a detachment of the National Guard came to assure their sovereign that the men were ready to die for their country and were warmly received. When he heard that a force of three thousand men had just been rallying support round the town under the leadership of Soult and Jerome, Napoleon suddenly decided: 'I will stay here until the army is reassembled. . . . Within twenty-four hours we will have a nucleus of from ten to twelve thousand men. With this little army I can hold back the enemy and give Grouchy time to join us, and the nation time to find its feet again.'

There was a general outcry; some declared that the Emperor had witnessed the rout of his army with his own eyes; what would be the use of ten or twelve thousand men, when all roads were open to the enemy and Grouchy's corps was lost? 'The citizens must be armed; Your Majesty's presence in Paris is necessary in order to keep the enemy in check and inspire and organise the devotion and zeal of patriots. When the Parisians see Your Majesty they will not hesitate to fight. If you stay away from them, a thousand rumours will be set going; they will say you have been killed, taken prisoner or surrounded. The National Guard and the Federates will lose heart and be afraid of being abandoned or betrayed, as they were last year, and will fight reluctantly, if indeed they fight at all.'[16]

---

[13] Flauhaut de la Billarderie, Joseph, Comte de (1785–1870). Illegitimate son of Talleyrand, attached to Bonaparte's staff, promoted general in 1813. From his liaison with Queen Hortense, a son, the Duc de Morny, was born. Married in England in 1817 to the daughter of Lord Keith, he was created peer of France in 1830, ambassador to London (1842–1848) and then Chancellor of the Legion of Honour during the Second Empire.

[14] Fleury de Chaboulon: *Mémoires*.

[15] Maret, Hughes, Duc de Bassano (1763–1839). He took part in the coup d'état of Brumaire and was Secretary General of the Consular Government. Faithful, devoted and hard working, he became Minister of State in 1811, and Minister for War in 1813, and again during the Hundred Days.

[16] Vaulabelle: *Histoire des deux Restaurations*.

'Very well,' Napoleon agreed, 'since you think it necessary, I will go to Paris; but I am convinced you are making me do a foolish thing.'

Before getting into his carriage, he dictated the official report of Mont-Saint-Jean, which was afterwards read to Bertrand, Drouot, Gourgaud and the aides-de-camp. 'We must tell France the whole truth, as we did after Moscow!' he said.

Next he sent some officers to inspect the surrounding positions and round up scattered detachments, entrusting to Bussy the task of preparing billets in Laon for the troops that were to reassemble there, after which he started for Paris, where he counted on reassuring the Chambers, pacifying public excitement, putting the city on a siege footing and ordering the reserves of his still powerful army to move in a north-easterly direction – all within two days.

✢　　　✢　　　✢

Napoleon and his suite arrived at the gates of Paris at about six o'clock on the morning of June 21; the town was still asleep, most of the shops were shut and his carriage reached the faubourg Saint-Honoré without attracting attention.

Caulaincourt[17] was waiting on the steps of the Élysée.

'Well, Caulaincourt,' said the Emperor. 'This is a momentous event. A lost battle. How will the country take this reverse? Will the Chambers back me up?'

Arrived in his study, he flung himself on the sofa.

'All our war material is gone. That's our most serious loss. We were winning. The army had performed prodigies; the enemy was beaten everywhere. Only the English centre stood firm. And then, at the end of the day, the army was suddenly seized with panic. It's inexplicable. . . .'

While his bath was being got ready, he talked without stopping, in a jerky voice, breathing heavily; he seemed on the point of giving way to exhaustion and despair; he had been in action for ten days

---

[17] Caulaincourt, Louis, Duc de Vicence (1773–1827). Formerly one of Bonaparte's aides-de-camp, he was successively Master of the Horse, Ambassador to Russia (1807) and, in 1813, Minister for Foreign Affairs. He returned to his post during the Hundred Days. Napoleon described him as 'a courageous and upright man'.

without sleep, on horseback all day long and tormented by dysuria.[18]

While his valets busied themselves, he enquired what rumours were current in Paris, and what effect had been produced by the campaign; then he asked for Joseph, Maret and Regnault de Saint-Jean-d'Angély to be sent for.[19]

'I intend to summon the two Chambers to a special session. I will describe the plight of the army; I will ask them to give me the means of saving the country; after that I will be off again, this evening or tomorrow.'

'The news of your misfortunes is already known, Sire,' said Caulaincourt sadly. 'There is great general agitation; deputies seem more hostile to you than ever before; and since Your Majesty condescends to listen to me, I must tell you that I fear the Chamber will not respond as you hope. I am sorry to see you in Paris, Sire. It would have been better not to leave your army; in it lies your strength, your safety. Your presence would have rallied your troops at Laon, or Soissons at least. Now that Your Majesty is not with the army, the Staff, the generals and the Guard will all hurry to Paris.'

'I have no army left, I have nothing but fugitives! I can find men, but how can I arm them? I have no more muskets. Yet, if we joined forces, everything could be put right. I hope the Chambers will support me and realise their responsibilities; I think you have misjudged their state of mind; the majority are good Frenchmen. I have only La Fayette, Lanjuinais, Flaugergues and a few others against me. They don't want me. I know that. I'm a nuisance to them. They want to work for their own interests; I won't let them; my presence here restrains them. If deputies are ill-disposed to me when I am here in Paris, they would be very much more so were I absent. Once measures have been taken and a national movement set going, I'll be off again, either this evening or tomorrow.'[20]

He had not had his boots off since the battle, but he was putting up a desperate struggle against fatigue and lethargy of mind; he talked for a long time with Caulaincourt, then with La Valette[21] who

---

[18] In his *Mémoires*, Ali notes: 'The Emperor suffered from a slight inconvenience: he had difficulty in passing water.' In 1821, the autopsy showed that there were small stones and traces of cystitis in the bladder.

[19] Regnault de Saint-Jean-d'Angély, Michel, Comte de (1761–1819). Administrator of the military hospitals in Italy, Councilor of State under the Consulate, Attorney General of the High Court under the Empire, and Minister of State during the Hundred Days.

[20] Caulaincourt: *Mémoires*.

[21] La Valette, Antoine (1769–1830). One of Bonaparte's aides-de camp, he married Emilie de Beauharnais. Postmaster General under the Empire and during the Hundred Days. Condemned to death in 1815, he escaped on the eve of his execution, thanks to the devotion of his wife, who lent him her clothes, and with the complicity of the English General Wilson.

had just arrived, relaxing his tense body in a warm bath the while. He never stopped attacking Ney and Grouchy.

A few moments later, Davout was announced, and ushered into the bathroom at once; as soon as he saw him, Napoleon raised and let fall his arm so suddenly that he splashed the Marshal's uniform.

'Well, Davout? Well?'

And he went on describing the mistakes Ney had made.

'He risked his neck to serve you!' growled Davout.

'What will come of it all?'

'I realise all must be lost, Sire, because if there were even four thousand men gathered together, Your Majesty would be at their head. We must take drastic measures. The most urgent is to prorogue the Chambers, otherwise the violent hostility of the Chamber of Representatives will paralyse all loyal feelings towards you.'

Napoleon got out of his bath and shaved; Joseph and Lucien had just arrived at the Élysée, and were present during his toilet and breakfast. Prudent and evasive, Joseph had presided over the Cabinet meeting in his brother's absence, apparently preferring to listen rather than to speak. Lucien was burning to take action, but he had not yet realised that his revolutionary eloquence would have no effect on a Chamber which was quite unknown to him after his years of exile. Joseph was sunk in gloom, for he had just had a conversation with Lanjuinais,[22] one of their opponents: it was Lucien who did most of the talking. He explained that the news of Waterloo was spreading like wildfire, and that there was great excitement; there was danger from the more determined members of the Chamber. 'La Fayette must be counted among them, he won't fail to stir up feeling against me,' remarked Napoleon; 'they imagine the Allies are only opposed to me personally, and they don't see that if they part from me they will destroy France.'[23]

Next he talked with Cambacérès, who was cold and serious, maintaining a prudent reserve. The archchancellor of the Empire had

---

[22] Lanjuinais, Jean (1753–1827). President of the Convention in 1795, afterwards deputy to the Ancients and senator from 1800. He voted against life Consulate and against the Empire. Created Count by Napoleon, whose deposition he voted for in 1814. He was president of the Chamber of Deputies during the Hundred Days.

[23] Marchand: *Mémoires*.

chosen his own line of action a long while ago. 'I would rather be forgotten,' he had declared at the time of the return from Elba. 'I hope the Emperor will leave me out.' He now lost himself in a maze of generalisations, reflecting bitterly that this military defeat would lead to his personal downfall. The man who had been amusingly nicknamed 'Ma Tante Urluru' by the pamphleteers was more conversant with the pleasures of the table, the arts of amorous intrigue of a special sort, and the subtleties of protocol than with the complicated science of politics.

Savary[24] and Peyrusse, the Emperor's Treasurer, stayed with him until nearly ten o'clock, when ministers grew impatient, and sent Davout to say they were awaiting His Majesty's pleasure; Napoleon told them to begin their deliberations with Joseph as president. The Marshal remarked that the Cabinet could not go into the problems of the moment in the presence of Prince Joseph alone: Napoleon followed him without another word.

All the ministers were present: beside the princes of the family, Joseph and Lucien, there were: Maret, devoted but vague; Cambacérès, as cautious as a monk; the shattered Caulaincourt; Carnot, still thinking of nothing but his country's safety, as in 1793; Gaudin,[25] with his clearcut ideas and strict honesty, more at his ease in his Exchequer than at the helm of the State; Mollien;[26] Davout, convinced that all was lost; Decrès,[27] ready to abandon ship, and lastly Fouché. Fouché was unfathomable, with his cadaverous, inscrutable face, whose detachment amounted to hostility. The four Ministers of State, all members of the Chamber, sat a little apart: Defermon,[28] Regnault de Saint-Jean-d'Angély, Boulay de la Meurthe[29] and Mer-

[24] Savary, Réné, Duc de Rovigo (1774-1833). Aide-de-camp to Desaix (1798) and then to Bonaparte (1800), he commanded the Consular Gendarmerie (1801), and replaced Fouché as Minister of Police from 1810 to 1814, later becoming Inspector General of the Gendarmerie during the Hundred Days.

[25] Gaudin, Martin, Duc de Gaète (1765-1841). Minister of Finance from Brumaire to 1814.

[26] Mollien, François (1758-1850). After being financial adviser to the First Consul, he was head of the Treasury from 1806 to 1814.

[27] Decrès, Denis (1761-1820). Admiral, Minister for the Navy since 1801.

[28] Defermon des Chapelierès, Joseph (1752-1831). Former member of the National Convention and the Five Hundred. Director of Finances under the Empire, then Minister of State.

[29] Boulay de la Merthe, Antoine, (1761-1840). Former deputy to the Five Hundred, Councillor of State and one of those who drafted the Code Civil.

lin de Douai,[30] as well as Berlier, secretary to the Cabinet – a strange mixture of fidelity and opportunism.

All these important personages listened while Maret read aloud the bulletin of the battle of Mont-Saint-Jean, 'so glorious yet so disastrous for the French armies', and then Napoleon took the floor:

'Our misfortunes are great. I have come here to put them right and initiate a great and noble movement. If the nation will rise, the enemy can be crushed; if instead of rising and taking drastic measures there is discussion, then all is lost. The enemy is in France. To save our country I must be given extraordinary powers and temporary dictatorship. In the interests of our country I could seize such powers, but it would be useful and more truly national if they were given me by the Chambers.'

Ministers lowered their eyes in embarrassment and fell silent; Napoleon asked them to express their views about the measures he considered indispensable. Carnot passionately advocated a declaration that the country was in danger, followed by a call to arms, and martial law in Paris, while they retired if necessary south of the Loire and kept the enemy occupied – until their forces could be assembled in sufficient numbers to drive him back across the frontiers; the voice of the Revolution was speaking, and the rolling of the drums of the year II echoed through men's memories.

Caulaincourt, Duc de Vicence, threw cold water on this sacred fire: he recalled the events of 1814, and assured his companions that the occupation of the capital by enemy forces would once more be decisive for the fate of the Empire; an immense national effort was necessary, and their safety did not depend on such or such a measure, but on the opinion of the Chambers and their solidity with the Emperor. Cambacérès and Maret agreed with him.[31]

Davout advised the dissolution of the Chamber and complete dictatorship:

'At such moments as this we cannot have two sources of power. There must be only one, and that strong enough to carry out all measures neces-

---

[30] Merlin de Douai, Philippe (1754–1838). Former member of the National Convention and the Committee of Public Safety, an outstanding legal expert, Minister at the Supreme Court of Appeal under the Empire.

[31] Cambacérès did not abandon his attitude of reserve. A few weeks earlier he had said to Napoleon with disarming candour: 'By God, Sire, I see people changing sides so easily, that a wise man cannot leave his own cottage without emotion.' Even if that cottage had in gold letters over the door 'Mansion of His Serene Highness the Duc de Parme'.

sary for resistance, and to control criminal or blind factions, whose intrigues and manoeuvres would hinder everything. The Chambers must be immediately prorogued, in conformity with constitutional law. It is perfectly legal. But, in order to lessen the effect this measure might have on the minds of over-scrupulous persons, it could be announced that the Chambers would be convoked in some town in the interior (to be chosen later) at a fixed time two or three weeks ahead, and subject to prorogation being renewed should circumstances still make it necessary.'[32]

Decrès, who had ruled over the Navy since 1801, and behaved in a servile and docile manner in the hours of triumph, though really 'hard and rather disobliging' as Napoleon knew, now seemed like a dismasted vessel; according to him it was a mistake to try and win over deputies; they were extremely hostile, and might be led into every form of excess.

Next Fouché asked with the utmost ingenuousness what was the purpose of this flood of words: would it not be better simply to trust to the Assembly, show good faith and merit deputies' esteem? Members could not refuse to support the Emperor's policy.

'Besides, Paris is quite calm,' he added smoothly.

'Calm,' rapped out Napoleon, 'calm. . . . Everything's quiet, according to him.'[33]

Fouché had his own reasons for doing everything possible to avoid prorogation, which would deprive him of the indispensable help of the deputies – who had responded so well to the advances of the emissaries he had sent to spread false news and calumnies.[34] If the Chamber were dissolved, or removed from Paris, the whole edifice would crumble.

But he did not have to wait long before he saw the debate take the turn he desired. The offensive was launched by Regnault de Saint-Jean-d'Angély, who had listened with a certain stupefaction while the Duc d'Otrante advocated an agreement with the Assemblies: in the course of an interview shortly before the Cabinet meeting, the Minister of Police had in fact assured his colleague that members were inclined towards Napoleon's deposition and that nothing but abdication could save the country and preserve the dynasty. Having enjoyed

[32] Davout: *Mémoires*, quoted by Houssaye.
[33] Ernouf: *Maret, Duc de Bassano*.
[34] 'I ought to have had Fouché hanged,' said Napoleon to Méneval before leaving Malmaison. 'I leave that task to the Bourbons.'

Napoleon's favour since the Italian campaign, it seemed impossible for Regnault to be won over by the factious party; his opinion ought therefore to be a deciding one – for nobody knew that he had secretly gone over to the Bourbons.[35] Now here he was, suddenly saying harshly that the representatives of the nation would not listen to the Emperor's objurgations, for they knew very well that he was no longer in a position to save France.

'I am afraid,' he said blankly, 'that a great sacrifice will be necessary.'

'Speak frankly!' burst out Napoleon. 'It's my abdication they want.'

'I'm afraid so, Sire, and however painful it may be to me, it is my duty to enlighten Your Majesty. I would even go so far as to say that if the Emperor does not make up his mind to offer to abdicate of his own accord, it is possible that the Chamber may dare to insist upon it.'[36]

Napoleon was stunned: he had just been trying to whip up energy and animate goodwill, and he found them ranged against his person. Lucien, who was boiling with impatience, said vehemently:

'Whenever I have been hard pressed, I have found that the greater the crisis the more energy had to be expended. If the Chamber will not support the Emperor, he will do without its help. The country's safety must be the first law of the State, and since the Chamber does not appear to be ready to join with the Emperor to save France he will have to save her alone. He must make himself dictator, declare martial law in France and summon all patriots and good Frenchmen to her defence.'

This was also Carnot's opinion: those two men, both coming from remote horizons, far away from the pomp and splendour of the Empire in its days of triumph, knew that the safety of France depended on severe and rapid decisions.

It was the Emperor's turn to draw conclusions from all this advice.

'The presence of the enemy on national soil,' he said, 'will I trust make deputies realise their duty. The nation did not appoint them to overthrow

[35] This man, who had been such a favourite of the Emperor's, had lost confidence in 1813, and assured the émigrés that 'if in due course the catastrophe now threatening the Government came about, he would be free of all commitments and devote himself to the interests of Louis XVIII.'

[36] Fleury de Chaboulon: *Mémoires*.

me, but to support me. I am not in the least afraid of them. Whatever they do, I shall always remain the idol of the people and the army. I have only to say a word to confound them all. But though I fear nothing for myself, I fear everything for France. If we quarrel among ourselves instead of acting in concert, we shall meet the fate of the Lower Empire; everything will be lost, although national patriotism, hatred of the Bourbons and attachment to my person still offer us inmense resources; our cause is by no means desperate.'

He went on to describe his plans in detail: the fortresses of the East and North, if well equipped and commanded, could hold out for more than three months. Brune of Toulon, Suchet and Lecourbe would fall back and defend Lyons. There were more than two hundred soldiers, pensioners, conscripts and National Guards in the regimental depots, ready to march. In a few days' time he would go in person to Laon and take command of the army – eighty thousand soldiers withdrawn from Belgium, and twenty thousand in Rapp's corps. With this army of a hundred thousand he would undertake to hold his own against the Allies, who hardly out-numbered them and were exhausted by the Belgian campaign and long marches. The defences of Paris would be strengthened and the conscription of 1815 would provide 160,000 recruits.

The energy of his exposition, the magic of his short concise sentences, his lucid reasoning, rich with figures and foresight, moved ministers to rally to the side of Lucien and Carnot. The switch-over was so violent that Fouché suddenly felt he was losing his footing, and a few days later he confided to one of the Royalists who already frequented his drawing-rooms:

'That devil of a man really frightened me that morning. As I listened to him I thought it was all going to begin over again; but fortunately it is not beginning again.'[37]

Martial law was therefore to be declared in Paris, and the Government and Chambers moved to Tours if need be; Davout would take command of the capital, Clausel was to be installed at the War Office, and the sharpshooters of Paris were to be reinforced. They were considering whether it was desirable for the Emperor to go in person to the Chambers and explain these decisions, and if so whether it would be suitable for him to go in uniform and without

[37] Villemain: *Souvenirs contemporains.*

ceremony, when an aide-de-camp placed on the table an envelope that had just arrived from the Palais Bourbon.

'The Chamber of Representatives declares that the independence of the nation is in danger. It declares itself to be in permanent session.'

'I ought to have got rid of those people before I left,' said Napoleon furiously. 'It's all over, they will be the ruin of France!'

And he brought the meeting to an end with a phrase which ought to have rejoiced the Duc d'Otrante: 'I see that Regnault did not deceive me; I will abdicate, if I must.'

But unable to bring himself to retreat before this handful of men whose pusillanimity he was well aware of, he quickly pulled himself together and attempted an outflanking movement. He asked Carnot and Regnault to go at once to the Peers and deputies and make an official announcement in his name.

'You will tell them that I have returned; that I have just called a Cabinet meeting; that after a signal victory the army had been engaged in a great battle; that everything was going well; that the English were beaten; that we had captured six flags, when a panic was created by mischiefmakers; that the army is now reassembling; that I have given orders for fugitives to be stopped; that I have come here to discuss matters with my ministers and the Chambers, and that I am at this moment taking the necessary measures to ensure the public safety.'

But while he was waging this last battle against ministers who were already disposed to abandon him, couriers from the army began to arrive at the Élysée; exhausted and overwrought, they ran straight into the gathering of important persons in the anti-chamber, and with their memories still full of the sinister episodes of the flight from Belgium, they gave a horrifying picture of the defeat. 'Then people said aloud that Napoleon was done for, and under their breaths that the only way to save France was for him to abdicate.'[38]

---

[38] Fleury de Chaboulon: *Mémoires.*

II

OPPOSITION FROM THE CHAMBERS

✠✠

The Chamber of Representatives – La Fayette – Lucien
Bonaparte's Mission – The Chamber calls for Abdication – Benjamin Constant – The Commission meets at
the Tuileries.

✠✠

> Bonaparte's advancing,
> I am on his side.
> But if he gets a trouncing,
> I'll not with him bide.
> (Song of the Hundred Days)

While Napoleon, carried away by his imagination, was laying project after project before ministers who had already made up their
minds to dissociate themselves from him, with a speed proportionate
to the fervour of their former zeal in serving the regime, the members
of the Chamber of Representatives, who had gathered at the Palais
Bourbon across the Seine in response to the news of the disaster of
Waterloo and Napoleon's return, were forming into noisy little
groups, reminiscent, as a witness said, 'of a hive of bees in a state of
total anarchy'.[1]

The 1815 elections, organised by Fouché, Minister of Police, and
ignored by Carnot, Minister of the Interior, had been the object of
a secret, unequal struggle between the frightened Bonapartists,
ghosts from the Revolution who had been kept at a distance since
the proclamation of the Empire, and the increasingly confident
Royalists. Members of the Convention like Barère, Cambon and
Drouet (the man who arrested Louis XVI at Varennes in 1791), La
Fayette, Lanjuinais, Flaugergues and Raynouard, were to be seen
taking their seats amid a confused roar of conversation, and waiting

[1] Thiébault: *Mémoires*.

to hear that the imbroglio of the Hundred Days had been settled on the battlefield of Waterloo. Opposite forty revolutionaries and a hundred Bonapartists, the Liberal section of the Assembly, consisting of about five hundred deputies, was preparing to champion a political formula which only needed news of a defeat to be launched.

On this morning of June 21, in a Paris beset by false rumours, stupefied by the heat and drained of men by the war, groups of deputies were collected in the corridors of the palace, partly drawn there by curiosity, but above all by the fear of seeing the fur caps of the National Guard suddenly appear, as they had on a certain evening of Brumaire. They huddled together for protection; they asked questions to keep their courage up; they jostled each other for attention. The feebler among them openly agreed with Sieyes: 'Napoleon has lost a battle, he needs us. Let's go along with him. It's the only way of saving ourselves. Once the danger is over, if he wants to play the despot, we'll join together and hang him. At the moment, what we must do is save him so that he can save us.'[2] The bolder spirits, who were advocating opposition to the bitter end, delightedly repeated a witty remark of La Fayette's: 'All I can see in Bonaparte is a soldier who has come from guard-room to guard-room until he reached the Tuileries.'

Twenty-three years after his appearance on the political scene, and still fully conscious of being the 'father of Liberty' and 'hero of Two Worlds', La Fayette once more felt called upon to play a leading part. Ever since 1802, when he voted against the Consulship and gave confused explanations about 'patriotic and personal motives' and 'hopes for the restoration of liberty', he had been openly sulking in his château at la Grange-Blénau. 'You think he's quiet,' said Napoleon at the Council of State in 1812, 'well, I tell you he's ready to start all over again.' And so he did! When he danced attendance on the Bourbons in 1814 in the splendid uniform of a field marshal of the time of Louis XVI, he got snubbed by a Court that was amazed by his nerve. He haughtily refused the peerage offered him by the Empire of the Hundred Days, but in May 1815 he accepted the votes of Seine-et-Marne electing him to the Chamber of Representatives, where he was Vice-President.

[2] Méneval: *Souvenirs.*

'In him blindness took the place of genius,' said Chateaubriand; this blindness prompted him to utter the astute words that were to destroy the Empire. Once again an Assembly's ignorance of the deeper feelings of the nation was to give it the opportunity to exercise a disastrous influence. Before going to the Chamber, La Fayette had run into Fouché, just as he was about to get into his carriage and drive to the Élysée for a Cabinet meeting.

'Well, General, of course there's not a moment to be lost,' declared the Duc d'Otrante.

'Yes, don't worry, I'm going to the Assembly.'

A malicious witness overheard this interchange.

'So you've already made your choice,' he said to Fouché when La Fayette had gone.

'It's very necessary,' sighed the Minister of Police.

'It's all up, and if we leave Napoleon to his own devices he will leave us to be divided up, or decimated like sheep.'

President Lanjuinais opened the proceedings at about noon; the hubbub that accompanied the reading of the minutes did not stop until La Fayette stood up and went into the bay, with his head held high, complaisantly presenting the elegant, aquiline profile of an embittered nobleman who had strayed among the mob, as in the tumultuous days of October, 1789. Slowly he climbed the steps of the tribune, and declared in solemn tones:

'If, for the first time for many years, I raise a voice which the old friends of liberty will still recognise, it is because I feel it is my duty to speak to you of the dangers threatening our country, which you alone at present have it in your power to save.

'Sinister rumours have been circulating; unfortunately they are now confirmed. The time has come for us to rally round the old tricolour flag, the flag of '89, of liberty, equality and public order; our sole duty is to defend it against foreign claims and disruption from within. Gentlemen, allow a veteran of this sacred cause, who has always been a stranger to faction, to submit to you some preliminary resolutions, the necessity for which I trust you will appreciate.

Clause 1. The Chamber of Representatives declares that the independence of the nation is in danger.

Clause 2. The Chamber declares itself in permanent session. Any attempt to dissolve it is a crime of high treason; whoever shall be guilty of such an attempt shall be a traitor to the country and immediately tried as such.

Clause 3. The regiments of the line and the National Guard, who have fought and will fight again in defence of the liberty, independence and the territory of France, have deserved well of their country.

Clause 4. The Minister of the Interior is invited to summon commanding officers and majors of the legions of the National Guard of Paris to Staff headquarters, with a view to deciding on a means of arming them and as far as possible bringing up the strength of this citizen guard, whose patriotism and zeal, tested for the last twenty-six years, offers a secure guarantee of the liberty, prosperity and tranquility of the capital and the inviolability of the representatives of the nation.

Clause 5. The Ministers for War, Foreign Affairs and of the Interior are invited to join this Assembly immediately.'

There was a burst of cheering. People shouted 'Divide!' and 'Seconded!' And La Fayette naively believed that he had just saved the country. 'Napoleon was preparing to get himself nominated dictator,' he wrote in his memoirs, 'and to dissolve the Chamber . . . his state coaches were already being got ready. . . . I went to see Fouché to make sure the facts were correct; they were confirmed by Regnault who came straight from the Élysée. I told them that I would steal a march on the Emperor.'

It was only afterwards, at Saint Helena, that Napoleon saw the Marquis's intervention in its proper perspective, and condemned it, blaming La Fayette for 'the unhappy outcome of the invasion of France'.[3]

The three first clauses of the motion were adopted; on the suggestion of Merlin de Douai it was decided that the fourth should be discussed in the presence of ministers and that the resolution should be sent to the peers and the sovereign. At this moment Regnault entered the chamber and demanded a hearing for a communication from the Government; it was listened to politely but frigidly. The Emperor's words, dictated before the effects of La Fayette's motion were known at the Élysée, rang false, and no orator came forward to ask questions; the deputies even refused to hear the official report of the battle read aloud. The people's representatives made no bones about opposing a sovereign whose fortune had deserted him: it was decided that the National Guard should be called

---

[3] 'He was a man without talents, either civil or military,' said the Emperor of La Fayette; 'a limited intelligence, a secretive character, dominated by vague, ill-digested and ill-conceived ideas of liberty.'

on to protect the nation's representatives, and once assured of that protection they boldly addressed a second injunction to ministers, requesting their presence at the Palais Bourbon.

Assembled under their president Cambacérès, the peers listened in evident agitation while Carnot read aloud the same message in a hesitant voice; but when the Chamber's resolution was brought to them, they followed the deputies' example and opted for the opposition.

'The Chamber of Representatives has set us a good example,' exclaimed Thibaudeau, one of the secretaries. 'We must lose no time in showing that we share their sentiments.'

'We ought to support the resolution of the Chamber,' amended another voice.

The Bonapartists protested feebly, and Cambacérès thought it advisable to disappear, on the pretext of going to the Élysée; after the motion opening hostilities against the sovereign had been adopted, the session was suspended. The way had been barred against any desperate attempt by the partisans of the regime.

Regnault and Carnot were back at the Élysée; they had had time to describe the coldness, truculence and hostility of the Assemblies before Napoleon received news of the motion passed by the Chamber and the defection of the peers. This second message from the deputies charged those ministers named by La Fayette to join the Assembly without delay.

The Emperor was pacing furiously up and down the council chamber, his cheeks patched with red.

'I'll send a few companies of the Guard to those rebels. . . . If they press me too hard I'll throw them into the Seine. . . .'

He ordered the ministers who had been sent for to turn a deaf ear to the summons. But Davout had been shaken by the deputies' firmness, probably suspecting that it had been engineered by Fouché, and he became suddenly cautious.

'The moment for action has passed,' he said. 'The representatives' resolution is unconstitutional, but it is an accomplished fact. Under present circumstances, we must not delude ourselves that we are contributing to another 18 Brumaire. For my part, I should refuse to be instrumental to such a thing.'

Napoleon knew perfectly well that only a violent reaction could thwart the plans of a Chamber that was determined to rebel against the sovereign, but he wanted to try negotiation and persuasion, nonetheless. He therefore authorised ministers to accept the deputies' summons. However, to avoid the impression that they were taking orders from a rebellious Assembly instead of from the legitimate sovereign, he decided to entrust them with a second message, and put his brother Lucien at their head, with the title of commissioner, representing the Emperor before Parliament. He vaguely hoped that the sight of the former president of the Five Hundred might evoke the spectre of Brumaire, give food for thought, and inspire a withdrawal on the part of the opposition; perhaps he was also counting on Lucien's fiery eloquence.

He took his brother aside into the park of the Palace, and outlined his mission as they paced to and fro; meanwhile the crowd that had collected outside the low wall bordering the Champs Élysées were shouting at the top of their voices 'Long live the Emperor!' and 'Give us arms!' Lucien pressed his brother to take the law into his own hands and drive the talkers out of the Palais Bourbon.

'It's not a question of a coup d'état but of a constitutional decree! You're within your rights!'

'The Chamber will resist. I should have to use force. And where is the force to do it? There are not even any soldiers left in Paris. At least we should need the troops Davout had orders to bring here from the regimental depots on the Somme. We have got to wait.'

'You deliberate when you should be acting! The deputies acted.'

'What can they do? They're only talkers.'

'Opinion is on their side. They'll announce your deposition.'

'Deposition?' cried Napoleon, startled. 'They wouldn't dare.'

'They'll dare everything!'

'I would attempt anything for France; I don't want to attempt anything for myself.'

Carnot, Fouché, Caulaincourt and Davout were awaiting the end of the interview; Lucien joined them with long strides, fuming with indignation.

'He's hesitating, he's temporising. . . . The smoke of Mont-Saint-Jean has gone to his head. He's a lost man.'[4]

---

[4] Villemain. *Souvenirs contemporains.*

'Off with you,' Napoleon urged. 'Talk to them about the interests of France, which must be dear to all representatives; when you return I will follow whatever course my duty dictates.'

✠   ✠   ✠

The deputies had been on their feet ever since morning, harassed by La Fayette and by Fouché's supporters, exacerbated by the noise, the heat and false rumours, alarmed by the goings and comings of the crowd in the Champs Élysées. When Lucien entered the house, followed by the Ministers of the Interior and Police, for Foreign Affairs and War, they hurried anxiously to their seats.

'Nominated commissioner extraordinary by His Imperial Majesty, I have come among you to agree with you on measures of safety; I herewith place His Majesty's message on the table, and request that you will form a secret committee to hear what ministers have to say.'

The public galleries were empty; the evening was approaching and the hall was melting into the shadows and lit only by the two torches on the tribune. The former president of the Five Hundred, with his pointed face, his obstinate forehead and his mobile, piercing gaze, had become the cynosure of all eyes. Some of the deputies still remembered with a thrill of terror a certain dialogue that had taken place in November, 1799, at Saint Cloud:

'Citizens, you are dissolved.'

'Soldiers, you are tarnishing your glory!'

And Murat's brutal order to his men:

'Get them out, the whole lot of them!'

But the man for whom the Prince of Canino was speaking that evening was not the victor of Rivoli; he was the vanquished general of Waterloo.

The imperial message began with an account of the battle of Mont-Saint-Jean, then went on to urge the deputies to join their sovereign and avert the misfortunes threatening their country: the Emperor advocated that a commission of five members be nominated, together with a deputation of peers, to act in concert with ministers, work out measures for the public safety, and embark on negotiations with the enemy.

As the minutes slipped by, members of parliament realised that an attempt to come to terms with them was being made, and regained their confidence; if that terrible man, built all in one piece, was prepared to relinquish a particle of his authority, he was no longer to be dreaded. As soon as Lucien stopped speaking, uproar burst forth. Questions and exclamations arose from the shadows, regardless of the exaggerated gestures of the president, Lanjuinais, as he tried to make himself heard.

Then Jay, former tutor to Fouché's children, an excitable publicist entirely devoted to the Minister of Police, mounted the rostrum. It was the Duc d'Otrante himself, sitting motionless and silent on his bench, who was speaking through his mouth.

'I do not disguise from myself the danger I shall be exposed to if the proposal I am about to make is not supported by the whole Chamber. But even were I to share the fate of the former deputies of the Gironde,[5] I would not shrink from doing my duty. Before submitting my proposal, Monsieur le Président, I beg to call upon ministers to say frankly whether they think France can resist the armies of Europe, and whether Napoleon's presence is not an invincible obstacle to negotiations and peace.'

Ministers sat in embarrassed silence, interchanging questioning glances. Fouché replied for his colleagues of the Cabinet that 'ministers had nothing to add to their previous report'.[6]

'In that case,' returned Jay triumphantly, having his answer in readiness, 'I will take those reports as a basis for my remarks.'

Paraphrasing Regnault's report, the deputy painted a sombre picture of the internal situation, which according to him proved that 'public liberty would never be established in France under a military leader'. Going on to deal with external affairs, he assured the Chamber that the Allied Powers were at war with Napoleon and not with France, that the army was beaten and incapable of further resistance, but would succumb gloriously, dragging the rest of the country with it into disaster and thus delivering it into the enemy's hands.

'And you, Prince,' he cried to Lucien, 'who have shown nobility of character in bad times and good, remember that you are a Frenchman, and

---

[5] Jay represented the department of the Gironde.

[6] A report on the military situation had been submitted to the deputies by Boulay de la Meurthe, and another on internal affairs by Regnault de Saint-Jean-d'Angély, on the 16 and 17 June respectively. Regnault's text, written by Fouché, caused great alarm in the Assembly.

that love of one's country must come before everything. Go back to your brother, tell him that the Assembly of the people's representatives expects a decision from him that will do him more honour in the future than all his victories; tell him that he can save France by abdicating; and, finally, tell him that his destiny will not wait, that within a day, perhaps within an hour, it will be too late. I call for the appointment of a Commission to go to Napoleon and demand his abdication, and to tell him that if he refuses the Assembly will pronounce his deposition.'

In a spirited and adroit reply, Lucien tried to prove that the report of June 17 was unduly pessimistic, that the rising of the Vendée had been suppressed, and that the country was whole-heartedly behind its sovereign; as for the army, it was mustering again after the battle, while important resources both in men and material still remained intact. And how much credit should be given, he asked, to the word of enemies who were hurling themselves against our frontiers?

'When victory deserted us for the first time, did they not swear before God and men to respect our laws and our independence? Do not let us fall a second time into the trap laid for our confidence, our credulity. In trying to separate the nation from the Emperor, their object is to disunite us, so that they may more easily conquer us and plunge us into abasement and slavery. I beseech you, citizens, in the sacred name of our country, rally round the leader whom the nation has recently so solemnly replaced at its head. Remember that our safety depends on our unity, and that you cannot separate from the Emperor and abandon him to his enemies without bringing disaster upon the State, breaking your oaths, and for ever tarnishing our national pride.'

La Fayette leaped to his feet:

'You accuse us of failing in our duty to our honour and Napoleon,' he cried. 'Have you forgotten what we have done for him? Have you forgotten that the bones of our children and our brothers everywhere bear witness to our fidelity, in the African desert, on the banks of the Guadalquivir, Tagus and Vistula, and on the frozen plains of Muscovy? During the last ten years and more, three million Frenchmen have perished for a man who still wants to go on fighting against all Europe today. We have done enough for him; our present duty is to save our country.'

Fouché's supporters took advantage of the hubbub caused by this apostrophe, and the emotion aroused by this reminder of tragic episodes in the Empire's history; they supported Jay in proposing that a deputation be sent to the Élysée to extract an abdication, using the threat of deposition if necessary. However, the motion was set

aside, from fear either of public opinion, or of a violent reaction from
detachments of the army billeted in Paris; a compromise decision
was reached, that five members of the Assembly should join ministers and a delegation of peers to implement the drastic measures
needed for the country's safety, without delay. A few malcontents
nevertheless shouted to Lucien that if Napoleon refused to submit his
deposition would be announced next day.

President Lanjuinais and the four vice-presidents, Flaugergues,[7]
La Fayette, Dupont de l'Eure[8] and General Grenier, were appointed
members of the commission. Davout, who was aware that the wind
was changing, thought it advisable to request leave to speak, and
made haste to declare:

'I hear that malicious persons are circulating a rumour that I gave
an order for troops to surround the Assembly. This report is harm-
ful to the Emperor and to his Minister, who is a good Frenchman.'

After making an identical report to the peers, who remained unmoved, Lucien left once more for the Élysée, while the upper Chamber was appointing its commission, consisting of Boissy d'Anglas,[9]
Thibaudeau,[10] Drouot,[11] Dejean[12] and Andréossy.[13]

✣   ✣   ✣

[7] Flaugergues, Pierre (1767–1836). Deputy to the Legislative Assembly in 1813, he
voted for the deposition of the Emperor in 1814. Vice-President of the Chamber of
Representatives during the Hundred Days, he voted for general conscription in 1815.

[8] Dupont de l'Eure, Jacques (1767–1855). Barrister, member of the Five Hundred,
deputy to the Legislative Assembly, then to the Chamber of Representatives in 1815, he
supported Napoleon II.

[9] Boissy d'Anglas, François (1756–1826). Member of the Committee of Public Safety
and president of the Convention after the 9 Thermidor, he afterwards had a seat among
the Five Hundred in the Tribunate, and finally the Senate. Created Count of the Empire
by Napoleon, he went over to the Bourbons and was created peer of France under Louis
XVIII.

[10] Thibaudeau, Antoine (1765–1854). Former member of the Convention, and then
of the Five Hundred, he was one of those who drew up the Code Civil. Exiled by Louis
XVIII, he left memoirs and the *Histoire générale de Napoleon*.

[11] Drouot, Antoine, Comte (1774–1847). He had fought at Fleurus and Hohenlinden.
Colonel of the Imperial Guard in 1808, he took part in the victories of Wagram and
Moskova. General, then aide-de-camp to the Emperor in 1813, he accompanied Nap-
oleon to the island of Elba. He had been nicknamed 'the Sage of the *Grande Armée*'.

[12] Dejean, Jean (1749–1824). Organiser of the Ligurian Republic, Minister for War
from 1802 to 1810, created peer of France under the First Restoration; during the Hundred Days he was Chancellor of the Legion of Honour.

[13] Andréossy, Antoine, Comte (1761–1828). General in the artillery, he took part in
the Italian and Egyptian campaigns, and was afterwards ambassador to London, Vienna
and Constantinople. Member of the Chamber of Peers during the Hundred Days.

During the evening, Napoleon sent for Benjamin Constant and received him at the Élysée. The writer, who had condemned the Empire at the height of its glory, had changed sides during the Hundred Days, and as well as accepting a post at the Council of State had consented to father the *Acte Constitutionel*, the charter of liberal Bonapartism. Considering him mainly as a man of letters, Napoleon spoke with the detachment of a historian seeking for the clue to a political intrigue; but beneath this attitude the irritation of a man of action frustrated by speechifiers was discernible:

'The issue no longer concerns myself, it concerns France. They want me to abdicate. Have they considered the inevitable consequences of such an abdication? I, and my name, are the centre around which the army is grouped; if you take me away, it will dissolve. If I abdicate today, there will be no army in two days time . . . The army does not understand all your subtleties. Do you suppose that metaphysical axioms, declarations of rights and parliamentary eloquence can stop them from breaking ranks? I could understand it if I had been rejected when I landed at Cannes; but abandoning me today is beyond my comprehension. . . . One cannot overthrow the Government with impunity when the enemy is only a few miles away. Does anyone suppose that the foreign invaders can be put off with phrases? To overthrow me a fortnight ago would have shown courage . . . , but now I am a part of what our foreign enemy is attacking, so that I am a part also of what France must defend. If she gives me up, she surrenders herself, admits her weakness, acknowledges defeat and encourages the conqueror's audacity . . . It is not liberty that is deposing me, but Waterloo; it is fear, a fear of which your enemies will take advantage. And what right has the Chamber to demand my abdication? It is overstepping its legal rights . . . it has not the authority. It is my right, my duty, to dissolve it.'

Constant noted that he was 'serious and calm' as he considered the probable consequences of his departure.

Separated from the Chambers, he was merely a military leader; the peaceful hard-working population in general no longer saw him as possessing constitutional power; but the army was still his, and the sight of a foreign flag always made the army rally round anyone ready to attack it. Even supposing this scattered army were to split, the part that remained faithful to him could be swelled by that numerous and vigorous class that is so easily roused because it owns no property, and so easily led because it has no intelligence. Organisation will not be found among such people, but plenty of resistance.[14]

While the two men paced slowly up and down the leafy alleys bathed in the evening light, murmurs were heard from the crowd collected in the Champs Élysées, and cries 'manifesting a sort of savage enthusiasm'[15] arose from the darkness.

'You see,' murmured Napoleon, 'these are not the people I have loaded with honours and riches. What duty do they owe me? I found them poor and I left them poor. But the instinct of nationality is alight in them, the voice of the country speaks through their mouths, and if I wish, if I allow it, the rebellious Chamber will cease to exist within an hour. . . . But no, it is too great a price to pay for one man's life; I did not return from the island of Elba to drench Paris in blood.'[16]

When Constant got home he noted down this last conversation:

I was convinced that, if he abdicated, which seemed to me probable in spite of his frequent vacillations, it would not be the result either of the advice of his timid friends, not of the threats of his inveterate enemies, but of his own dislike of extreme measures, and even more of a feeling of inner exhaustion and lassitude. I might have attributed some of the credit for this abdication to myself, along with many others; for one can describe a tête-à-tête as one chooses; but it was Bonaparte alone, and his memories and his antipathies, and perhaps his regrets for having so greatly abused his unique opportunities, and his surprise at having misjudged a class which had been docile for so long that he believed he could always dominate it while despising it – such were in my opinion the causes of that self-surrender, which appeared to bring him a sort of relief and repose during the following days.

When Constant left, Queen Hortense was announced; she had been waiting since morning, and knew all about the defeat in Belgium, having heard a description of the battle from King Joseph himself, and discussed it with the Bertrands.[17] The Grand Marshal's wife, an Irishwoman, born Dillon,[18] kept repeating distractedly:

---

[14] [15] [16] Benjamin Constant: *Mémoires sur les Cent Jours.*

[17] Bertrand, Henri, Comte (1773–1844). Officer in the Engineers, he served in Italy and Egypt, where he was promoted colonel and then general. Aide-de-camp to the Emperor in 1804, Governor of the Illyrian provinces, Grand Marshal of the Palace on the death of Duroc in 1813, he followed the Emperor to Elba and St. Helena.

[18] Her father, Arthur Dillon (1750–1794), had been deputy for Martinique at the States General. This French general of Irish extraction commanded the army of the North, then that of the Centre in 1792, and was guillotined during the Terror.

'Why did we leave Elba! What will become of the Emperor?'

In great agitation, Josephine's daughter rushed to meet her step-father, with the Countess Bertrand's last words still echoing in her ears: 'The English are free and enlightened; they are the only race capable of welcoming the Emperor and understanding him.'

'What have they told you?' asked Napoleon bluntly.

'That you have been unfortunate, Sire.'

He did not reply, but went into his study; she followed him. He sat down at a table, opened a few letters mechanically and threw them down without reading them. He only looked up when dinner was announced.

'I suppose you've already dined?' he asked. 'Will you keep me company?'

He ate in silence, except for a few unimportant and disconnected remarks, then he went into the drawing-room where he found his mother and brothers, whom he took into the park for a last conversation. Afterwards, at St. Helena, he remembered sadly what an ordeal that evening had been.

Would the French people ever know how much suffering the night before that final decision cost him, a night of doubts and anxiety? Two courses were left him: to try and save the country by violence, or to surrender to general pressure. . . . He had to take the one he followed; both friends and enemies, the well-meaning and the malevolent, they were all against him. He was left alone, he had to give in; and once the deed was done, it was done; he was not one for half measures; besides, sovereignty is not a thing to be taken off and put on again like a cloak. The other course demanded unusual strength; it might have created great criminals and severe punishments; blood might have been shed and can it ever be known whither it might have led? It would have needed a terror, as in 1793, to save the Empire by putting a stop to defection.[19]

Lucien and Joseph left the Élysée a little before midnight, to attend the meeting of the commission appointed by the Chamber. At the Tuileries they found the eight Cabinet ministers, four ministers of State and ten representatives of the Assemblies. Cambacérès presided. In the hall of the Council of State, in this deserted palace associated with the finest hours in French history, which in spite of temporary abandonment symbolised the sovereign's autocratic

---

[19] Las Cases: *Mémorial*; Montholon: *Récits de la Capitivité*; Gourgaud: *Journal*.

glory, some of those present felt it to be a solemn moment, others a dangerous one. Without precise agenda or well-defined mission, ministers confined themselves to proposing urgent solutions to meet the invasion and deal with internal disturbances.

This by no means suited those who had come there solely to talk about abdication; with La Fayette as spokesman they put forward the demands of the Assembly and the necessity to agree to every sacrifice, however painful, for the country's safety. The Marquis coldly emphasised the fact that deputies insisted on abdication or deposition.

'If Napoleon's friends had believed his abdication necessary for the safety of France, they would have been the first to demand it of him,' retorted Lucien.

'Now you are talking like a true Frenchman,' said La Fayette ironically. 'I'm delighted. I adopt that idea and convert it into a motion. I demand that we all go to the Emperor and tell him that, after all that has passed, his abdication has become necessary in the country's interests.'

Cambacérès put a stop to this offensive by gravely insisting that he could not call a vote on a proposition of this sort; the discussion then continued until three in the morning, when the harassed and confused members of the commission separated, after passing a resolution that: 'the country's safety requires the Emperor's consent to the Chambers' appointing a commission charged with negotiating directly with the allied powers, on condition that national independence and the universal right of all nationalities to the constitution they judge suitable be respected; these negotiations should be supported by the development of the whole of the national forces; ministers should propose measures to provide men, horses and money, as well as those needed to contain and repress the enemies within the country.'

When the vote was being taken, protests were heard because the word 'abdication' did not figure in the resolution; Fouché's were the most persistent. As they left the royal palace in the pale light of dawn, he said to his colleague Thibaudeau: 'We must settle this question today.'

It was the 1815 version of his saying of Thermidor: 'We must strike tomorrow.'

III

ABDICATION

✛✛✛

The Chamber in session – The abdication – The
Executive Commission – The Emperor's hesitations –
Davout's mission – Carnot's visit – The Emperor
leaves for Malmaison.

✛✛✛

On the morning of June 22, a decisive battle began between the
Emperor and members of parliament.

At his levée, Napoleon gave audience to some of his faithful supporters, who had come to the palace less to organise resistance than
to repeat what the Chambers had said: Joseph, Cambacérès, Regnault, Caulaincourt, Savary and La Valette in fact spoke of nothing
but abdication. Indefatigably, the Emperor repeated his arguments
for maintaining inviolable unity, and rallying all the national forces.

'They think they'll save themselves by ruining me,' he said again,
'but they'll discover how mistaken they are.'

The Chamber had assembled at about nine o'clock, and as time
pressed they began to grow bolder. They listened to General Grenier's report on the night's meeting at the Tuileries, and were annoyed
to hear that the commission had not confined their discussion to the
subject of abdication. Reassured by the absence of reaction on
Napoleon's part, however, members who were yesterday ready to
beat a retreat at the first roll of a drum, now agreed upon a plan of
action.[1]

A certain Duchêne demanded that the Emperor be invited to
abdicate 'in the name of the safety of the State'; the imperturbable
La Fayette openly advocated deposition, while Sebastiani, the hero

---

[1] La Fayette was to say later that 'the Emperor could have had the most influential
members of the Chamber arrested during the night,' and that 'by not doing so he showed
irresolution'.

of Constantinople, distinguished himself by relentlessly insisting on an immediate decision being extracted from the sovereign. In consideration for his feelings, and possibly to avoid some furious reaction which might upset everything, a suggestion made by General de Solignac[2] was accepted, and the ultimatum allowed His Majesty an hour's delay. Lucien was bursting with indignation; in one of the corridors he ran into La Fayette, who exploded:

'Tell your brother to send us his abdication, or else we'll send him his deposition.'

'And I shall send La Bédoyère to you with a battalion of the Guard!' Lucien retorted.

While de Solignac was hurrying to the Élysée to inform the Emperor that he had been granted an hour's grace in which to relinquish the crown, Davout ascended the rostrum and announced that he had news of the army; he had difficulty in gaining the attention of several deputies, who were whispering, exchanging glances, and going in and out of the hall like conspirators. The Assembly listened abstractedly to the Minister for War's remarks; their thoughts were all centred on the Élysée, as if the fate of the man engaged in his lonely struggle there was more important for the country's safety than the fact that the English and Prussians were marching along the roads of France.

'They wouldn't listen to me,' the Marshal had to admit pathetically, when he returned to the palace.

Regnault, who was hurrying to and fro between the Élysée and the Palais Bourbon, gave a frank account of the temperature of the Assembly, who were now shouting angrily and calling for arrest. When Napoleon heard the ultimatum brought by General de Solignac, he flew into a rage:

'Since they want to force me, I will not abdicate. The Chamber are all Jacobins, and ambitious men whom I ought to have denounced to the country and sent packing. But it's still not too late.'

He was striding up and down his room, throwing out jerky, violent remarks, or muttered words that escaped the ears of listeners. Lucien again tried to plead the cause of dissolution, reminding him of past events that were both so recent and so remote:

---

[2] General de Solignac had taken part in the 13 Vendémiaire, 18 Fructidor and 18 Brumaire, but had fallen from grace during the Empire.

'You didn't do so badly by following my advice on the 18 Brumaire. The country approved what we did; they acclaimed you; although it is true that we had no legal right to take measures which amounted to no more nor less than revolution. What a difference today! You have complete power. Foreign troops are advancing on Paris. Never was a dictatorship, a military dictatorship more justifiable.'

'My dear Lucien, it is quite true that on the 18 Brumaire we had no backing but the people's safety; yet, when we asked for an act of indemnity, we were greeted by immense acclamations. Today, the law is entirely on our side, but I must not use it.'[3]

He had made his choice, and it was too late to embark on a different course. His mistake, during those fatal days of June 1815, was not to have followed the advice of the faithful and intelligent La Bédoyère, and presented himself to the Chambers, booted and spattered with the mud of Waterloo, before they had time to put their heads together. His authority and his presence would have made the extreme solution advocated by Lucien unnecessary. But this man who grasped a situation so quickly when he could see and touch it, had been content to make up his mind from the judgements of such men as Regnault, who was already won over to the enemy, Joseph Bonaparte, who was unable to take a wide view of politics, or Caulaincourt, Maret and Boulay de la Meurthe – officials anxious to think along the same lines as their sovereign, able assistants only used to carrying out orders.

'Very well', he said, suddenly becoming calm, 'let it be as they wish. The future will show if their way has served France better!'

Then, turning to Fouché who was listening with an impassive and remote air, he added smiling:

'Write and tell those good people to keep calm – they'll get what they want.'

Fouché seized a sheet of paper, scribbled a few lines and sent them to the Assembly, addressed to his faithful Manuel.[4] Napoleon, whose very glance had so often made him fear for his liberty and even his life, was no longer formidable; this pale plump man, tightly buttoned

---

[3] Roland Bonaparte: *Lucien Bonaparte et sa famille*, quoted by Houssaye.

[4] Manuel, Jacques (1775–1827). A young advocate, noticed by Fouché when senator for Aix. Sent to the Chamber of Representatives by a constituency in the Basses-Alpes, his gift of oratory, his liveliness and intelligence at once made an impression. According to a contemporary: 'His words expressed the thoughts of the Duc d'Otrante, sitting silent and motionless in the ministerial seats.'

into his famous uniform, was now no more alarming than the great man who died in Thermidor. Robespierre, Napoleon. . . . How many brilliant but dangerous chapters there had been in the career of the Duc d'Otrante; the plot against the Incorruptible, hatched in the safety of an impregnable retreat, had paved the way for another contrived by the Empire's Minister of Police from within the fortress of his ministerial office; this time there was no need to utter the former threat: 'You will die if he does not die.' His accomplices had prepared the ground.

There was no time to lose, for it was after twelve o'clock. Napoleon turned to his brother: 'Prince Lucien, write!'

This short phrase, which had so often been heard in bivouacs and palaces all over Europe, echoed sadly in this study, where, among several distressed supporters, one professional traitor, and his crestfallen brothers, Napoleon was tackling the last crisis in his political career, with the speed of action that characterised all his decisions.

'Frenchmen, when I embarked on the war in support of national independence, I counted on united effort and determination and the co-operation of all national authorities; I was justified in hoping for success, and I defied all the declarations of the allied powers against me.

Circumstances seem to me to have changed. I offer myself as a sacrifice to the hatred of France's enemies. May they prove sincere in their declaration that their quarrel is only with me personally. My political life is over, and I proclaim my son Emperor of the French, under the title of Napoleon II.

Present ministers will form a provisional council of government; the interest I feel for my son inspires me to invite the Chambers to pass a law organising the regency, without delay.

Be united, all of you, in the interest of public safety and so that you may keep your natural independence.'

Lucien handed the draft of this declaration to the secretary, Fleury de Chaboulon, who made fair copies while shedding a few of those tears that come rarely to the young; then Fouché, Caulaincourt and Decrès were delegated to take the document to the Chamber of Representatives, and Carnot, Mollien and Gaudin to the peers. They made haste, but the occupants of the Palais Bourbon were in such a fever that they hardly allowed them time to cross the Seine; the adjutant-general of the National Guard burst into the Élysée a few minutes after they had left, and announced that the most hostile section of the Assembly was just going to propose deposition.

'These good people seem to be in a great hurry,' said Napoleon banteringly; 'tell them to keep calm; I sent them my abdication a quarter of an hour ago.'

His trials were not over. The debates in the Chambers reached a lower level even than could have been expected from men who had been for the last twenty years chafing under the unrelenting control of their leader. It is true that Fouché declared, with apparently sincere emotion: 'The representatives of the nation must not forget, in the course of the coming negotiations, to guard the interests of the man who has presided over the destiny of our country for so many long years,' but the name of Napoleon II was suppressed from this piece of oratory. The Assembly followed his example, and decided to entrust executive power to a commission of five members, three deputies and two peers. The Duc d'Otrante, Carnot and Grenier were elected on the spot. This was a rebuff for Napoleon, and Fouché, who as president of the commission was about to become temporary master of France, murmured in Pasquier's ear in a satisfied tone: 'We've done quite a lot of work in less than twice twenty-four hours.'[5]

In the Chamber of Peers, painful scenes were taking place: they were not above flinging abuse at the lonely man in the Élysée, now that he was no longer an object of terror. First there was a tragic monologue from Ney, who had returned at full speed from Belgium to declare that Davout's report on the state of the army was false; he described the total defeat of the troops with complaisance, and finally demanded in passionate tones that negotiations should be opened up with the enemy. He was giving the expected signal for a political sauve-qui-peut and general change of front that did much harm to Lucien's intervention in favour of the King of Rome.

'Our concern must be to avoid civil war,' declared the Prince de Canino during the evening session of the Chamber of Peers, 'and to prove that France is an independent nation, a free nation. The Emperor is dead, long live the Emperor! The Emperor has abdicated, long live the Emperor! There must be no interval between an Emperor who dies, or abdicates,

[5] Pasquier: *Mémoires*.

and his successor. Any interruption is anarchy. I demand that, in conformity with the *Acte Constitutionel*, the Chamber of Peers, (who have
sworn fidelity to the Emperor and the constitution, and who not long ago
before France and the whole of Europe once more proclaimed that constitution at the Champ de Mai), that this Chamber of Peers unanimously
and spontaneously declares before the French people and foreign nations,
that they recognise Napoleon II as Emperor of the French. I will set the
first example: I swear fidelity to him.'

It was indeed a question of oaths! Wounded in their self-esteem
by this reminder of promises they would rather forget, the peers
looked about for excuses, alibis and grievances. Louis Le Doulcet,
Comte de Pontécoulant,[6] exerted himself and launched an attack on
the Emperor's brother.

'I ask the Prince: what right has he to speak in this Chamber? Is he a
Frenchman? I do not recognise him as such. . . . He is a Roman prince,
and Rome is no longer part of French territory. . . . However great my
respect and devotion for the Emperor, I resolutely declare that I will never
recognise a child as king; or anyone who does not live in France as sovereign.'

There was an outburst, however, from young La Bédoyère, who
was indignant at the duplicity of all these servants of the Empire who
were now eager to be rid of both father and son at one blow. Vehemently attacking those he called the 'faithful adorers of power', he
said with pitiless mockery:

'I have seen them round the throne, sitting at the feet of their sovereign
in his days of glory; they went away when he was in trouble. And now they
reject Napoleon II because they cannot wait to be dictated to by foreigners, whom they already speak of as allies, or perhaps friends. . . . Woe to
those base generals who have already abandoned him, and are perhaps at
this very moment contemplating fresh betrayals! What has become of all
those oaths, that enthusiasm, those thousands of electors who expressed
the will of the people?'

Annoyed by this attack, the Assembly became stormy, but could
only find two rejoinders in its defence. Old Marshal Massena, Duc
de Rivoli and Prince d'Essling, shouted:

---

[6] Pontécoulant, Louis Le Doulcet, Comte de (1764–1853). He showed his political
prudence by belonging in turn to the Legislative Assembly, the Convention, the Committee of Public Safety and the Five Hundred. Senator and Count of the Empire, he
was a peer during the Hundred Days and the Restoration, and ended, as might be expected, by rallying to the monarchy of July.

'Young man, you forget yourself!'

And the Comte de Lameth added ironically:

'He thinks he's still in the guard-room!'

La Bédoyère and Lameth were to experience the fates reserved for brave and prudent men respectively: the former was shot and the second, Baron and peer of France by favour of Napoleon, ended as a deputy under Louis XVIII. Clutching the tribune, La Bédoyère braved the storm; the noise could not frighten this generous young man, who had been one of the last to leave the battlefield of Waterloo on June 18. He let his scornful gaze travel over the seats crowded with dukes, counts and barons of the Empire, prefects, ambassadors and marshals, and said crushingly:

'My God! Are we never to hear anything but ignoble opinions in this place?'

He was called to order, and finally had to give way to the Comte de Ségur, who asked for a regency to be set up, and then to Cornudet, who favoured a provisional government. Last came Lameth, whose interpretation of the concern of the majority of the peers took the form of a platitude:

'Whatever title the government is to have, it must be nominated.'

'If the Emperor had been killed,' Flahaut tried to intervene, 'surely his son would suceed him? He has abdicated, he is politically dead; why then should his son not succeed him?'

Decrès, who had had time to change sides while crossing the Seine, leaped to his feet and shouted:

'Is this the moment to consider individuals? We must put our country first. There is not a moment to be lost. I demand that the debate be closed.'

There was applause for a suggestion which put an end to regrets, indignation and platitudes alike: to the feebler spirits, silence seemed an opportune weapon, and the Chamber of Peers had no desire to press ahead. They therefore contented themselves with nominating members to sit on the executive Commission. Caulaincourt and Quinette[7] received 52 and 48 votes respectively. Quinette, member of

---

[7] Quinette, Nicolas (1762–1821). Handed over to the Austrians by Dumouriez, he was exchanged with Madame Royale in 1795. He joined Bonaparte after the 18 Brumaire, was prefect under the Consulate, councillor of State under the Empire, and peer of France during the Hundred Days.

the Convention and the Committee for Public Safety, created Baron de Tochemont by the Emperor, beat Lucien, who only received eighteen votes.

✢ ✢ ✢

If Napoleon had been under any illusions as to the attitude to be adopted by the sixty-one generals of the Empire and eleven chamberlains sitting in the Peers, they were soon to be disappointed. He did not conceal his bitterness from the deputies who came to notify him that his abdication had been accepted, and to express the nation's gratitude. He told them frankly:

'I desire my abdication to bring happiness to France, but I am not hopeful: it leaves the State without a leader, without political guidance. The time lost in overthrowing me would have been better employed in putting France in a condition to crush the enemy. I advise the Chamber to reinforce the armies immediately; he who wants peace must prepare for war. Do not leave this great nation to the mercy of foreigners; take care lest your hopes prove false; this is the danger. Whatever my personal situation, I shall always be content if France is happy. I commend my son to France. I hope she will not forget that I have only abdicated in his favour.'

Lanjuinais replied in vague terms that 'the sovereign's wishes concerning his son would be conveyed to the Assembly'.

Napoleon felt the defection of the Peers keenly, and repeated to their representatives, led by Lacépède:

'I have only abdicated in favour of my son; if the Chambers do not proclaim him, my abdication will be null and void. I will reclaim all my rights. . . . After the step you are now taking, the Bourbons will be brought back. . . . You will soon be shedding tears of blood.'[8]

Next day the Chamber retaliated with a decisive blow at the sinking regime; Fouché's liegeman, Manuel, proposed the adoption of a motion recognising that 'Napoleon II had become Emperor of the French as a result of the abdication of Napoleon I and in conformity with the Constitution of the Empire', followed by a clause specifying that: 'In a decree dated yesterday, the Chambers expressed their

[8] Thibaudeau: *Histoire de Napoléon.*

wish and intention to nominate an Executive Commission, in order
to give the nation the guarantee needed for their liberty and repose,
by means of an administration possessing the entire confidence of
the people.'

Not only was there no mention of formal proclamation of the
heir to the throne, but the council of regency desired by Napoleon
was actually replaced by a provisional government, responsible only
to the nation. An overwrought Assembly, flushed with importance
by its victory over the sovereign and the approach of enemy forces,
greeted this specious proposition with expressions of delight. They
even shouted 'Long live Napoleon II', although the motion for
which they had just voted made it possible for the imperial child to
be set aside as soon as the all-powerful provisional government
might think it desirable.

Two days later, in fact, the Executive Commission was to publish
'in the name of the French people' and in opposition to its critics, a
decree that 'since Napoleon II has not yet been recognised sovereign
of France by any power we cannot negotiate with foreign nations in
his name, and the Commission believes it to be its duty to act pro-
visionally in the name of the French people, in order to deprive the
enemy of any pretext for refusing to accept negotiations.'

Alone at the Élysée, deprived of power, and suddenly overtaken
by the calm succeeding the storm of the preceding hours, Napoleon
appeared crushed by the violence of the attacks on him, and the
multiplicity of schemes being hatched against his person, his regime,
and what he sometimes proudly described as his dynasty. And, in
spite of the encouragements showered on him with typically Parisian
good humour, by the suburban tradespeople, Federates, and the
crowd of students mixed with workmen who gathered round the
palace, 'inveighing against the nobility and the Bourbons' according
to one witness, he resigned himself to leaving the outcome of events
in the hands of providence. As Villemain wrote: 'One sensed the
vacillation of strength and the self-doubts of genius.' Aware of his
own hesitancy and the diminution of his faculties after the super-
human efforts of the Hundred Days, during which he had been
obliged to take over all functions, control everything and prepare
everything, he now gave way to fatigue and resignation.

As he was to admit afterwards at St. Helena, 'In these circum-

stances I knew I could no longer be sure of ultimate success: I had
not the confidence of the old days. And my steps were no longer
attended by that good fortune which had once loaded me with favours, but instead by a harsh destiny, always prompt to avenge any
advantages I managed to snatch from it by force'.

The cynical tergiversation of men whose fortunes had been made
and families enriched by him, hurt him more than the uncertainty
of his own fate, and he could not reconcile himself to the thought
that 'they were deserting him just as easily as they had accepted him'.
He had expected support, or at least passive consent, and he hoped
his partisans would be ready to sacrifice themselves in honourable
battle rather than stand aside in favour of the men of the Restoration.
Alas, his marshals would soon be dancing attendance at the King's
door, and his peers hurrying to the Tuileries and shamelessly presenting their requests to have their titles confirmed.

The imperial era had been destroyed by its own greatness; Napoleon had played his part until the final cue: he had braved the savage
forces of the Revolution, converted the people's thirst for violence
into warlike ardour and made the sons of sansculottes into the pio-
neers of a new world, while at the same time giving France institutions
which would defy the passage of time. Now that the tragedy of
Waterloo was over, the footlights were being extinguished at the end
of a drama whose inspiration had astonished, enraptured and then
confounded a nation that had suddenly become in a great hurry
to regain its balance and enjoy the sweets of peace – a nation that
watched the departure of the man it had already made into a legendary hero with no sense of guilt. 'That fantastic hero will remain the
real personage; the other portraits will disappear.'[9]

✤   ✤   ✤

Fouché and the members of the Commission would have felt reassured by Napoleon's sudden isolation, had there not still remained
one last obstacle to be surmounted: the great man had to be got rid
of, and his person disposed of, in spite of the opinions of the army
and the man in the street. But it was the events in the streets that
were to force them to act harshly.

Grouchy's army, which had not been engaged in the Waterloo

[9] Chateaubriand. *Mémoires d'outre-tombe.*

campaign, had just reassembled near Laon – sixty or seventy thousand men in all – and the soldiers were indignant at the news of the abdication. Although Soult had been at pains to emphasise in his order of the day that the abdication had been voluntary, the veterans of Napoleon's campaigns were attached to their leader by almost religious devotion, and they began talking about treason, and angrily spreading the rumour that 'le Tondu'[10] had been driven out of his palace by unknown politicians.

Even in Paris, although they had been accustomed for the last twenty-five years to the schemes of the speechifiers and parties jockeying for power, the working classes scented a trap, and openly manifested their disapproval by forming into processions and marching to the Élysée; the general excitement found vent in shouts of 'Long Live Napoleon!' 'Down with the Bourbons!' and 'Down with the priests!' 'A large crowd kept surrounding the garden,' noted Queen Hortense, and 'were as eager to see their unhappy sovereign as others were to be dissociated from him.'

Popular agitation is always alarming, and Fouché felt it necessary to move fast. Through Bertrand, Napoleon had asked for passports and ships to take him to the United States; at the same time he instructed his bookseller, Barbier, to collect some volumes and despatch them to Le Havre and America; he must clearly have come to a decision. But Fouché was still afraid that Lucien's influence, supported by demonstrations in the streets when the moment came, might drive the former sovereign to some dangerous change of plan. If a second 18 Brumaire was to be prevented, this man must be got rid of without delay.

On June 24, Duchêne, deputy for the Isère and a friend of the Duc d'Otrante, proposed that the ex-Emperor 'be invited in the name of the nation to leave the capital, where his presence can only cause trouble and be a source of danger to the public'. Then a rumour was hawked around the Élysée itself that an attempt on Napoleon's life was being planned; the Guard was reinforced so as to make him believe that they were trying to save him from a death like Ceasar's, at the hands of his own friends. He turned a deaf ear, for he foolishly went on hoping that they would come and beg him to save the country; meanwhile he killed time by interminable conversations with his

[10] The nickname given to Napoleon by his soldiers.

mother and brothers and any members of the household who might be wandering through the sleeping palace.

Queen Hortense was brave enough to force an entrance and offer him some advice; she had inherited from her mother that feminine intuition which often takes the place of commonsense, and also a gift for dealing with Napoleons' brusqueness.[11]

She told him that the situation was critical, and that if he wanted to go to Austria or Russia there was no time to be lost.

He changed the conversation by asking Hortense what were her own plans, and whether she would retreat to her property in Switzerland. Then he mentioned the possibility of living in retirement at Malmaison, and added:

'If they won't let me stay in France, where do they want me to go? To England? My life there would be ridiculous, and uneasy too. Even if I kept quiet, they wouldn't believe it. Every fog would be suspected of tempting me to the coast. At the first glimpse of a green coat disembarking from a ship's boat, some would leave France in a hurry, others would declare war on her. I should compromise everyone, and by dint of saying: "Here he comes," they would tempt me to come.'

But a little later, when the net was closing round him and he had to abandon his dreams and give orders for his journey, he talked freely to Caulaincourt, who was in favour of his taking refuge in Russia, and broached new plans, dictated less by choice than constraint. 'Austria? Never; they have hurt me too deeply by keeping my wife and son from me. As for Russia, I should be surrendering to a man. In England I should at least surrender to a nation.'

To speed a departure which was becoming urgent, Fouché sent Marshal Davout to the Élysée. It was a provocative choice; the sight of this marshal of the Empire, Duc d'Auerstaedt and Prince d'Eckmühl, made Napoleon's blood boil, and he furiously attacked the deputies, ministers and the five 'emperors'.

'You hear those shouts,' he said, stretching his arms towards the gardens. 'If I wanted to put myself at the head of those people, who instinctively feel the country's true need, I should soon have done with all these men who only have the courage to act against me when they see me defenceless. They want me to go? That will cost me no

[11] Queen Hortense: *Mémoires*.

greater effort than anything else. Fouché deceives everyone, and will be deceived himself in the end, and caught in his own net. He's fooling the Chamber, but the Allies will fool him and it will be his doing when they bring back Louis XVIII.'

The meeting had been frigid, and Davout, created marshal in 1804 and one of Napoleon's most brilliant lieutenants, left in hostile silence.

✤   ✤   ✤

Departure was not merely a matter of going away and leaving all the resources of power to Fouché, it also meant making an irrevocable decision, and descending from the most glorious throne in Europe to become General Bonaparte, Europe's prisoner.

At first he was in favour of taking refuge in the United States,[12] and he got Bertrand to find out how the land lay from Decrès, Minister for the Navy. But the Grand Marshal was given an evasive answer; the matter must be referred to the Executive Commission before the two frigates anchored in the Basque Roads, the *Saale* and the *Méduse* could be put at the disposal of the Emperor and his companions, and pronounced in a fit state to embark on such a long sea journey with any hope of success. The truth was that Fouché had no intention of replying in a hurry: Napoleon's person was a trump card, which it suited him to keep in his pocket. After Decrès' rebuff, Bertrand returned to the attack on June 24 and was told that the Commission had not yet come to a decision.

Suspecting a trap, Napoleon, who had arranged to be kept posted with news of the Allied advance, now began to fear that he would find himself caught in Paris, in the middle of a possible Royalist rising: something must be done, and that same evening he said to Hortense:

'Malmaison belongs to you; I should very much like to go there, and you would give me pleasure if you would stay there with me. I will leave tomorrow, but I do not wish to occupy the Empress's suite'.

Josephine's daughter hurried away to install her children in a safe

[12] Napoleon believed he would be warmly welcomed in a country that had been at war with England from 1812 to 1814.

refuge, and then went to Rueil to make preparation for the Emperor's
stay; she thus unhesitatingly renounced all hope of protection from
the allied sovereigns.

But Malmaison could only be a stage of the journey: all vain projects must be given up, and the Parisian palace and its familiar setting abandoned in favour of the hazards of travel and inns. His all
too vivid recollections of the flight of 1814, along the hostile roads
of the Midi, prompted him to take extra precautions this time: the
Grand Marshal saw to the preparations for the journey while Napoleon put his private archives in order. There was so much to do in
so short a time, and so many intimate details to arrange! He was
surrounded by an anxious throng – Madame Mère, with her grave,
unhappy face, his brothers, concerned with their own departure, his
attendants, uneasy and apprehensive, and the officers, as excited as on
the eve of a battle. Etiquette went by the board, and doors were opened
to those who came to collect the crumbs of the final distribution; a
collection of gold boxes was stolen from the Grand Marshal's apartments, and a wad of bearer bonds from the Emperor's study.

Everyone was thinking of the difficulties of embarking on so
lengthy an undertaking as a voyage to America, over hostile roads
and across a sea ploughed by English ships, and doing his best to
provide himself with resources for the journey. . . .

As for Napoleon, the signing of the abdication left him without
means, and he had therefore to make sure of sufficient revenues to
support himself and those who had offered to share his exile: the
Bertrands, who had a way of accepting everything without turning
a hair, and who were used to the luxurious establishment of a
high officer of the Crown, the Montholons[13] and Gourgaud,[14]

[13] Montholon, Charles (1783–1853). Born into a family of the Ancien Régime, Chamberlain and Count of the Empire, minister plenipotentiary at Würzburg in 1811, he
rallied to Napoleon when he returned from Elba and was made aide-de-camp. His marriage to Albine de Vassal had cost him his post at Würzburg.

[14] Gourgaud, Gaspard (1783–1852). Educated at the Military Academy, he took part
in all the campaigns of the Empire and gained promotion at Austerlitz, Friedland and in
Spain. As a brave, hot-blooded aide-de-camp, he distinguished himself repeatedly to
impress his sovereign, and was made a Baron of the Empire when still only a captain
during the Russian campaign. The Emperor saw him swim across the icy Beresina, for
which he was mentioned in dispatches; Napoleon, who was not insensible to spectac-
ular courage, made him his first aide-de-camp on his return. Colonel in 1814, he joined
the Bourbons on Napoleon's advice, but hurried to the Tuileries after the return from
Elba, and re-entered his service.

(both unprovided for), Las Cases,[15] Planat, de Résigny and Saint-Yon.

Napoleon's first concern was for his family: his brothers, who had caused him so much trouble during his years of power but had rallied to him with Corsican devotion in his hours of adversity. Jerome pocketed a hundred thousand francs, Joseph seven hundred thousand, Lucien claimed the two hundred and fifty thousand he said he had spent on putting the Palais Royal in order for his own occupation during the Hundred Days. Hortense found herself being offered over a million in timber shares, which she was never to cash, however. Then the list of servants for his future establishment was presented to Napoleon, and studied attentively by all his companions. Bertrand had claimed from the Commission 'the wherewithal to furnish a town house and a country house, and a few officers,' as well as furniture, silver and books.

Meanwhile, Marchand the valet, wandering through the deserted appartments of the palace, was the only one who was thinking of his master's material comfort; he collected a few familiar objects, furniture, portraits, ornaments and silver from the smaller rooms, and safely stowed away the medal cabinet and uniforms of state, lace and some other objects of value. King Joseph was entrusted with the Emperor's correspondence with European sovereigns, documents which Napoleon hoped to make use of one day to prove that the kings who drove him from his throne and separated him from his son were once at his feet.[16]

That evening, Marchand was given a more delicate mission: he took invitations to three women, to come to Malmaison on the following day for a final interview. They were the Countess Walewska,[17]

[15] Las Cases, Emmanuel (1766–1842). An emigré who returned after the 18 Brumaire, former naval officer and compiler of a much admired atlas, he was made chamberlain in 1809.

[16] In April 1815 Napoleon had arranged for the letters received from foreign sovereigns since the year VIII to be collected and copied, with a view to using them against princes who refused to acknowledge him after the return from Elba. While at St. Helena, he several times expressed his desire to publish these documents 'so as to put these sovereigns to shame, and show the whole world what abject homage was paid me by these vassals when they had favours to ask of me or were begging me for their thrones.'

[17] Walewska, Marie (1789–1817). The pretty Polish countess was the heroine of what seems to have been Napoleon's most faithful liaison. Her son by the Emperor became Napoleon III's minister.

Madame Pellapra,[18] and Mademoiselle Duchâtel.[19] Last of all Laffitte,[20] and Peyrusse the Treasurer, were also ordered to come to Rueil.

While Napoleon was going through his papers and throwing letters and petitions which might have compromised their writers into his study fire, Carnot was announced. This former member of the Tribunate had voted against the Empire and heaped abuse on the Emperor; while Napoleon was master of Europe he had shut himself up in a studious retreat, living on the pension he received from the Treasury; but at the time of the defeat in Russia he resumed service as governor of Antwerp, and after the return from Elba accepted the Ministry of the Interior. Honest, hard-working and sincere, he fell an easy prey to unscrupulous politicians. 'He is readily influenced and misled,' Napoleon said of him. The Duc d'Otrante, director of the Commission, is said to have inspired this ingenuous man's visit to the fallen sovereign, but whatever the original purpose of the visit, the 'Organiser of Victory' was suddenly overcome by emotion.

'Don't go to England,' he said. 'They hate you too much; you would be insulted by prize fighters.[21] Don't hesitate to go to America. From there, you can still make your enemies tremble. If France is to fall under the yoke of the Bourbons again, your presence in a free country will be a support to national opinion.'[22]

Napoleon embraced him with genuine emotion, and went with him to the stairs: 'Goodbye, Carnot, if only I had known you sooner!'

Returning to his study, he dictated an official request to the Commission for the two frigates anchored at Rochefort to be put at his

[18] Pellapra, Françoise, wife of a banker. A frivolous coquette, she was mistress also to Murat and the Duc de Berry. Though her son was born before her liaison with Napoleon, she claimed that he was the fruit of the Emperor's love.

[19] Duchâtel, Marie-Antoinette (1782–1860). Lady-in-waiting to the Empress, she had a brief affair with Napoleon, thanks to Murat.

[20] Laffitte, Jacques (1767–1844). Brother-in-law of Marshal Marmont and one of the most influential bankers in Europe. He was governor of the Bank of France and deputy for Paris in April 1815. He contributed loans to support the imperial policy of the Hundred Days. He was the faithful and discreet trustee of the exiled Emperor's funds.

[21] Boxing was all the rage in England, and the heroes of popular fights with bare fists, such as Kickman, Sutton, Mendoza the Jew and Cribb were treated as heroes. Men of the world liked to be seen about with well-known pugilists, who gave lessons in boxing in the fashionable districts of London.

[22] H. Carnot: *Mémoires sur Carnot*.

disposal for his voyage to the United States, then he got ready to go to Malmaison.

The carriage and its six horses was waiting in front of the palace; but the news of his move had spread like wildfire, and an excited crowd had collected to protest, and was shouting: 'Don't abandon us!' The Emperor thought it best to go out discreetly by one of the garden doors, leaving the state coach to his aides-de-camp. At Chaillot, he moved over from the Grand Marshal's carriage to his own, and drove off towards Rueil at a brisk pace. As he left, he saw men working on the Arc de Triomphe. It was his farewell to the capital.

The Commission was sitting at the Tuileries when news of his departure was brought to Fouché. The former Minister of the Imperial Police immediately proposed that General Beker, deputy for Puy-de-Dôme, should be appointed commanding officer of Napoleon's guard at Malmaison. It was a calculated choice: Beker had been in disgrace since 1810.

IV

MALMAISON

The man who, although still strong in possession of the remains of an
army that had been invincible for twenty years and a name which electrified the multitude, set aside power rather than dispute it by means of the
massacre of civil war – has, on this occasion, deserved well of mankind.

Benjamin Constant.

Hortense had made haste to put the little château in order, particularly the wing containing the library and council chamber, which
was to be for her step-father's use, while his suite occupied the rooms
on the second floor. It had been foreseen that twenty-five men of the
Guard and one officer, lodged in the servants' quarters, would make
up the military establishment of the illustrious visitor – an indispensable precaution, for this fat, pale man was now merely an outlaw in
his own country. A whim of fate had brought him back to the scenes
of his youth, to keep tryst with ghosts of the past. 'At the sight of
those abandoned gardens, those uninhabited rooms, those faded
galleries where routs had once been held, those rooms where songs
and music were no longer heard, Napoleon may well have lived
through his whole career.'[1]

But what a contrast between that portly figure, harassed by a
fortnight constantly on the move, with the tired countenance, ironic-

---

[1] Chateaubriand; *Mémoires d'outre-tombe*.

ally described by one of his visitors as a 'boiled calf's head,' and the serene beauty of nature in festive mood!

However, the time had not yet come to give way to the memories that haunted every room of the charming house; Napoleon was clinging to the insane belief that there would be another turn of fortune's wheel in his favour. Pinning all his hopes on the army now returning from Belgium, he drew up a proclamation[2] intended to restore confidence to the exhausted soldiers, and to let barracks and bivouacs hear a voice and a name which could evoke wonder-working memories of the battlefield and of victories:

'Soldiers! A few more efforts and the coalition will be dissolved. Napoleon will recognise you by the blows you strike.

Save the honour, the independence of the French nation; continue to be, until the last, such as I have known you for the last twenty years, and you will be invincible!'

Shortly afterwards, Jacques Laffitte arrived, and was shown into the library, that corner room which General Bonaparte liked to compare to 'the sacristy of a church,'[3] where he had arrived at the most important decisions of the Consulate, in the friendly, youthful atmosphere of a Court that informally combined serious discussion with plays performed in the little theatre or games of prisoner's base. The ha-ha was crossed by a light bridge, leading into the peaceful park where the birds fluttered in the lilacs and swans glided on the pond; the light played on the mahogany furniture and the Jacob armchairs. Laffitte had been the witness, even the engineer, of France's financial recovery, as the governor of the First Consul's chief creation – the Bank. The money troubles of those in power were an open book to him, and his word was worth millions; he had managed Louis XVIII's funds while he was a refugee at Ghent, and he afterwards took just as much trouble to keep the fortune of the exile at St. Helena intact. Napoleon now proposed to entrust him with eight hundred thousand francs in cash, and three millions in gold, which had been set apart in the cellars of the Tuileries by the Treasurer

---

[2] Sent to Fouché to be inserted in *Le Moniteur*, this noble and at the same time bitter document was buried in a dossier; the new head of the government was not at all inclined to let the tired soldiers hear their Emperor's voice.

[3] Fontaine: *Journal*, quoted by M. L. Biver.

Peyrusse, along with what was left of the treasure from the isle of Elba – five millions in all.

'I do not know what is in store for me,' said the Emperor. 'I am still in good health and I have fifteen years more ahead of me. I sleep and wake up when I want to; I can ride four hours on end and work ten hours a day. My food does not cost much. I could live very well anywhere on a louis a day. We shall see.'[4]

The banker was not a little surprised to find this man who had turned the last page of his tumultuous career only two days before, and was still faced with many obstacles, suddenly relaxed and full of projects.

Several times during that day Napoleon talked about his departure, about the safe-conducts he was awaiting, and the frigates at Rochefort, to which Decrès had sent a special messenger in all haste announcing the arrival in secret of a new minister from France to the United States, accompanied by a suite of twenty persons. As to his ultimate destination, he was obviously still hesitating. One moment he would be persuaded by Caulaincourt to land on the English coast in a boat and claim the protection of British laws, but at the same time he would ask the Minister for the Navy for a list of American ships at present in French ports. Later, much later, Decrès prided himself on his reply:

'You see that there's a ship at le Havre; her captain is in my anteroom; my post-chaise is at my door; it's just going to start. I can answer for him. Tomorrow, if you wish, you can be out of reach of your enemies.'

Caulaincourt then produced antedated passports for the United States.

'You seem to be in a great hurry to see me go,' teased Napoleon.

The Duc de Vicence spoke of the urgent need to come to a decision; enemy forces were advancing on the capital, and there was every reason to fear their relentlessness and hatred.

'I've abdicated,' Napoleon interrupted. 'It's the duty of France to protect me!'

During that afternoon there was a moment of panic when General Beker arrived, for Hortense believed he had orders to arrest the

<hr>

[4] Jacques Lafitte: *Mémoires*.

Emperor. He brought a note from the Minister for War, and was ushered into the study. This stern Alsatian's face was not a familiar one: a soldier since 1788, adjutant-general during the Consulate and a general of the Empire, he had proudly pinned the cross of Saint Louis beside the badge of the Legion of Honour in 1815.[5] Having been unemployed since 1810, he had just been entrusted by Fouché, through Davout's agency, with an order to carry out this unexpected mission, which he now proffered in some embarrassment:

The Executive Commission has chosen you to take command of the Emperor Napoleon's guard at Malmaison. The honour of France demands that care should be taken for his personal safety and the respect due to him. The interests of the country require that malicious persons should be prevented from using his name to excite a disturbance. The character you are known to possess is a guarantee, for the Government and for France, that you will carry out this twofold aim. I invite you to go at once to Malmaison, make yourself known to the Guard, and do everything necessary to carry out this twofold aim.

Paris, June 25
at four o'clock in the afternoon.
Davout.

Three hundred grenadiers and infantrymen had already moved into quarters at Rueil to carry out Beker's orders. 'This is an unexpected development, and I don't like the sound of it,' Napoleon grumbled when Savary told him the news. When he read the order signed by Davout he flew into a rage.

'They should have given me official notice of a procedure which I regard as a matter of form, not as a measure of surveillance to which it was useless to subject me.'

'I'm an old soldier, Sire,' stammered Beker, 'and I have accepted this mission solely in order to protect you. If it does not meet with Your Majesty's consent and entire approval, I will withdraw immediately.'

Mollified by these marks of respect, Napoleon spoke to him in a kinder and more conciliatory style:

[5] Beker, General Leonard Nicolas (1770–1840), brother-in-law to Desaix, created Comte de Mons by Napoleon; he commanded the Guard of the Chamber of Representatives, and was deputy for Puy-de-Dôme. Deprived of the honour of serving His Majesty since 1809, in his own words, he was impatiently awaiting the moment when 'his health should be equal to his devotion'.

'Set your mind at rest, General, I am very pleased to have you with me. If the choice of an officer had been left to me, you are the one I would have preferred, because I have long recognised your loyalty.'

He took Beker over the little bridge into the park and asked him about the present mood of the capital, the subject closest to his heart at the moment. Beker assured him that what was left of the army remained faithful to the Emperor's person, and that the tradesmen and people of Paris were demanding someone to lead them against the invaders. They talked for two hours on end, and Napoleon condemned the attitude of the Chambers.

'Your Majesty could retire to Metz or Strasburg with a picked contingent of the Guard,' suggested Beker. 'Those two positions could hold out for several months. . . . In any case it would have been extremely embarrassing to Your Majesty's father-in-law if, after abdicating in favour of the Prince Imperial and sacrificing yourself for the safety of our institutions, you should surrender to him.'

'You don't know what these people are like,' grumbled Napoleon.

But he was particularly eager to hear about the excited mood of the public and the rebellion in the Assembly.

'There's no enthusiasm left,' he sighed. 'It's all used up, demoralised. How can one count on people who are ready to surrender to the enemy after losing a single battle!'

He paced up and down, a prey to doubts, in the darkness of that beautiful June night; before returning to the château he spoke about the possibility of going to America, and the risks he would run of falling into the hands of his enemies, French or otherwise.

'If they would give me the two frigates I have asked for I would leave for Rochefort at once. But I must find some suitable way of getting to my destination without falling into enemy hands. . . . I am anxious to leave France so as to avoid such a disaster, the odium for which would fall on the French nation.'

Next day, June 26, was given over to memories; the solitude of the château – once too small to hold the swarms of visitors – made it possible for him to take a walk in the familiar park, among the abandoned flower-beds and rare trees.

This house had cost him 'all he possessed' in 1799, and the ghost of Josephine haunted every grove, arousing a procession of images in his memory: business dinners during the Consulate, musical evenings, readings from Bernardin de Saint-Pierre, visits from Percier and de Fontaine to submit their plans, or Redouté, to paint the glory of Josephine's roses, comedies in the little theatre, performed by actors whose names were Hortense, Louis, Eugène, Caroline and Savary. He lived again through the days of his rise to power, as he gazed at the lime walk, the roses in full bloom, the elms and beeches.

'Poor Josephine,' he said to Hortense. 'I cannot get used to living in this place without her. I seem to see her all the time, emerging from an alley or picking the flowers she loved so much. But she would have been very unhappy now. . . . She had more charm that anyone else I ever saw. . . . Get a portrait of her painted for me, I would like to have it in a locket.'

Meanwhile, in Paris, Fouché was advancing prudently along the path of negotiation: on June 25, Bignon,[6] Secretary of State for Foreign Affairs, requested Wellington to provide a safe-conduct for Napoleon 'who desired to go to the United States'. This met the Emperor's wishes, while at the same time being a move to gain the goodwill of the Allies by letting them know the fugitive's plans; and since a copy of the dispatch would be sent to Lord Castlereagh,[7] the British fleet would have a chance to prepare for pursuit.

When, on June 26, Beker sent Davout another request from Napoleon for frigates, Fouché did not wait for a reply from the English, which could not fail to be negative, but rapidly dictated an order designed to gain a little more time:

The Minister for the Navy will give orders for the two frigates in the port of Rochefort to be armed ready to convey Napoleon Bonaparte to the United States.

If he desires, he will be given a sufficient escort as far as the place of

---

[6] Bignon, Louis (1771–1841). Diplomat entrusted by Napoleon with the administrative organisation of Prussia and Austria from 1806 to 1809, and afterwards of Poland. Member of the Chamber of Representatives during the Hundred Days, he temporarily took over Foreign Affairs and signed the convention of Paris.

[7] Castlereagh, Robert, Marquess of Londonderry (1769–1822). Secretary of State for War (1807) and Foreign Secretary (1812). A relentless enemy of Napoleon's, he contributed to the policy of encirclement that led to the overthrow of the Empire. He committed suicide by cutting his throat during a fit of insanity. Napoleon said of him: 'Lord Castlereagh, pupil of Pitt, probably believes himself his equal, but in fact merely apes him. Yet, such is the way things happen in this world, Pitt for all his genius has constantly failed where the incapable Castlereagh has succeeded.

embarkation, under the orders of General Beker, who has been charged with providing for his safety.

The Minister for the Navy will issue the necessary orders to safeguard the immediate return of the frigates after disembarkation.

The frigates will not leave Rochefort roads until the safe-conducts have arrived.

This apparently favourable decision had the advantage of removing the Emperor from Paris, while at the same time keeping him within reach at Rochefort, immobilised on a warship, and, if circumstances made it necessary, in a position to be handed over to the highest bidder. Beker took a copy to Malmaison and communicated it to his august prisoner.

It is difficult to believe that Napoleon was deceived by this offer, and he said bluntly:

'I don't want to go to Rochefort unless I can be sure of embarking at once. I would rather be arrested here.'

This was, in fact, his third attempt to get his departure for America authorised, and he guessed that the Commission's tergiversations had the sole object of forcing him to await the conquerors' decision, out of range of Paris, the army and his supporters; he also understood human nature well enough to suspect that Fouché intended to use his person as a trump card and bargaining counter, in the final contest with the invaders.

On June 26, a French courier was in fact galloping towards Wellington's headquarters; he would not be back in Paris for several days, as the British Commander-in-Chief was sure to consult his Minister and his ally Blücher before dictating his reply. As he signed the decree, on the same day, Fouché could thus be sure of a delay in which to perfect his schemes.

By a strange coincidence, as he watched the army manoeuvres in the peaceful setting of Malmaison, Napoleon was giving way to the desire to temporise, and beginning to hope that some change in the situation might allow him to take up arms again or put himself at the head of the opposition. The miniature war he was planning to wage against the final clause in Fouché's order, immobilising the frigates until the arrival of safe-conducts, therefore gave him the necessary respite; as he afterwards confided to Las Cases: 'I was hoping that the imminence of danger would open people's eyes, that they would

Le Marquis de La Fayette

Le Maréchal Ney, Duc d'Elchingen,
Prince de la Moskowa

Fouché, Duc d'Otrante

Lucien Bonaparte, Prince de Canino

Hortense Bonaparte, Reine de
Hollande

Joseph Bonaparte, Roi d'Espagne

Le Comte Emmanuel Auguste
Dieudonné de Las Cases

Le Maréchal de Camp Baron
Gourgaud

Château de la Malmaison, a view from the gardens

The room used by Napoleon in the prefecture of Rochefort

The house in which Napoleon stayed at Ile d'Aix

Captain Frederick Lewis Maitland

Admiral Lord Keith

Robert Banks Jenkinson, 2nd Earl of
Liverpool

Lord Bathurst

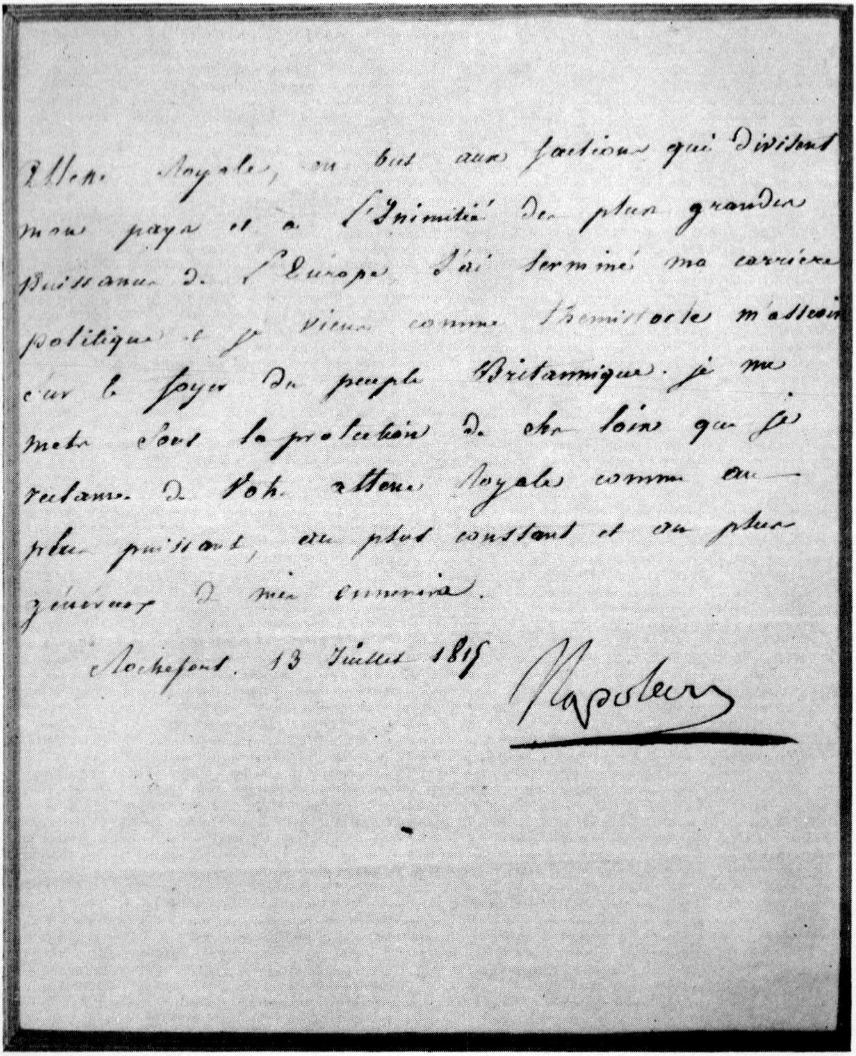

Altesse Royale, en but aux factions qui divisent mon pays et à l'inimitié des plus grandes puissances de l'Europe, j'ai terminé ma carrière politique et je viens comme Themistocle m'asseoir sur le foyer du peuple Britannique. je me mets sous la protection de ses loix que je réclame de Votre altesse Royale comme au plus puissant, au plus constant et au plus généreux de mes ennemis.

Rochefort. 13 Juillet 1815

Napoleon

Napoleon's letter to the Prince Regent

Part of Napoleon's letter of protest from the *Bellerophon*, August 4, 1815

Napoleon at the gangway of the *Bellerophon*, from a painting by Sir Charles Lock Eastlake

again turn to me and I could save the country: it was this that made me linger on at Malmaison for as long as I could.'[8]

Savary and La Valette were chosen to gallop to Paris and discuss with the Commission the cancellation of the restrictive clause. As the new Government was in session, the emissaries had to wait before they could approach Fouché.

'I cannot take it on myself to let him go without precautions for his security,' he said. 'I want to safeguard my responsibility; I should never be forgiven if I acted without foresight.'

Savary retorted that Napoleon absolved the Commission from all responsibility, and realised the risks involved in hastening his departure. Carnot and Caulaincourt then intervened. Carnot was agitated, but had been entirely won over to the Duc d'Otrante's ideas.

'We do not want to obstruct the Emperor's departure,' he grumbled, 'far from it; we want to ensure that we shall never see him again!'

Then he slipped away at the heels of his present master. Left alone with his former colleague, Caulaincourt became more pressing.

'Tell him to go,' he begged; 'add that I entreat him to, and that the sooner he does so the better.'

But these exhortations, however sincere, and coming from a man whose honesty Napoleon appreciated, could not take the place of a safe-conduct, and on the following day the Emperor sent Savary to the Tuileries again, choosing him rather than the Grand Marshal because he knew him to be more direct, more outspoken and less ready to be satisfied by evasive answers: having suffered from the hatred of the Royalists ever since the unhappy affair of the Duc d'Enghien, the Duc de Rovigo would be sure to prove a convinced advocate of his cause.

On the morning of June 27, Fouché changed his plans: he was now determined to let Napoleon leave France as soon as he reached Rochefort. Why this sudden volte-face? Did he suspect that the Allies had been kept informed by official dispatches, and were about to perform prodigies of speed so as to get their hands on their old enemy, or did he simply want to remove the Emperor, lest his presence should jeopardise the political situation when the proposal to

[8] Las Cases: *Mémorial*, May 26, 1816.

recall the Bourbons was put before the Chambers that very same day?
However that may have been, Decrès received an urgent note in the
course of the morning, which caused him to jump into his carriage
and hurry to Malmaison. Fouché had written as follows:

Monsieur le Duc, the Emperor's departure is urgently necessary. The
enemy is advancing, and may already have reached Compiègne. The Commission requests you to go at once to Malmaison and insist on the Emperor's departure, as we cannot answer for any movement that may take
place. As for the condition set out in Clause 5 of yesterday's decree,
relating to safe-conducts, the Commission authorises you to regard it as
cancelled. All the other conditions are confirmed.

The Duc d'Otrante
June 27, in the morning.

P.S.   It is important that the Emperor leaves incognito.

This disturbing postscript may well have revealed fears of a popular rising in the Emperor's favour, just when Fouché was about to
propose to the deputies that Louis XVIII be recalled, but it probably inspired those at Malmaison with fears of a police coup, which
would be facilitated if Napoleon travelled incognito.

While Decrès was driving towards Rueil to encourage Napoleon
to make a discreet departure, the first dispatches from the French
plenipotentiaries charged with making contact with the enemy arrived on Fouché's desk. On June 26, at ten o'clock in the evening,
the envoys – La Fayette, Sebastiani, Pontécoulant, d'Argenson,[9]
Laforest[10] and Benjamin Constant – wrote as follows:

From conversations with Blücher's two aides-de-camp, it definitely
emerges that one of the chief difficulties concerns the person of the Emperor. They think that the powers will insist on guarantees and precautions
to prevent his ever again reappearing on the world's stage. They maintain
that the nations they represent demand safeguards against his enter-
prises. It is our duty to point out that his escape before negotiations have
been concluded would be regarded as an act of bad faith on our part, and
could vitally compromise France's safety.

[9] Voyer d'Argenson, Marc (1771–1842). Prefect of the Empire and member of the
Chamber of Representatives during the Hundred Days.
[10] Laforest, Antoine, Comte de (1756–1846). Diplomat, plenipotentiary at Lunéville,
Ambassador at Berlin (1805–1808) and Madrid (1808–1813). He temporarily took over
Foreign Affairs under the First Restoration and had definitely gone over to Louis
XVIII.

'The most urgent matter of all is to prevent Napoleon from leaving!' exclaimed Fouché.[11]

He immediately alerted Decres and Davout:

Monsieur le Duc, according to dispatches received this morning, the Emperor cannot leave our ports without a safe-conduct. He must wait for this safe-conduct in the roadstead. Consequently, yesterday's order holds good in its entirety, and the letter we wrote you this morning cancelling clause 5 is null and void.

Monsieur le Maréchal, the circumstances are such that it is essential for Napoleon to make up his mind to leave for the Ile d'Aix. If he does not do so, you must keep him under such close surveillance at Malmaison as to make his escape impossible. You will therefore put at General Beker's disposal such police and troops as are necessary to guard all approaches to every part of Malmaison. . . . These measures must remain secret as long as possible.'

Fouché was playing his cards with the utmost care, and Napoleon had become a hostage with his back to the wall: he was to be forced to journey to Rochefort without any guarantee of being allowed to embark, or else to remain at Malmaison as the prisoner of the Executive Commission.

Astounded by this order, Beker galloped to Paris to sound out the intentions of the Minister for War, but he found the offices empty and the corridors deserted. Berlier, the secretary to the Commission, handed him a written pass and pressed him to travel to Rochefort with Napoleon.

The Executive Commission directs all civil and military officers to allow free passage to Count Beker, Lieutenant-general and deputy to the Chamber of Representatives, on his way to Rochefort accompanied by his secretary and a servant. They are expressly enjoined not to allow them to be delayed, nor to put any obstacles in M. le Comte de Beker's way, but on the contrary to give him any assistance he may need.

'So I have become your secretary!' exclaimed Napoleon when he read this document.

He shrugged his shoulders and went off to attend to something else. At the end of the morning, a little before luncheon, he was visited by the father-in-law of Méneval, his former secretary, who was holding a fair-haired boy of about ten by the hand.

[11] Thibaudeau: *Mémoires*.

'Hortense,' he said, 'look at this child. Who is he like?'

'He's your son, Sire. He's the image of the King of Rome.'

'You think so? Then it must be so. I thought I was hard-hearted, but the sight of him has moved me.'

The child was Léon,[12] born of Napoleon's love affair with the very pretty and too compliant Éléonore Denuelle, reader aloud to Caroline Murat.

'When I get to America, I will send for him.'

To America! What a lot of difficulties lay in the way of a voyage which was now the object of his dreams: Fouché and his activities, Royalists talking of assassination, Blücher swearing to all and sundry that he would have Bonaparte hanged at the head of his troops. Metternich was already jubilant: 'They've captured Napoleon's hat. It is to be hoped that he'll be taken himself in the end.'[13] The hat which the Austrian chancellor had been almost compelled to collect at Dresden, still haunted his dreams and he talked of nothing but vengeance. Wellington alone maintained the detachment befitting a great Englishman, and said haughtily that it was not in his power to grant safe-conducts, but that if the sovereigns wanted to put Napoleon to death they must choose an executioner who was not the British Commander-in-Chief. 'Put to death.' This was the issue under consideration at Malmaison, in Fouché's gilded study, Wellington's tent and Blücher's camp.

One evening later, at St. Helena, Napoleon was to wonder at what period of his career he was thought to have been happiest; he seldom returned to his failures, but if he had wished to recall the darkest moment of his downfall, it would surely have been those gloomy hours of June 1815, spent, by a cruel irony, in the setting of his triumphant youth with Josephine. The last page of his reign as an enlightened despot had been turned, his friends were scattered or fled, his faithful supporters were becoming few, and he had fallen from his lonely splendour to become a man trying to protect himself against ambushes, an impotent pawn in the hands of those he despised because they had too often given him cause for suspicion.

---

[12] Denuelle de la Plagne, Léon, Comte (1806–1881). Illegitimate son of the Emperor; he was brought up by Méneval's father-in-law. His contemporaries often mentioned his surprising resemblance to Napoleon.

[13] A berlin belonging to the Emperor had been captured at Waterloo.

'I will go to the United States. They will give me land, or I'll buy some, and we'll cultivate it. I shall end up as man began; I shall live on the produce of my fields and flocks.'

'That's all very fine, Sire,' murmured a young secretary, 'but do you think the English will leave you in peace to cultivate your fields?'

'Why not, what harm can I do them?'

'Has Your Majesty forgotten how you made England tremble? . . . The Americans love and admire you; you would have a great influence on them, and perhaps could involve them in undertakings fatal to England.'

'What undertakings? The English know very well that Americans are all ready to die in defence of their native soil, but that they dislike making war outside their own country. They have not yet succeeded in seriously disturbing the English; one day, perhaps, they will be the avengers of the seas, but that time – which I might perhaps have brought closer – is at present a long way off; the Americans grow up slowly.'

'The Allies will force the Americans to send you away from their country, even if they do not make them hand you over to them.'

'Well then I shall go to Mexico – to Caracas in California.'

'And what about the English fleet?'

'If I can't elude them, they will take me; their Government is worthless, but they are a great nation, noble and generous; they will treat me as I ought to be treated.'[14]

On the morning of June 28, Napoleon dictated a letter for Davout to Beker:

After having communicated to the Emperor the Government's order relating to his departure for Rochefort, His Majesty has charged me to inform Your Highness that he renounces this journey, in view of the fact that, communications not being free, there are no sufficient guarantees for his personal safety. Moreover on his arrival at that destination, the Emperor considers he would be a prisoner, since his departure for the Ile d'Aix depends on the arrival of passports to go to America, which will probably be refused him.

As a result of this interpretation, the Emperor is determined to await his arrest at Malmaison, and until a decision on his fate has been made by the Duke of Wellington, Napoleon will therefore remain at Malmaison, in

---

[14] Fleury de Chaboulon: *Mémoires.*

the persuasion that no action unworthy of the nation and its Government will be taken against him. . . .

Napoleon was trying, by pure strategy, to force Davout to take a momentous and historic responsibility; his request to remain in retreat at Malmaison, without official assurances, would in fact be extremely embarrassing to Fouché and his colleagues.

'What have I to fear here?' said Napoleon ironically. 'I am safeguarded by French honour.'

He understood them so well, these men he had been manipulating for more than ten years, who had only left his orbit to fall into that of the Duc d'Otrante! However, the result surpassed his expectations. Davout, who had become 'the arm of that policy whose soul was Fouché,' according to Villemain's excellent phrase, was heard shouting at General Flahaut, who had come to try and get the Commission to provide safe-conducts:

'General, your Bonaparte doesn't want to leave, but we must certainly get rid of him; his presence is inconvenient and annoying; it prejudices the success of our negotiations. If he hopes we shall take him back, he's wrong; we want no more of him. Tell him from me that he must go, and if he doesn't leave at once I shall have him arrested, I will even arrest him myself!'

Youth is the age of audacity, and Flahaut came of good stock. Mere general and aide-de-camp though he was, he flung in the face of the Prince d'Eckmühl, Minister of War, words which touched this Marshal of France on the raw:

'I would never have believed, Monsieur le Maréchal, that a man who was at Napoleon's feet eight days ago, could talk in such a way today. I have too much self-respect, and I respect the Emperor too much, to repeat your words to him; go to him yourself, Monsieur le Maréchal, it will come better from you than from me.'[15]

Furiously angry, Davout reminded the young man that he was speaking to the Minister for War, and ordered him to retire to Fontainebleau and await orders.

[15] Davout, Louis-Nicolas, Duc d'Auerstaedt, Prince d'Eckmühl. Defender of Hamburg in 1813, he only surrendered it to Louis XVIII in April 1814; he retired to his estates during the First Restoration. He rallied to the Emperor in March 1815, and accepted the post of Minister for War with reluctance. The thought of the reprisals he could expect when the Bourbons returned seems to have dictated his exaggerated behaviour during those uncertain days.

'No, Monsieur, I will not go; I will not abandon the Emperor; I shall be faithful to him till the last as so many others swore to be.'

'I shall have you punished for your disobedience!'

'You no longer have any right to do so. From this moment I tender you my resignation. I could never serve under your orders without dishonouring my epaulettes.'

Flahaut returned to Malmaison, angry and depressed, and confessed what had happened.

'Let him come!' growled Napoleon. 'I'm ready to offer him my neck, if I must.'

Then he resumed his preparations for departure; he had not forgotten his experiences of 1814 and his dramatic journey across hostile provinces. Madame Mère and Cardinal Fesch were urging him to leave; a few high officials of the old Court were braving the Commission's wrath by remaining in attendance: Maret, Savary, La Valette, the Duchesse de Vicence (who brought exhortations from her husband with an air of great mystery), Lallemand, La Bédoyère, (who was eager to join his former sovereign in the New World) and even Talma, fat and solemn in his tight uniform of the National Guard.[16] The Duchesse de Vicence entreated the Emperor to get away without losing any time.

'But I cannot go without a passport and ships,' said Napoleon angrily; 'otherwise the mayor of the first village we come to would arrest me! It would be quite enough to tell him that I had valuables with me. He would write to Paris; Fouché wouldn't answer; events would take their course, and that would be the end of me.'

And he added to Maret, who was also insistently begging him to leave:

'The best thing I could do for all of you, for my son and for myself, would be to throw myself on the mercy of my soldiers. My appearance would electrify the army; they would blow the enemy to blazes. . . . But if on the contrary you leave me here with my sword rusting, they will laugh at you, and you'll have to go, hat in hand and welcome Louis XVIII. We must make an end of it all.'

---

[16] Talma, François (1763–1826). Tragedian admired by Napoleon, who made him act before the sovereigns at Erfurt. When people said that he had taken lessons from this member of the Comédie Française, the Emperor replied laughing: 'If Talma was my master, it proves that I played my part well.'

Maret spoke of the opposition there would be from those in power and the dangers of a new campaign.

'Ah well, I see; I always have to give in,' Napoleon grumbled. 'And it's true, as you say, that I ought not to take responsibility for such a business. I must wait until the voices of the people, the soldiers and the Chambers recall me. But why does Paris not send for me? Haven't they noticed that the Allies are ignoring my abdication?'

Corvisart, Napoleon's doctor, now arrived to introduce one of his pupils, Maingault, who was ready to follow the Emperor to America; he walked in the park with his illustrious patient for a good half-hour. When he had gone, Napoleon handed Marchand a small bottle of reddish liquid, telling him to let no-one see it.

'See that I have it on my person, either attached to my jacket, or to some other part of my clothes, but always in such a way that I can get at it easily.'

The Prussians were not going to be allowed to take him alive!

Then Peyrusse, his treasurer, and Noel, his notary, made him sign papers authorising the sale of certificates representing a capital of a hundred and eighty thousand francs, destined for the expenses of the journey. They were followed by the Countess Walewska, with little Alexandre, but she wept so bitterly that Queen Hortense had to lead her away and give her luncheon, so that she should not make a public scene.

In the middle of all this bustle, agitation and weeping, Napoleon preserved an air of calm detachment that quite disconcerted the others. He wandered through the park, admired the lime avenue where he had often strolled during the Consulate, and the groves where he had worked as he walked, followed by a solemn and attentive Talleyrand. He sat down beside Hortense and the Comtesse Bertrand, who tried in vain to hide their reddened eyes.

'How beautiful Malmaison is! It would have been pleasant to stay here, don't you think so, Hortense?'

Between two interviews, he plunged into Humboldt's *Voyages to the equinoctial countries of the New World*, as if he were trying to furnish his memory with extra information. Perhaps he already saw himself launched on a new life.

'I want to start a new career,' he confided to a visitor, 'I should like to leave some work behind, some discovery worthy of me.'

The career of the scholar philosopher may well have seemed Utopian, in this château where the panic of some combined with the confusion of others, where devotion was at odds with self-interest, and which might at any moment be involved in the fury of battle. The thunder of enemy guns rent the air from the direction of Gonesse and Nanterre; this familiar sound woke Napoleon from his American dreams, and he bent frequently over the map where blue and red pins marked the positions of the armies.

During the afternoon of June 28, an officer of the National Guard came to announce the approach of the Prussians, who might easily attempt a surprise atttack, as the Emperor was known to be at Malmaison.

'Ah!' exclaimed Napoleon laughing, 'I've let myself be outflanked!'

He sent Gourgaud and Montholon to scour the park and reconnoitre the situation; at the same moment Beker received an order from Davout to burn the bridge at Chatou so as to cut the road by which Blücher's hussars were approaching. The battle was coming closer, and in his excitement General Gourgaud declared that he would blow the Emperor's brains out rather than let him fall into enemy hands alive.

Blücher's encircling movement, and the fact that French regiments were falling back on Paris, made the former sovereign's departure an urgent matter for the Government: ministers of the Commission and members of the Assemblies all knew that if Napoleon remained at Malmaison he must either fall into the hands of the Prussians, who would not hesitate to execute him, or else be persuaded by popular feeling to lead a movement of armed resistance. Disgrace, or danger!

The Peers sent a deputation to the Tuileries expressing their fears. But they were preaching to the converted. The Duc d'Otrante listened to them patiently; he had already laid his plans and wrote that evening to Decrès:

Because of the long delay since safe-conducts were asked for, and the fears for his personal safety resulting from the present situation, we are resolved to regard clause 5 of our order of the 26 of this month as cancelled. The frigates will therefore be at Napoleon's disposal. There is now no obstacle to his departure. The interests of the State, and his own, make it imperative that he should leave as soon as he receives the notification you will convey to him of this decision. Monsieur le Comte Merlin is to join you in this mission.

P.S. It is very important that you start for Malmaison with M. Merlin immediately on receipt of this order. Comte Merlin will come and find you.

This note reached Decrès that same night. At two in the morning he grew tired of waiting for Merlin (who had been afraid of an ambush and refused to open his door to the Government's messenger) and again approached Fouché, who chose another envoy in the person of Boulay de la Meurthe, temporary Minister for Justice. The two men arrived at Malmaison at dawn on the 29th. Napoleon was roused from his bed and received them in his dressing-gown. They explained that the advance of the Prussian army justified their fears for the safety of the château, that it was necessary to the interests of the State that he should leave without delay, and handed him passports for all those who intended to accompany him. He thanked them and sent them away, assuring them that he would start on his journey that day.

Was he really resigned to flight? If he still hesitated to take to the road, and cut the last bridge between himself and the capital, it was because he was counting on the intervention of chance in destinies such as his own. He had ordered these ministers about far too long, and controlled their every action, for him not to cherish persistent dreams of taking the whip hand once more, as with restive horses after they have shied. As he short-sightedly watched little Decrès taking his awkward, embarrassed departure, with his unpleasant mission accomplished, he may perhaps have remembered some of the crushing remarks he had once heaped on the head of his over-zealous Minister for the Navy.[17] A single success, he believed, and they would all be at his beck and call as before, these inefficient rather than hostile officials.

A moment came on that morning of June 29, when he saw the possibility of victory looming against the backcloth of panic and defection. After Decrès had left, he was heard to murmur:

'I've done everything they wanted. Here are the letters from the provisional Government and the Ministry for the Navy. The

---

[17] 'You may refrain from comparing me to God. There is so much eccentricity and irrespect for me in the phrase that I would like to believe you were not thinking what you wrote. I pity your lack of judgement.' Napoleon to Decrès, May 22, 1808.

difficulties they have made over providing me with two armed frigates have kept me here until this moment. It's their fault if I have not left sooner, but I shall leave today.'

There was general relief. But Maret and La Valette arrived from Paris with fresh news, which in his capacity as Postmaster General, La Valette had extracted from official communications and couriers' reports: news of the withdrawal of the French troops both infantry and cavalry from Belgium, the Prussian advance between Senlis and Soissons, and the inexplicable absence of the English army. At the same moment shouts were heard from a detachment of a line regiment outside the walls: 'Long live the Emperor!' Napoleon silently went and looked at his map, and altered the position of several pins representing troop movements with a tense expression on his face.

'France ought not to submit to a handful of Prussians! I can still halt the enemy advance and give the Government time to negotiate with the Allies. After that I will leave for the United States and end my days there.'

Rapidly disappearing up the concealed staircase leading from his library to his bedroom, he astonished his companions by returning a few minutes later dressed in the uniform of the Guard, booted and with a sword at his side. He sent for Beker and declared impulsively:

'The enemy will reach the gates of Paris tomorrow. You believe all is lost! But only give me back the command of the army, not as Emperor but as a general. I will crush the enemy in front of Paris. Go and take my request to the Executive Commission. Explain that I have no intention of reclaiming power. On my honour as a soldier, a citizen and a Frenchman, I promise to leave for America on the very day I defeat the enemy!'

Petrified at first, but soon won over by the ardour of his words, Beker agreed to take the message to the 'five emperors' at the Tuileries. While he was galloping towards Paris their leader's enthusiasm infected his companions, and they began making rapid preparations to leave for the front. Hortense was the only one to give way to panic, and dare to ask: would he have adequate support? 'No,' cried Napoleon, 'but nothing is impossible to the French!'

More than a hundred thousand men were stationed beneath the walls of Paris, equipped with five hundred pieces of ordnance, and if the enemy were surprised it might turn to defeat. Blücher, drowsing on his laurels, had no more than fifty-seven thousand soldiers at his disposal, and Wellington was taking it easy at two days' march from the capital.

But the Executive Commission were much more afraid of an imperial victory than of an allied triumph. Beker got a cool reception from Fouché, who refused to let his colleagues get a word in edgewise.

'Is he making fun of us?' he hissed. 'Set him at the head of the army again! He has very probably spared the Commission that task already; he may have slipped away after you left, and perhaps he is at this very moment addressing his soldiers and reviewing them.'

Then he let fly at the unfortunate messenger and berated him as if he had been a corporal.

'Why did you undertake such a mission, when on the contrary it was your duty to urge the Emperor to hasten his departure, in the interests of his own personal safety, which we can no longer guarantee? For the enemy is advancing rapidly on Paris, and this morning's reports from our generals speak of large scale desertions from the army. Look here! Read these letters from Grouchy, Vandamme and others; you'll see whether this long delay is not exposing His Majesty to the danger of falling into enemy hands.'

He was silent, staring at Beker, who was being looked at in no friendly manner by the other members of the Commission; then, the policeman in him coming to the surface, he enquired smoothly:

'Tell me, who was with the Emperor when he entrusted you with this message?'

Beker mentioned several names, in particular Maret's.

'I see who is to be thanked for this,' sneered Fouché. 'But tell the Emperor that his offers cannot be accepted. All hope of negotiation would have to be abandoned. It is of the greatest possible urgency that he leaves at once for Rochefort, where he will be safer than he is here.'

Beker said that Napoleon had spoken with evident sincerity.

'And do you suppose we are on a bed of roses here?' cried Fouché. 'We cannot possibly alter any of the dispositions we have made.'

Then, seizing a sheet of paper, he scribbled a note to Maret and handed it to Beker:

The provisional Government, being unable to accept the proposals just made by General Beker on behalf of his Majesty, on account of considerations that you must yourself appreciate, I beg you, Monsieur le Duc, to use the influence you have always exercised on his mind to advise him to leave without delay, since the Prussians are now marching on Versailles.

Fouché had been unable to resist a passing dig at Maret, whom he had detested for so many years.

✤   ✤   ✤

Beker reached Malmaison a little before five o'clock; he found a scene of great animation in the main courtyard, and the equerry on duty called out to him: 'The Emperor is going to rejoin the army.'

Napoleon was waiting in the library. Beker gave an account of his interview, described the crowd of important officials dancing attendance on their new masters, and handed him Fouché's note.

'Those men do not understand either the state of affairs or of public feeling if they refuse my proposal. . . . I have no alternative now but to leave. Give orders for my departure. When they have been carried out, come and let me know.'

Afterwards he talked alone with Joseph, who had also resigned himself to exile, and who was by nature cool-headed, in spite of his younger brother's harsh opinion of him. The former king of Spain had made arrangements to travel to the United States discreetly and with a small suite; a large part of his property having been deposited in safety, he could lead the comfortable, philosophical life that attracted him so much more than his sinecure as a reluctant monarch. The two brothers probably discussed plans for establishing themselves on the other side of the Atlantic; we have no exact records, but later on there was a question of substantial sums being sent to England and America by members of Napoleon's suite, and Joseph probably took with him considerable funds, some of which were to be for the Emperor's use. Napoleon had now changed into a chestnut-coloured frock-coat and blue breeches, and seemed impatient to be off and make the final break. He embraced Hortense, who was in tears,[18] and received several of the officers of the tiny garrison of Malmaison.

[18] Queen Hortense wanted to give him her diamond necklace, but the Emperor would only accept it in exchange for a note for 200,000 francs signed by himself, and also gave her Josephine's wedding-ring.

'We realise that we shall not have the happiness to die in your service,'[19] stammered one of the soldiers.

These tearful demonstrations must have irritated this cool-headed man, who was far less concerned with intimate feelings than with political and military calculations, and who was fighting for his liberty and life. From his mother, he knew well, he need fear no embarrassing emotionalism. Like the women of antiquity, she was made of the same stuff as her formidable son, and would, until the last moment, reply in the heroic style expected of her.

'Goodbye, mother.'

'Goodbye, my son!'

A few tears trickled down Madame Mère's almost unfaded cheeks, as she started on the road for Italy and became an exile for the second time.

It only remained for Napoleon to take leave of the dead. He spent some minutes alone in Josephine's room, with its pale blue ceiling, red hangings and gilded bronzes, where the woman who had been the passion of his youth had ended her days. The angels still watched from the ceiling, but the swans on the great bed no longer guided the beautiful sleeper through the night. He had only to rest his hand on a piece of furniture or material and close his eyes, to hear the laughter and voice of that greatly desired woman.

'I have not passed a day without loving you. I have not passed a night without clasping you in my arms. . . . No woman was ever loved with more devotion, ardour and tenderness. . . . only death could break a union formed by sympathy, love and true feeling.'

Death had done its work. He tore himself away from his thoughts, softly shut the door of the temple of his youthful love, and went downstairs to his study with an impassive countenance.

A little after five o'clock, Beker came to announce the time of departure. The imperial carriages, loaded to capacity, were waiting in the main courtyard. Since the pass issued by the Commission specified that Napoleon must travel incognito as Beker's secretary, an ordinary four-seated barouche had been brought round to the

---

[19] All the devotion shown him was not similarly disinterested; Generals Piré and Chartran, who had come to assure the Emperor of their fidelity two days earlier, now bluntly demanded money and made such a scene that the Grand Marshal gave 12,000 francs to the former and 6,000 to the latter.

south gate, opening on to the road from La Celle to Saint-Cloud. Napoleon put on a curious round cap, traversed the council chamber and entrance-hall, crossed the wooden bridge and walked rapidly towards the gate. He only stopped once, to have a last look at the château's charming façade. Reaching the iron gates, he quickly got into the carriage and sank wearily back on to the seat. Bertrand sat on his left, Beker and Savary opposite; then Ali[20] whipped up the horses. They moved swiftly along the road through the woods towards Rocquencourt and Saint-Cyr.

[20] Saint-Denis, Louis, known as Ali (1788–1856). A former groom, he became mameluke in 1811. He used to sleep at the foot of the Emperor's bed, and carried his field-glasses on campaigns. He had accompanied Napoleon to Elba and shared his exile in St. Helena.

V

THE ROAD TO EXILE

✦✦

Tours and Niort – Beker's dispatch to the Commission –
Rochefort – How to break through the English squad-
ron – Will Napoleon surrender to the English? – The
Commission insists on Napoleon's departure.

✦✦

Between Malmaison and Rambouillet not a word was uttered: lulled
by the trotting of the horses and the rumbling of the wheels, the
Emperor was plunged in a reverie that was not far from stupor, and
his companions did not dare break the silence.

Determined to leave in a dignified style, as a sovereign travelling
incognito, Napoleon's chief fear was that he would be pursued like
an adventurer. On the box, the trusty Ali occasionally caressed the
handles of his pistols; the Emperor and his companions were armed
with swords, and in the locker of the calash Marchand had stowed
twenty thousand francs in rouleaus. Four swords and a few handfuls
of gold was very little with which to brave 'the winds and fortune'.

The travellers had been divided into two convoys: following the
Emperor's simple yellow calash, but at some distance, came the
imperial coach occupied by General Gourgaud, whose duty it was
to divert any manifestations of sympathy or hostility upon himself;
next came Marchand's carriage, with four servants and a woman
purveyor. Other vehicles containing the Montholons, the Las Cases
and Madame Bertrand, were to take a different route through
Orleans and Angoulême, 'allowing the population the benefit of any
illusions that might be inspired by the sight of the Emperor's coat
of arms and liveries'.[1]

On the way to Saint-Cyr, Napoleon's carriage crossed the park of
Versailles by the paved road running beside the Trianon. The park

[1] Montholon: *Récits de la captivité.*

and its rose-pink marble 'folly', which had witnessed the grandeur and downfall of another dynasty, must have provided the sovereign on his way to exile with food for reflection!

At Rambouillet, although he had only been in his carriage for a few hours, Napoleon expressed a desire to stop and have a rest; the gates were opened, he ate his supper rapidly and retired with General Bertrand; but when his valet had undressed him he suddenly became uneasy and decided to pass the night in the château. Was he still hoping for a courier? Did he think there might be a rising just as the Allies were investing the capital? Or was it simply that the possibility of some nocturnal escapade in the neighbourhood of Paris and on bad roads, made him prefer the protection of the walls of François I's grim dwelling?

While the generals were settling themselves in chairs, as if they were on a campaign, he drank some tea and dropped off to sleep, waking at daylight, fresh and alert. He chatted for a few minutes with the caretaker of the estate,[2] a veteran of the Egyptian campaign, who owed him his job, and ordered Bertrand to choose some books and maps from the library and have them all sent to Rochefort.

At about eleven o'clock he got into his carriage, without having received the hoped-for summons. However, a crowd had been collecting outside the iron gates of the park, and the calash set off towards Chartres to cries of 'Long live the Emperor!'

They were expecting danger, but they merely met with surprises. At Vendôme the Emperor was recognised by the postmistress, as 'uncle Louis XVI' had been at Varennes, but he was cheered, not denounced. A little later, tormented by thirst, he was seen nibbling some cherries Ali had bought, and throwing the stones out of the window. Finally, there was the comic episode of the dull-witted gendarme who knocked on the door of the inn at night, frowning with suspicion, only to be stopped by Saint-Denis, who was keeping watch weapon in hand, and hauled over the coals by Savary, a former inspector-general of the gendarmerie.

Gradually the heat finished what discouragement had begun, and the travellers became as weary in body as in mind; from time to time

---

[2] Hébert, who was bequeathed a legacy of fifty thousand francs in his will. He also gave him ten thousand francs in cash at the time of his journey into exile, to compensate him for the probable loss of his post as caretaker.

Beker would take out his snuff-box and offer it to the Emperor, who took a pinch, gazing in silence at the miniature on the lid: it was Marie-Louise, rosy and fair-haired, with her fixed, Viennese doll's smile.

They reached Tours at about midnight, and the prefect, the Count de Miramon, a former chamberlain, came to talk to his fallen sovereign; Napoleon was living in dread of some hostile attempt fomented by Fouché, and he asked him if he had heard of any couriers arriving from Paris. Miramon reassured him, and they set off again on a long stage ending at Poitiers, which they reached at about eleven. Defeated by the heat of the first day of July, the party stopped for lunch at the post-house just outside the town, and Napoleon dispatched a note to the maritime prefect at Rochefort, to try and get information about the position of the frigates off the Ile d'Aix. He left again at four and entered Niort just as night was falling. Shortly before they reached the town, the travellers got out to enjoy the cool evening air; a farmer casually walked a little way with them, observing the Emperor closely.

'Who are these gentlemen?' he asked Ali.

'Some important officials on their way to Niort', was the evasive reply.

'Well, I don't know,' the good man muttered, 'but it seems to me I recognise one of them; I'm certain I've seen him somewhere.'

'That's quite possible, Monsieur'.

This amazing man had been seen in so many different places since 1793 that it was hardly surprising that a French peasant should follow him on foot along the roads of Saintonge.

After two days' driving the travellers were dog-tired, and Napoleon decided to spend the night at the Auberge de la Boule d'Or, outside the town; before retiring, he asked the prefect to call on him at dawn. He arrived at the appointed time, in a great state of astonishment and begged the illustrious traveller to move into the prefecture. As the soldiers had already recognised their leader beneath the frock coat of Beker's 'secretary', and were shouting 'Long live the Emperor', there was no point in preserving his incognito, and Napoleon accepted the offer. After breakfasting in private he received a naval officer from Rochefort called Quérengal, who told him that the maritime prefect was ill and unable to come and meet the barouche, but was sending General Beker information about the English blockade:

The roadsteads are almost entirely blocked by an English squadron.[3] It seems to me that it would be extremely dangerous for our frigates and those on board to try and force a passage. It will be necessary to await a favourable moment, which will not occur for some time at this season. The blockade puts an end to all hope of our succeeding in getting our ships away.

Although it emanated from a timid opportunist,[4] this outburst seriously obstructed the plan formed in Paris, and Napoleon decided to apply to the Commission again, through Beker. On his suggestion the dispatch of July 2nd ran as follows:

The Emperor arrived last night at Niort, very tired and extremely worried about the fate of France.

Though he has not been recognised, Napoleon has been well aware of the interest and anxiety with which people have asked for news of him on the journey. These demonstrations have caused him to say, more than once: 'The Government does not understand the mood of France; they were in too great a hurry to remove me from Paris, and if they had accepted my final proposal the situation would have been different. I could still, in the name of the nation, exercise considerable influence in politics, by supporting the Government's negotiations with an army for which my name would have served as a rallying-point.'

Arrived at Niort, His Majesty was informed by the marine prefect of Rochefort that the English squadron had redoubled its vigilance since June 29, making it impossible for ships to get away. This being the case, the Emperor desires the Minister for the Navy to authorise the captain of the frigate he is to board to communicate with the officer commanding the English squadron, if extraordinary circumstances should make this step necessary, both for His Majesty's personal safety and to spare France the sorrow and shame of seeing His Majesty taken from his last refuge and handed over unconditionally to his enemies.

---

[3] The *Bellerophon* was alone from July 3 to 6. It was only joined by the *Myrmidon* on July 7. The frigates could have got away between the 3rd and 6th.

[4] Bonnefoux, Casimir de. Entered the navy in 1779 and had been maritime prefect at Boulogne. Remaining at his post after the abdication of Fontainebleu, he hastily hoisted the white flag, and gave an ostentatious welcome to the Duc d'Angoulême in July 1814. He was a Chevalier de St. Louis, and had not forgotten Napoleon's refusal to confirm his rank as ship's captain in 1800, 'because he had asked to serve on condition that he did not go to sea.' (Letter 5121 of Napoleon's I's *Correspondence*.)

While Beker was copying out this dispatch, the prefect Busche came to announce that, according to information from Paris dated June 30, an important battle had taken place between the French and the Allies beneath the walls of Paris. Napoleon at once ordered Beker to add a paragraph to his letter.

We are anxiously awaiting news from Paris. We hope the capital will defend itself, and that the enemy will give you time to see some result of the negotiations begun by your ambassadors, and to reinforce the army so as to cover Paris (this sentence and the next have been dictated by the Emperor). If, in this situation, the English blockade prevents the frigates getting away, the Emperor is at your service, as a general whose sole desire is to be of use to his country.

Napoleon believed that this appeal would confront the members of the Commission with a choice involving their honour: their changing decisions' left their former sovereign no alternative in the last resort, except to communicate with the British squadron and seek refuge on an enemy ship, rather than fall into the hands of the Royalists and Louis XVIII's functionaries, unless regret for what they have done, and alarm at enemy demands, should make them accept his offer to take command of the army.

It was difficult to make a complete break with a past such as his, and his welcome at Niort made the fugitive hesitate once again between departure and some impulsive action; the prefect's courteous attentions; the enthusiasm of the second regiment of hussars, billeted in the town, and of the population, hopes based on the army of the Loire – all combined to set him planning his campaign. Joseph would be arriving soon, and then General Lallemand,[5] who had been carried away by the acclamations of the hussars, and was eager to establish a liaison with Generals Lamarque and Clausel, who were commanding in the Vendée and the Gironde. After a moment's

[5] Lallemand, Frédéric-Antoine (1774–1839). He had fought in the Italian and Egyptian campaigns. Created baron in 1808 and general in 1811, he took part in the defence of Hamburg (1813–1814). Rallying to the Bourbons at the Second Restoration, he followed the Emperor after the return from Elba, sat in the Chamber of Peers during the Hundred Days and fought at Waterloo where he was wounded. He accompanied Napoleon to Rochefort and asked for hospitality on the *Bellerophon* from the English, who interned him at Malta. Condemned to death by the French in his absence, he took refuge in Turkey, then Egypt and finally the United States. He returned to France in 1830 and was reinstated in the army.

hesitation, Napoleon realised how many concealed snares were involved in this plan, now that a provisional Government was installed at the Tuileries, and that any movement in the provinces might be interpreted as a reckless attempt to start a civil war just as enemy forces were spreading over the northern part of the country.

'I am nothing any more, and I can do nothing more,' he repeated to them all, to put a stop to their suggestions.

But in the evening there was a reception at the prefecture, at which the authorities and other important people were present, and military bands played, while the crowds in the streets sang the choruses of marching songs. To calm the visibly mounting excitement, Napoleon issued an announcement that he would continue on his journey at four o'clock next day.

He left at the appointed time, turning his back on chimeras which might perhaps have led him in front of a firing squad in the moat at Vincennes.

For the last time in his life he travelled as a sovereign: saluted by the prefect on the steps of the prefecture, escorted by riders with drawn swords, and acclaimed by the crowds pressing against the iron gates in the light of dawn. Along the flat roads of the Charente, edged with elms and tamarisks rustling in the breeze from the ocean close by, the carriage rumbled towards Rochefort, and at eight o'clock on the morning of July 3 they passed the postern of Vauban's ramparts and reached the prefecture.

Casimir de Bonnefoux, heir to a title of the Ancien Régime, and maritime prefect under the Empire and the First Restoration, was a man whose conduct was guided by prudence.

'I thought you were ill?' said Napoleon in surprise when he saw him.

'No longer, Sire, and I should have been deeply grieved not to receive you in person.'

'That is characteristic of you, Monsieur de Bonnefoux; I should have been very sorry myself.'

Both men were on their guard: the prefect, who was quite aware that a Bourbon would soon be climbing the steps of the throne the Emperor had just descended, and Napoleon, who had not forgotten the other's eagerness to put himself at the service of the son of the Comte d'Artois only a year previously. As, like most naval officers,

Bonnefoux had been quick to rally to Louis XVIII in 1814, and as the Hundred Days had been too short a space to admit of a purge of the services, it so happened that the Emperor's departure was to be arranged by an official who had twice gone over to the Bourbons.

While the prefect was showing Napoleon the apartments which had been decorated in honour of the imperial journey of 1808, and used by the Duc d'Angoulême in 1814, the Emperor enquired about the state of the sea and the position of British ships. Through the window of his bedroom he was soon gazing at the winding course of the Charente, slowly rolling its yellowish waters towards the sea; his objective was close, but the elements could be more easily conquered than those in power on this July day, when the capitulation of Paris gave France to the Bourbons, and the administration to the Royalists.

Napoleon had only envisaged making a short halt at Rochefort before going on to the roadstead, but after listening patiently to the maritime prefect's explanations, he felt the need of hearing other opinions. Savary, Bertrand, Beker and Bonnefoux therefore formed themselves into a council, and were joined by several naval officers and Admiral Martin,[6] a former prefect living in retirement near Rochefort.

The sailors were pessimistic, and Napoleon listened to their remarks with a certain amount of irritation; throughout his reign he had always detested empty arguments and half-measures.

To avoid committing themselves, the sailors persistently added wind and weather to the threat by English ships, thus accumulating objections and finally falling back on a solution worthy of shopkeepers: that the departure should be made on a neutral ship, either an American vessel or a Danish cargo-boat. Admiral Martin was the only one to defend a more acceptable plan: the *Bayadère*, a corvette

---

[6] Vice-Admiral Comte Pierre Martin, born in Canada, had been head of the naval division of the Italian army, and commanded the Mediterranean fleet before he was maritime prefect at Rochefort. He had been forced to retire from office by Decrès after the affair of the Aix fire-ships. The navy had tried in vain to get him reinstated after the death of Latouche-Tréville; but owing to Decrès's detestation of him the petition never reached Napoleon.

'If we had had Admiral Martin to command us,' said Admiral Cosmao, the brave captain of the *Tonnant*, 'we should not have had to face this engagement, or if we had we should most certainly have won it.'

lying at Royan in the Gironde and commanded by the son[7] of Baudin, member of the Convention for the Ardennes.

'I know Baudin,' he said, 'he's the only man capable of taking the Emperor safe and sound to America.'

Napoleon would have to go by boat to a point on the coast, south of the Seudre, and thence to Royan on horseback. It was decided to send a courier to Baudin at once.

The position of the British squadrons justified every attempt: the admiral who was keeping watch over the coast from Brest to Arcachon, and at the same time provisioning the Royalists in the Vendée, had but two ships at his disposal, beside three frigates and a dozen small boats; only the *Bellerophon* could be spared to block the Basque Roads and its three entrances. By itself, this old ship, a veteran of Aboukir, would have been quite unable to prevent the escape of two reputedly swift frigates like the *Saale* and the *Méduse*, and its captain was to admit afterwards that it was not impossible for the escape to be effected.[8]

It seems probable that Bonnefoux exaggerated the difficulties unnecessarily in order to temporise; this sailor, who was no fool, had read between the lines of the dispatches from Paris, and guessed at the predicament of the provisional Government, and the importance of the ex-sovereign's person to the Allies and Royalists. Ever since June 27, Decrès' orders had revealed anxiety and vacillation. Everyone in both camps, in Paris and at Rochefort, was trying to gain time. To Bonnefoux, far away from the Tuileries and its intrigues, one thing alone was clear: he had been ordered to have the vessels ready to put to sea twelve hours after the Emperor's arrival at Rochefort, but only 'if the position of enemy ships makes it possible to do so without endangering the frigates'.

Since Trafalgar, the shadow of English sails had, alas, often

---

[7] Baudin, Charles (1784–1854). Under the Directory he had taken part in an expedition to explore the southern hemisphere. Inactive under the Restoration, he returned to service in 1830 and was Minister for the Navy in 1841, then Admiral of France in 1854, shortly before his death.

[8] The position of the British ships in Basque Roads is known. From June 27 to 30: *Bellerophon, Cephalus* and *Myrmidon*. July 1: *Bellerophon*. July 2: *Bellerophon* and *Phoebe*. From July 3 to 5: *Bellerophon*. From July 6 to 8: *Bellerophon, Myrmidon* and *Slaney*. July 9: *Bellerophon* and *Myrmidon*. July 10: *Bellerophon, Myrmidon* and *Falmouth*. July 11: *Bellerophon* and *Myrmidon*. July 12: *Bellerophon, Slaney, Myrmidon* and *Cyrus. Slaney* and *Myrmidon* were corvettes with twenty guns each.

troubled the sleep of French Admirals; the exemplary sanctions enforced by the Emperor against the commanders of the fleet had made them wary and often driven them to join the opposition. Bonnefoux thus felt somewhat embarrassed in guaranteeing that the frigates could get out of the channels without being subjected to fire, but he tried to make his lukewarm position more defensible by using arguments about wind and tides. He therefore explained that 'by day the wind blew from the sea and by night from the land, but that it was not felt three leagues out to sea'. This being so, the English squadron, ceaselessly ploughing the waves between Brittany and the Gironde, would seldom find the winds in their favour. And how could Bonnefoux talk of a 'calm' when he could see so many English ships cruising in the channel?

In this way, five precious days were lost, so giving time to the enemy flotilla to regroup in front of the Basque Roads and tighten their blockade.

Having failed to hit on a satisfactory plan, the Emperor's party set about organising his 'Household', which greatly annoyed General Gourgaud. 'His Majesty consults me about the organisation of his Household, telling me that Montholon and I are to be aides-decamp. He at once makes me write a draft of this organisation, and asks me if I know Monsieur de Las Cases, and in what way he could be useful; His Majesty wants to make him his cashier; I say that he would be good at the head of the Cabinet, that he is a scholarly man and could replace Monsieur de Bassano.'[9]

The respective functions of all those who faithfully linked their fortunes to the Emperor's had already been defined at Malmaison, after anterooms and offices had been emptied by the abdication. Count Bertrand would remain Grand Marshal; Savary, Lallemand, Montholon, Gourgaud, Résigny and Planat would be aides-de-camp, Las Cases chamberlain, and young Emmanuel, his son, a page. But, feeling that whatever the outcome of the voyage he would soon have to part with some of his officers, Napoleon probably felt it necessary to make a second choice. Las Cases had already made himself indispensable, and Napoleon was sounding Gourgaud's feelings in order to find out the reactions of the other officers, should the future author of the *Mémorial* embark in place of one of them.

[9] Gourgaud: *Journal*, July 4, 1815.

On July 5 Prince Joseph arrived, had a conversation with his brother, and begged him to leave: orders were given to load the baggage on board the frigates, but during the evening Bonnefoux received a report from Baudin which left the decision once again in the balance. The captain of the *Bayadère* was delightedly preparing to welcome his former sovereign:

The Emperor may rely on me. I was opposed to his attempt to reascend the throne, both in principle and in practice, because I thought it would be disastrous for France, and indeed events have only too well justified my anticipations. Today, there is nothing I am not prepared to undertake in order to spare our country the humiliation of seeing her sovereign fall into the hands of our most implacable enemy. My father died of joy when he heard of General Bonaparte's return from Egypt. I should die of grief at seeing the Emperor leave France, if I believed that he could do anything more for her by remaining. But he must leave, and live an honourable life in a free country, rather than die a prisoner among his enemies.[10]

He offered to take Napoleon to America, either on one of his corvettes, the *Bayadère* or the *Infatigable*, or on an American vessel, the *Pike*.

'In case of a meeting with the enemy, I would make it my business to bar their way with the *Bayadère* and the *Infatigable*. Whatever superiority they might possess, I am sure I could stop them.'

To ensure a successful getaway, he concocted a very clever plan: for several days no ships would be allowed to leave the Gironde, then, once a considerable flotilla had collected, the signal to put to sea would be hoisted, and the English would be unable to stop and search so many ships at once. Napoleon replied through Bonnefoux that he approved of this manoeuvre, but that he wished to wait. Waiting had become the order of the day. While the Emperor paced the balcony of the prefecture, gazing at the hill of Tonnay-Charente in the distance, contemplating the dockyard humming with activity below, or scrutinising the low-lying country bordering the river Charente, watched over by enemy ships, his Household kicked their heels in corridors and anterooms. Gourgaud visited the port, which had become prosperous as a result of improvements undertaken under the Empire, and now provided work for a population genuinely attached to the regime. Savary negotiated bills of exchange, thus

---

[10] Baudin to Bonnefoux in Verdon Roads, July 5 at 4 a.m.

enriching the imperial privy purse by a hundred thousand francs, and Las Cases signed a charter with Captain Besson, of the Danish ship the *Magdeleine*, for the transport of a cargo of brandy to America. Besson's solution was now in favour: he had promised to take the Emperor and four members of his suite aboard and to shield the illustrious traveller from English searchers, by hiding him in a padded cask. 'The Emperor felt it undignified to be found hiding in the hold of the ship, if he should be captured,'[11] but it was a card that it might be necessary to play when the moment came.

Although the Emperor still wore his chestnut-coloured frock-coat, he adhered to the formalities of the Tuileries: the same strict etiquette governed daily life, and no-one was admitted to his presence without having first sought and obtained an audience. 'The Emperor hardly sees anyone but Bertrand and Savary, and we are reduced to rumours and conjecture,' complained Las Cases, who was already collecting material for his *Mémorial*. There was however one detail which alarmed the fugitives: the provisional Government had refused the Grand Marshal's request for furniture for the American establishment, and Barbier, the imperial librarian, had not been authorised to dispatch the books from the Trianon which would have formed an indispensable basis for a studious life; this decision might be an indication that the wind was suddenly changing, and that the pursuit of the ex-sovereign, currently described as 'the Usurper', could have a great many unpleasant surprises in store, as soon as a new administration had taken over ministerial departments.

Electrified by the presence of the man they had seen at the height of his power[12] in 1808, the population of Rochefort paid no attention to Royalist rumours, on the contrary, a delegation of inhabitants and soldiers asked for an audience so as to entreat the Emperor not to abandon France. He replied simply that such a decision was no longer possible, 'that his advice, opinion and his services had been scorned and rejected, that the enemy was in Paris, and that he would merely be adding the horrors of civil war to a foreign invasion'.

✢   ✢   ✢

[11] Marchand: *Mémoires*.
[12] Napoleon had given orders for important operations which had benefited the town, notably the draining of the marshes.

It is astonishing to read of those days wasted in tentatives and audiences, at a time when danger was approaching, when the white flag floated from village belfries, and a handful of Royalists could have roused the whole town. What reasons could this man of action, who knew so well how to make the most of time, have had for postponing his inevitable departure? 'The reasons for our staying at Rochefort until the evening of July 8, when we embarked for the frigate *Saale*, were a mystery that I have never succeeded in fathoming,' wrote Count Montholon afterwards, 'for I shall always refuse to believe that we remained five days at Rochefort merely to wait for packing cases or waggons, sent to La Rochelle by mistake, and containing objects used by the Grand Marshal on the isle of Elba.'[13]

Of course, to embark there and then on the frigates, when the opposition was gaining ground with the speed of the telegraph, might mean handing himself over to the tender mercies and vengeance of Louis XVIII, but it was the solution advanced by the courageous Baudin, and the strategem devised by Besson. Alas, such an adventure might have suited Joseph, who was more of a philosopher than a king, for whom liberty was well worth confinement in a cask, and who had thoroughly organised his departure, after putting his diamonds and his papers in safety and reducing his suite to three discreet and faithful followers. But how could Napoleon, with his Household of more that sixty persons, escape incognito, or in disguise? What a subject for English caricaturists, and what a chapter for historians! He deluded himself with the tenacious hope that safeconducts might arrive from London, enabling him to cross the ocean, and above all to leave France on ships flying the tricolour, with a certain amount of ceremony instead of like a ruined banker. And he still did' not' rule out the more and more precarious possibility of a popular rising, a summons from the army and a return to power.

When the chances of such a dramatic dénouement grew less he could always fall back on that last resource, that act of blind folly: to surrender to his enemies the English. He had been thinking of this ever since Paris, he had talked about it to Carnot and Caulaincourt,

[13] Montholon: *Récits de la captivité.*

and at Niort he had renewed his request for permission to communicate with the commander of the British squadron.[14]

The Corsican ogre on the banks of the Thames! Already in 1814 he had directed Caulaincourt to sound the British Foreign Secretary during the negotiations of the treaty of April 11, so as 'to find out whether the English government would see any inconvenience in giving me a refuge in England, with the same guarantee that every English citizen possesses and with entire and absolute liberty,[15] Lord Castlereagh informed the Prime Minister of this strange initiative, commenting shrewdly: 'I did not think it possible to encourage the alternative which Caulaincourt has assured me Bonaparte has mentioned several times, namely a refuge in England.'

On the island of Elba, a few months later, aware of being the centre of interest for all the courts of Europe, and the target of all plots, Napoleon confided to the British commissioner his desire to 'end his days in England'.

A report from Beker to Bonnefoux, written at Niort, proves that the idea gained ground:

It was agreed that if there remained no other course to the persons concerned than to surrender to the English, the minister would stipulate that the captain of the frigate should leave them free to do so. The minister has forgotten this arrangement. Be so good therefore as to let me know whether it is your intention that, once embarked on the frigate, the captain would permit parleying with the English and the conveyance of the passengers on to English ships.

As for Countess Bertrand, she never stopped taking advantage of the influence over Napoleon given her by her position as wife of the highest officer of the crown, and the intimacy with the master of the Tuileries that had been attributed to her, to plead the cause of English hospitality with enthusiasm. This daughter of an Irishman cannot have taken such a course without due reflection. In any case her efforts do not seem to have had much effect on the policy of waiting that was the order of the day, and a paragraph of Marchand's mem-

[14] Perhaps he was thinking of the fate of Pasquale Paoli, the champion of Corsican independence, who had taken refuge in England after his defeat, and enjoyed a comfortable pension and a peaceful retreat. But Paoli had been a friend to the English, and they had rewarded him out of gratitude.

[15] Caulaincourt's archives.

oirs exonerates the Countess from a mistake that might have brought an avalanche of reproaches on her head:

The Countess Bertrand did not conceal her desire for the Emperor to be in England, and had no doubts about his being received there with solemn ceremony. She did me the honour to talk to me about this, but her feelings had no influence at all on the decision taken by His Majesty. At St. Helena, the Emperor read a little book called: *Souvenirs de Mme Durand, dame d'annonce chez l'impératrice Marie-Louise*, and finding this accusation there he took a pencil, made a mark in the margin and wrote 'false'.[16]

All the same it seems probable that his suite joined their reproaches to those of the Countess, and, chiefly for personal reasons, tried to make the Emperor feel guilty whenever he seemed disposed to choose one of the possible plans: a secret flight would have obliged Napoleon to part at once with his much too large retinue of officers, women and servants whose fate would have been precarious.

If left alone, the Emperor would not have hesitated as to the course he should follow; even at Niort he had said: 'As soon as Marchand arrives, I shall go to Rochefort and embark on the first ship I find there sailing for America, where the others can join me.' He was dissuaded from this plan, and was joined by women and children – that was the trouble.[17]

During the evening of July 7, Beker received a dispatch from the members of the Commission, in reply to his report from Niort. The indignation of these statesmen had been increased by Napoleon's extraordinary proposal to take over the command of the army again, at the very moment when French forces were having to retire south of the Loire. They could already imagine this incorrigible man mounting his horse and haranguing the troops, who were at present only a few leagues away from him. The orders were accordingly curt:

Napoleon must embark without delay. The success of our negotiations largely depends on the allied powers' desire to be certain that he has embarked, and you do not realise to what extent the safety and tranquillity of the State are imperilled by all these delays. If Napoleon had made his decision at once, we have before us a report from the maritime prefect of Rochefort saying that it would not have been impossible for him to leave

[16] Marchand: *Mémoires*.
[17] Marchand: *Mémoires*.

on the 29th.[18] The Commission therefore holds you responsible for Napoleon's person; you must use all measures of force that may be necessary, while treating him with due respect. See that he reaches Rochefort without delay and embarks at once. As for his offer of his services, our duties to France and our agreements with foreign powers make it impossible for us to accept it, and you must not refer to it again. Finally the Commission finds that there would be disadvantages in Napoleon's communicating with the English squadron, and cannot grant the permission requested in this respect.[19]

This document, signed by Fouché, Carnot, Grenier, Quinette and Caulaincourt, is damning to its authors: they recognised that the Emperor might have escaped on June 29, but not on July 7; by expressly refusing to let him take to an English ship they were condemning him to delays on a frigate flying a French flag – delays which would hand him over to the Royalists of tomorrow or to his foreign enemies.

'They want to keep me imprisoned on a frigate,' he grumbled.

Then, turning to Beker, he asked pointblank:

'What do you think about it? Everyone here has given their advice, except you.'

Fouché's liegeman was on tenter-hooks, as his reply shows:

The only advice I dare give Your Majesty is that you should make a decision and carry out your chosen plan at once, as quickly as possible. As the fate of France is unfortunately settled, Your Majesty must expect agents to be sent in pursuit of you. From this moment the situation has changed, Sire. The power I hold from the Commission ceases, and Your Majesty will risk fresh dangers whose issue it is difficult to foresee.

'But, General, come what may, you are surely not capable of handing me over?'

'Your Majesty knows that I am ready to give my life for you; but in these circumstances my life would not save you. The same people who crowd under your windows every evening, and force you to show yourself, would perhaps be uttering shouts of a different sort if the situation

[18] Report from Bonnefoux to Decrès: 'The two frigates will be ready tonight, but for the last three or four days an enemy squadron composed of two frigates and two corvettes has been cruising constantly off the entry to the Antioche channel: this creates a difficulty, but I do not believe it to be insuperable.' June 29, 1815.

[19] In his capacity as Minister for War, Davout had written to Beker that 'he had just instructed the officers commanding the troops at Rochefort and La Rochelle to assist in carrying out these orders.'

changed. And then, Sire, I repeat, your liberty, which is already threatened, would be completely compromised. I beg you to reflect on the urgency of the situation.'[20]

'Very well,' said Napoleon, 'give orders to make the boats ready to go to the Ile d'Aix. I shall be close to the frigates there, and in a position to embark whenever the winds are at all favourable to our getting away.'

[20] Montholon: *Récits de la captivité.*

VI

ON THE ILE D'AIX

✚✚✚

On board the *Saale* – The Ile d'Aix – Further orders from the Commission.

✚✚✚

Next day, at dawn, Gourgaud galloped to Fouras to confer with the captains of the French ships. 'I consulted Captains Philibert and Ponée', he said. 'They once more assured me that by day the wind blew from the sea, and by night from the land; but that three leagues off shore there was none; that the English ships were spread in echelon across the bay, keeping watch between Les Sables and the Gironde, and that there was small hope of being able to get away.' On July 8, the *Bellerophon*, cruising off the Basque Roads, had been reinforced by the *Myrmidon* and the *Slaney*.

Gourgaud returned to Rochefort at about three o'clock and saw looks of consternation on every face in the corridors of the prefecture; the Emperor had now decided to embark at Fouras, and this decision, necessarily leading either to confrontation with the enemy squadron or to a parting with his suite, should he adopt the more adventurous course, did not appear to be to everyone's taste.

It was four o'clock when Napoleon unobtrusively left the maritime prefecture, by the terrace leading to the river Charente. While the carriages of his suite were being cheered by the crowds collected in the streets and in the Place Colbert, he took his place in Bonnefoux's carriage, offering him his own in exchange. The prefect put up a stout resistance against this compromising gift.

He would only accept a gold box with the imperial monogram when he was assured that it was quite empty.

While the carriages of the official convoy were jolting along the narrow streets of the town, Napoleon's own was rumbling through the outer suburbs towards the La Rochelle road. As far as the turning to Fouras, this is a flat road, edged with canals full of reeds beaten down by the wind; large oxen were grazing in fields flooded with harsh sunlight, and a few low houses stood with their backs to the sea, merging into the monotonous landscape.

At present these houses were deserted, for a crowd had collected on the beach at Fouras; moved and silent, they were more impressed by the comings and goings of officers in uniform than by the solemnity of the moment. They held their breaths when they saw appearing, on the summit of the low sand dune overlooking the north beach, the Emperor's thickset silhouette, surrounded by his officers. They realised now that the hazards of war had given this wretched hamlet the chance of a spectacle worthy of antiquity; an Emperor of the French fleeing from his country on the shoulders of a simple sailor;[1] the stormy waves seemed to oppose his departure, and behind lay the dark bulk of a ship flying the enemy's White Ensign, and the slender shapes of the frigates still sporting their tricolours.

When the sailors had carried all the passengers to the boats, Napoleon stood up and waved his hand to the crowd: 'Goodbye, my friends!'

The ten oarsmen bent over their sculls, but the violent wind hurled itself against the fragile barges and drove them back towards the shore. The watching crowd shouted 'Long live the Emperor', but their words were carried away; they waved handkerchiefs and hats. The heavily laden boats reared on the crests of the waves, and then dropped suddenly into the troughs, covering their occupants with water. An hour and a half later they had still only drawn level with the frigates in the Fosse d'Enette, and the Ile d'Aix lay several miles off towards the setting sun. No longer sheltered by the land, the oarsmen were toiling against the waves without making appreciable headway; Napoleon therefore decided to go on board the *Saale* instead of making for the island. The log-book of the frigate notes that he arrived on deck at half past seven, followed by Bertrand, Savary, Lallemand and Gourgaud.[2]

---

[1] He was carried to his boat on the shoulders of a young sailor from Fouras, called Beau.

[2] The Emperor's baggage had been embarked on July 6 – five trunks full of silver, clothes, medicines, maps and food.

Captain Philibert[3] received his former sovereign with all military honours except the regulation salvos, which would have alerted the British; the officers saluted him sword in hand, and the crew were drawn up on the starboard side of the deck. All this was gratifying, but Napoleon soon guessed what lay behind this official welcome. It was true that the Captain received the Emperor hat in hand, fell in with his wishes and showed him over the ship, but even a simple character like Ali, the false mameluke, could not help noticing that Philibert 'was so apathetic and indifferent by nature that it seemed impossible to expect anything of him. . . . He was far from delighted at the arrival of the distinguished and unfortunate man who had taken refuge on board his ship.'

Napoleon pretended to be favourably impressed by the preparations which had been going on since June 27; provisions for four and a half months had been taken on board, the crew was complete and they could put to sea at any moment. The only embarrassing feature was that Philibert had had the windows of the poop decorated with fleur-de-lis.

After dining expeditiously, Napoleon retired to his cabin.

In the small hours next morning he sent for Gourgaud and asked him about the wind: it was now four o'clock and from one to three o'clock it had blown from the north. Dressing quickly, the Emperor went on to the bridge and questioned Luneau, the sub-lieutenant, who was on anchor-watch.

'Where is the enemy, and from what direction is the wind?'

'The wind is slight but adverse, Sire; as for the enemy, we have not been able to sight him so far, as the sun is not yet risen, but I can see two suspicious-looking sails in the direction of Chassiron.'[4]

Napoleon scanned the horizon and paced the damp deck for a little while, pondering his decision, then he suddenly announced: 'We will go to the Ile d'Aix!'

It was only five o'clock when Gourgaud came hurrying for orders, followed by Philibert; the ship's boat made for the island, whose fortifications could just be seen. Beker, informed at the last moment, appeared on the bridge in his turn and called angrily for a second

---

[3] Philibert, Pierre (1774–1824). He had served at Boulogne and in the campaigns of Martinique and Santo Domingo. His frigate was launched in 1810 and carried forty guns.

[4] Gérard Pesme: *Les Dernières Heures de Napoléon à l'île d'Aix.*

boat. At the same moment the brig *Épervier*, arriving from Port-des-Barques, dropped anchor close to the *Saale*.

It was Sunday, and the population of the Ile d'Aix, intrigued by the comings and goings of launches and longboats, had collected near the landing-stage and outside the postern of the fort. Violently anti-English since the Day of the Fireships,[5] the island families still remembered the imperial visit of 1808; a glance from their sovereign and one or two orders after inspecting them had transformed their existence, and converted the spit of land they inhabited into the main bastion of maritime defence between Bordeaux and La Rochelle.[6] It was therefore amidst cheers that Napoleon now inspected the forts, ramparts and batteries, and reviewed a company of the fourteenth regiment of marines. Shouts of 'To the army of the Loire,' and 'Do not leave us!' were heard. As Beker admitted, he seemed still to be 'at the height of his power'.

Restored to equanimity by finding these outposts of his last defences in such good order, he returned on board the *Saale* at about eight o'clock in time to receive the last official documents brought by the maritime prefect, who reached the frigate at about nine; an order from the Executive Commission and two letters from the Minister for the Navy.

A letter from Decrès, addressed to Bonnefoux on July 6, should have been communicated to Napoleon at once:

It is of the utmost importance that the Emperor leaves the soil of France as soon as possible. The interests of the State and the safety of his person make this absolutely necessary.

If circumstances do not permit of his leaving on the frigates, perhaps it would be possible for an advice-boat to slip through the English blockade, and if this measure is acceptable to him, you must not hesitate to put one at his disposal, so that he can leave within twenty-four hours. If he does not approve of this measure and prefers to go on board one of the British ships or directly to England, it is suggested that he addresses a formal and definite request in writing, and in this case you will at once put a boat un-

[5] On April 11, 1809, the English Admiral Gambier, with a fleet of seventy-six ships disposed between Aix and the mainland, had surprised eleven ships and four frigates under Admiral Allemand and destroyed them by means of fireships.

[6] 'I approve the two fortifications protecting the approaches to the defences of the village of Ile d'Aix ... They will have escarpments, counter-escarpment, glacis and covert-way' ... Saint-Cloud, March 26, 1808.

der a flag of truce at his disposal, to go to whichever of these two destinations he chooses. . . .

I cannot too often repeat that his departure is of the greatest possible urgency. However, he should not leave on an advice-boat for the United States, or under flag of truce for the English squadron or England, according to his desire, without making an explicit request in writing. And this restriction, which General Beker will make known to him, should bring it home to him that one of the chief motives for his urgent departure is founded on interests for his own personal safety. . . .

An order from the Commission was sent with this letter. It left no choice to the fallen sovereign, for they were now determined to get rid of him by fair means or foul:

Clause 1. The Minister for the Navy repeats the orders he gave for Napoleon to embark immediately on the two frigates destined for this mission.

Clause 2. If, as a result of contrary winds, the presence of the enemy, or for any other cause whatever, his immediate departure should be prevented, and if it seems possible that Napoleon could be successfully conveyed on an advice-boat, the Minister for the Navy will give orders for one to be put at his disposal without delay, on condition that the said advice-boat leaves within twenty-four hours at the latest.

Clause 3. But if, because of the difficulties that a contrary wind might cause him on an advice-boat, Napoleon prefers to be immediately taken, either on board an English ship, or else to England, the maritime prefect of the fifth arrondissement will provide the means, in return for a written request, and in that case a flag of truce will at once be put at his disposal.

Clause 4. In any case, the officer commanding the vessel destined to convey Napoleon must not, on pain of treason, disembark at any point on French soil.

Clause 5. If the officer commanding the vessel should be forced to put in to the French coast, he must take all necessary measures to prevent Napoleon disembarking; if need be he will ask for help from the civil and military authorities.

Clause 6. General Beker, who has been responsible for Napoleon's custody and person, must not leave him until he is outside the channels, and, if Napoleon asks to be conveyed on board an English ship or to England, he must not leave him until he has either been taken on board the said ship or disembarked in England.

July 6, 1815.

This order was signed by Fouché, Carnot, Quinette, Grenier and Caulaincourt – by the grace of Napoleon, Duc d'Otrante, Comte

Carnot, Comte Grenier, Baron Quinette and Duc de Vicence – and it was the last official act of a body who were to stand aside in favour of the new masters of France on the following day, July 7. After driving Napoleon to surrender to his most implacable enemy, they had every intention of leaving him the full responsibility for his final gesture.

After luncheon, which was a gloomy meal, the maritime prefect disappeared to wait for further dispatches in his office at Rochefort, while Napoleon and his companions passed recent events under review and once again discussed the rival merits of Baudin and the *Bayadère*, the American ship, resistance on the Ile d'Aix, and joining forces with General Clausel at Bordeaux. But there was one unalterable circumstance on which their decision must be based – the twenty four hours ultimatum imposed by the Commission, and due to expire with the resumption of central power by the Royalists. Napoleon was silent; three of the courses before him seemed to him worthy of him: to put himself at the head of the army; to leave France openly, with safe-conducts from the Allies; or to trust to the generosity of the English people. The first two were paved with difficulties, which he recoiled from both on account of his personal safety and for the peace of France; he must therefore cease temporising and make up his mind to approach the captain of the *Bellerophon*, and find out how London would respond to such a surprising gesture.

That same evening, he gave orders to Savary and Las Cases to get themselves conveyed to the great ship, which was being watched through a telescope from the signal station, and ask for the British Government's official reply to his request for a passport. Las Cases would pretend he understood no English, and thus be able to discover the enemy's views.

LONDON AND THE FALL
OF BONAPARTE

✚✚

England and the War – The blockade by sea during the
Hundred Days – Lord Keith – Hotham's mission to the
shores of the Vendée – Maitland in Basque Roads – The
British Admiralty organises Bonaparte's capture.

✚✚

Las Cases wondered how he would be received by the English. . . .
We must not forget that Napoleon had left Elba on February 26 and
that the news did not reach Vienna until the evening of March 6.
The Congress, after losing whole months in subtleties of protocol
and in receptions, had spent the previous evening enjoying a sumptuous display of tableaux vivants held by the Empress of Austria
in the severe drawing-rooms of the Hofburg, and representing the
marriage of Maximilian and Marguerite of Burgundy. Never did a
party have such a dismal aftermath!

During the night of March 6–7, a meeting of the plenipotentiaries
of the allied powers had taken place in Metternich's study: they had
sat up until three in the morning, and the Chancellor was dropping
with sleep. At six, his valet brought him an express dispatch from
the Imperial and Royal Consul General at Genoa. So insignificant a
personage could hardly be sending important news, and Metternich
threw the envelope unopened on his bedside table; at half past seven,
unable to sleep, he decided to break the seal:

The English commissioner Campbell has just entered the harbour to
enquire whether anyone had seen Napoleon at Genoa, as he had disappeared from the island of Elba. The answer being in the negative, the
British frigate put to sea again without delay.

At a quarter past eight the Emperors of Austria and Russia had
been alerted, and by ten o'clock the ministers of the allied powers

were again gathered in Metternich's study, making plans to resume the war.

'Do you know where Napoleon is making for?' asked Talleyrand ingenuously.

'The dispatch does not say.'

'He will land somewhere on the Italian coast and then make haste into Switzerland,' sighed the Frenchman.

'No!' cut in Metternich. 'He will go straight to Paris!'

While the couriers were leaving with mobilisation orders, the plenipotentiaries, under the aegis of the Prince de Bénévent, were signing the declaration outlawing Bonaparte – for it was by this common surname that they now referred to the man who was the Emperor of Austria's son-in-law and the ex-sovereign of the one-time bishop of Autun. Here is the text of the declaration:

By breaking the convention that established him at Elba, Bonaparte has destroyed the only legal title on which his existence depended; and by re-appearing in France with plans for disturbances and upheavals, he has deprived himself of the protection of the law and has manifested, before the whole world, that there can be neither peace nor truce with him.

The powers consequently declare that Napoleon Bonaparte has placed himself outside the pale of civil and social relations, and delivered himself up to public vengeance as an enemy and disturber of world peace.

They declare at the same time that . . . they will employ all their means and will unite their efforts to protect Europe from any possible attempt that might threaten to plunge their populations once more into the disorder and misery of revolution.

The Tsar Alexander, his friend of the Tilsit meeting, signed with alacrity, after guaranteeing 'that he would spend his last rouble and his last man', on defeating this spectre from the past – words that must have caused considerable relief to the British delegate, whose country had for years borne the expense of the war against Napoleon.[1] Metternich coolly followed suit, thus subscribing to a measure that authorised the summary execution of his sovereign's son-in-law. 'History provides no example of a similar rejection by the whole human race,' wrote Talleyrand to his niece.

At Westminster they did not wait until March 13 to discuss the deplorable events that were occurring between the south of France

---

[1] More than seven hundred million pounds!

and Paris. Although London was plunged in gloom at the thought that everything was beginning again, His Majesty's opposition opened fire in the Commons, and criticised in advance every warlike measure the Cabinet might decide upon. And the most active section of English opinion, that which listened to what the Liberals had to say, did not hesitate to agree with Burdett[2] that it would be a monstrous action to make war on a nation so as to impose a government upon her that she did not want.

In Vienna the coalition was forming again however, and Talleyrand joined Russia, Austria and Great Britain in a quadruple alliance to attack on all fronts.

On the shores of the Thames there were some who understood the matter differently, and Sheridan[3] set the fashion for elegant Liberal society by deriding the resolutions of the Congress, speaking of 'crowned scoundrels cutting up Europe like carcass-butchers, and cruelly maltreating their subjects who had rescued them from Napoleon, and silencing us by the dirty bribe of a crown for Hanover ... for there never was a sillier saying than that of Fox, about Hanover being as dear to us as Hampshire.'[4]

In the Commons, on April 3, Whitbread[5] challenged the Cabinet, and sharply criticised the decision made by Wellington, British delegate to the Congress of Vienna, to involve the country by signing the shameful declaration of March 13: in his view the authority of Parliament itself had been undermined by the General's attitude. This motion was rejected, and on April 6 the Cabinet threw the sovereign's influence into the balance by addressing to the House a message from the Prince Regent asking for a vote of considerable military supplies. Lord Liverpool,[6] speaking in his turn, summarised

---

[2] Sir Francis Burdett (1770–1844). Liberal M.P. and friend of Byron.

[3] Sheridan, Richard Brinsley (1751–1816). Dramatist and politician.

[4] Lord Broughton, *Recollections of a Long Life*.

[5] Whitbread, Samuel (1758–1815). Son of a brewer and Liberal M.P. since 1790. He distinguished himself by his speeches against the war, and in favour of liberating the American slaves and religious freedom. He had campaigned for the recognition of Napoleon after the return from Elba, on the basis of 'peace at any price'. He committed suicide in July 1815.

[6] Lord Liverpool (1770–1828). Prime Minister in 1812, after the assassination of Perceval, and until 1827. His opposition to many liberal measures, the severity with which he repressed popular risings and the part he played in the movement against Queen Caroline, made him unpopular.

Anglo-French relations since the Consulate, and ended by saying that there was no point in drafting a declaration of war against France, since hostilities were merely being resumed.

Lord Castlereagh, the Foreign Secretary, was more adroit: he drew a disturbing picture of the triumph of Napoleonic dictatorship and its consequences on a manner of life dear to every Englishman: 'We must be compelled to depart from, and turn our backs on that ancient social system which we were anxious again to enjoy; when the military character would not be predominant, but would be merged in the general mass of the community, and take its place and order among the other ranks of society.'

In spite of attacks from the opposition, the Cabinet secured a considerable majority, enabling the Prime Minister to assure the public forthwith that His Majesty's Government had no intention of carrying on an interminable war merely to impose any particular regime on France, while Castlereagh added that he was repelled by the idea of entering France with the intention of re-establishing a sovereign who had been abandoned and betrayed by his soldiers and his subjects. A great Liberal nobleman, Lord Lansdowne, went further still: when Fouché made secret overtures to London, he replied to the Duc d'Otrante that England was by no means set on re-establishing Louis XVIII in preference to any other form of government.

But although England had thus loudly declared that she would refrain from exerting pressure on the decisions of the French nation, she still had to get rid of Bonaparte.

Events moved quickly. On May 23, the Prince Regent asked Parliament to vote credits to support the efforts of the continental powers; the opposition grew restive, but the Government won its point, with the support of the Irish leader Grattan, who expressed himself in the Commons in a phrase with a prophetic ring: 'the name you have established, the deeds you have achieved, and the part you have sustained, preclude you from a second place among nations; and when you cease to be first, you are nothing'.

Once again, persuaded by her ministers that the safety of Europe and liberty depended on the bravery of her soldiers and sailors, England took up arms.

✤   ✤   ✤

The Royal Navy, object of her interest and pride, had been idle since the summer of 1814; her ships now had to be refitted, and their command reorganised. Thus it was that Lord Keith, who had returned to civilian life in July 1814, received an order from the Admiralty on April 28, 1815, asking him to come to Plymouth, hoist his flag on the *Ville de Paris* and take over the functions of Commander-in-Chief of the Channel fleet.

Youngest son of the tenth Lord Elphinstone, George Keith Elphinstone was born into an ancient and noble family in 1746. At the age of fifteen he embarked as midshipman under the future Earl of St. Vincent, conqueror of the Spanish fleet.

After a short spell in the East India Company, he returned to the King's service to fight in America, and was elected to the House of Commons in 1780. The events of the French Revolution inspired him to go to sea again, in the Mediterranean, with a difficult but brilliant captain, Horatio Nelson, serving under him. We find him in the forefront of the capture of Toulon – where a young artillery officer called Napoleon Bonaparte distinguished himself – and afterwards at the Cape of Good Hope; and on his return to London he received a peerage with the title of Baron Keith of Stonehaven Marischal. In 1797 he helped put down a mutiny in the Royal Navy, a dark page in the history of a body of men celebrated for their discipline, and in 1801 he carried out the landing at Aboukir, thus dealing a fatal blow to General Bonaparte's plans. He passed through all the mysterious grades of the naval hierarchy, becoming in turn an admiral of 'the blue', 'the white' and 'the red', with his barony converted into a viscountcy in 1814, at a time when he had swelled his fortune by substantial captures at sea. He retired with the lucrative post of Commander-in-Chief of the Channel Fleet.

This command was a pleasant sinecure at Plymouth: the French fleet was recuperating after being disabled at Trafalgar, and its admirals confined themselves to making war on merchant vessels and capturing their crews. Lord Keith's task was merely to organise a systematic blockade of the enemy coast, and this he carried out until the abdication at Fontainebleau in April 1814. With the return of peace in July, he said goodbye to the fleet and prepared, at the age of sixty-eight, to enjoy retirement on his country estate. The landing at Golfe-Juan snatched him from such dreams: he was urgently recalled to Plymouth, where his three subordinates, Admirals Sir John Duckworth, Sir Ben Hallowell and Sir Henry Hotham were awaiting him.

Without a moment's delay he drafted his first secret instructions, sending the blockading squadrons back to their stations, to board enemy ships and supply the Royalists of the Vendée, this last operation being specially entrusted to Admiral Sir Henry Hotham, with H.M.S. *Superb* and H.M.S. *Bellerophon*.

He spent the month of May 1815 sending encouragements to the captains cruising in the Channel and the Bay of Biscay between Boulogne and Spain, within range of shore batteries, and reinforcing the blockade of the ports. On the 25th he received an alert that gave him cause for thought: he was informed that an American ship was about to put to sea from Le Havre, with what was described as 'Bonaparte's treasure' on board. This affair had no further consequences, because, instead of escaping to America, Bonaparte was again in the news, and Keith had to resume shipping arms to the Whites in the Vendée. 'I send them arms, shoes, cannon, and a little money now and then,' he wrote to his wife; 'but there are rogues Royal as well as Imperial!'

On May 30, Sir Henry Hotham[7], cruising off Quiberon, thought it advisable to sent the *Bellerophon*,[8] commanded by Captain Maitland,[9] to prevent the departure of a corvette suspected of carrying instructions from Paris to the Antilles. A conscientious naval officer, Maitland took advantage of this mission to reconnoitre the Basque Roads, and noticed that two large frigates, the *Saale* and the *Méduse*, the corvette *Bedoyère* and the brig *Épervier*, were all lying in the shelter of the Ile d'Aix.

When he reported this discovery to his chief, the latter sent him orders to join up with the frigate *Eridamus* and the corvette *Cephalus* and blockade the roads by tacking to and fro in sight of the Chassiron lighthouse.

[7] Hotham, Sir Henry (1773-1833). Nephew of Lord Hotham, he distinguished himself at Trafalgar.

[8] The *Bellerophon*, of 1713 tons and 74 guns had been launched in 1786 and had been under fire at Aboukir and Trafalgar.

[9] Maitland, Frederick Lewis (1777-1839). He had served under Lord Howe and Lord St. Vincent, and taken part in the Egyptian campaign with Abercromby. He was made a C.B. after Napoleon's surrender and K.C.B. and rear-admiral in 1830. He died on his flag-ship off Bombay.

It was now only a matter of waiting.

On June 19, the day after Waterloo, every ship, and Lord Keith himself, were in a state of expectation, and the Commander-in-Chief wrote to his wife in a light vein: . . . 'Bonny[10] having no ships. I hear the Rascal is strong and our purse weak. I think matters cannot remain much longer as they now are. We must begin or make peace.'

On the following day the Admiral was able to beguile his impatience by the mock-heroic capture of a frigate flying the French flag carrying reinforcements from Martinique, which had sailed off course near Plymouth. A wretched lot of reinforcements, it must be said: 'Half of the quarter men cried out "Vive l'Empereur", the other half "Vive le Roi".' Our captains told them they must determine who was to be uppermost, or they would fire, and a few shots decided in favour of Louis.'[11]

The news of Waterloo reached Keith on June 22. Maitland heard it on the 28th, from a captured vessel. However crushing Bonaparte's defeat might be, it had no effect on Admiralty orders.

Rumours of every description were spread by neutral ships leaving the Channel and Atlantic ports. On the evening of June 19, an American ship was stopped by an English one and gave a reassuring report: 'The Royalists . . . have taken Nantes and Bordeaux. . . . The French frigate *Hortense*, reported the fastest sailer in the French Navy, has received sudden orders to prepare for sea. . . . People say she is intended to take off Bonaparte in the event of defeat. . . . The inhabitants of Brest are generally averse to Bonaparte and long for peace and the Bourbons. . . . The Commandant and the military there were in dread of an attack from the English.'

As for Maitland, still keeping watch off the islands of Ré and Oléron, he trembled with joy when he received a letter from an anonymous correspondent, on the evening of June 30, informing him explicitly that Napoleon had just arrived at Bordeaux and was planning to get away by way of the Gironde or the Teste, that the troops in this town had been reinforced, that the Grande Armée had been destroyed and the Allies were beneath the walls of Paris. The writer begged him to keep a very close watch on the American vessel

---

[10] Keith spelt it thus, or 'Bony', instead of the more usual 'Boney'.
[11] Lord Keith's *Journal*.

Susquehanna of Philadelphia, about to sail from Bordeaux, and on United States ships in general.

But Maitland did not want to quit his post and leave the exit from Rochefort free; he dispatched the *Myrmidon* towards Bordeaux and the *Cephalus* to Arcachon, and made arrangements for the old *Bellerophon* to remain, day and night, at less than three miles distance from the Charente coast. Events were to reward him for his shrewdness.

On June 27, Lord Melville, First Lord of the Admiralty, addressed a dispatch to Lord Keith marked 'Secret and personal,' warning all ships engaged in watching the French coasts to be ready for action:

Reports have reached H.M. Government from various quarters that in the event of adverse fortune it was the intention of Bonaparte to escape to America. If there is any truth in these statements he will in all probability make the attempt now, unless he should be forcibly detained in Paris. If he should embark in a small vessel from one of the numerous ports along the coast of France it may be scarcely possible to prevent his escape; but if he should wait till a frigate or sloop of war can be fitted out for him, you may receive information of such preparation and may thereby be enabled to watch and intercept her. At any rate it is desirable that you should take every precaution in your power with a view to his seizure and detention should he endeavour to quit France by sea.

Lord Keith made haste to pass on this report, vague as it was, to the officers patrolling the ocean, through Sir Henry Hotham, who had not stirred from Quiberon Bay. A single phrase in the Admiralty dispatch set the tone of this manhunt; it was quite definitely a question of 'seizure' and 'detention'.

On July 1, Croker,[12] secretary of the Admiralty, was in a position to explain the intentions of his superiors: the chiefs of the Royal Navy were laying down in advance rules of behaviour for the captain who should have the 'good luck' to lay hands on Bonaparte:

In reference and addition to my letter of yesterday relative to Napoleon Bonaparte, I am commanded by my Lords Commissioners of the Admiralty to acquaint your Lordship that a proposition reached H.M. Government

---

[12] Croker, J. W. (1780–1857). According to Chateaubriand he 'belonged to the school of Pitt but had fewer illusions'. He was a 'director of one of those establishments whose weight is felt to the ends of the earth', and he kept his post at the Admiralty until the reign of William IV. Endowed with a certain literary gift, he was one of the founders of the *Quarterly Review* and was to be involved in Dr. O'Meara's troubles at St. Helena.

last night from the present rulers of France demanding a passport and safe-conduct for Bonaparte and his family to proceed to America. To this proposition H.M. Government have returned a negative answer; and it now seems more probable than ever that Bonaparte will endeavour to effect his escape, either to England, or what is more likely to America.

Your Lordship will therefore repeat to all your cruisers the orders already given, with further directions to make the strictest search of any vessel they may fall in with; and if they should be so fortunate as to intercept Bonaparte, the captain of H.M. ship should transfer him and his family to H.M. ship and there keeping him in careful custody should return to the nearest port of England with all possible expedition. He should not permit any communication whatsoever with the shore, and he will be held responsible for keeping the whole transaction a profound secret until their Lordships' further orders shall be received.

On the ship's arrival at a port in which there is a flag officer the captain is to send to acquaint him with the circumstances, strictly charging the officer sent on shore with his letter not to divulge its contents; and the flag officer will immediately forward the said letter to me for their Lordships' information; and if there should be no flag officer at the port at which the ship may arrive, the captain is to send his letter to me with a strict injunction of secrecy to the officer who may be the bearer of it.

The interest of this dispatch, here quoted in full, lies in one very significant detail: the Executive Commission had in fact requested passports and safe-conducts for Napoleon and his suite, but without explaining that the Emperor wished to embark from the Ile d'Aix, which would have revealed his temporary refuge.

London could therefore expect him to leave from any one of numerous ports on the French coast; because of this uncertainty, Lord Keith made haste to change the disposition of his ships, as is shown by his report to the Admiralty on July 3:

I request you will be pleased to inform their Lordships that in consequence of your letter of the 1st inst. relative to the expected departure of Bonaparte for America, I have sent out for the purpose of intercepting him, with orders in strict conformity to their Lordships' directions, the *Swiftsure* to the north of Cape Finisterre, the *Vengeur* in the trade of the Channel thirty leagues to the westward of the island of Ushant, and the *Glasgow* off Brest, with directions to Captain Duncan to take under his orders upon arrival there the *Esk*, *Prometheus* and *Ferret*, and to cruise with them and the ship he commands between ten leagues to the southward and ten leagues to the westward of the island of Ushant, and from twenty to forty leagues to the southward and westward of that island.

I have also sent out the necessary orders to the squadron off Brest and directed Captain Lloyd to send either the *Liffey* or *Erne* with a despatch containing similar instructions to Rear-Admiral Sir Henry Hotham.

Maitland had not waited for these dispatches, which did not reach him until July 7, to concentrate his attention on the movements going on in the Basque Roads. On July 1 he had the good fortune to speak a ship from Rochefort, and hear that the *Saale* and the *Méduse* had filled up with powder and were making ready to put to sea, and that several persons in civilian clothes, supposed to belong to Bonaparte's suite, had arrived at the Ile d'Aix (it seems probable that they were couriers sent by the Minister for the Navy and the maritime prefect of Rochefort to the commanding officers of the ships). 'Upon the whole there was little doubt,' notes Maitland, 'of its being his intention to effect his escape, if possible, from that place in the frigates.' He therefore at once anchored the *Bellerophon* as close as possible to the enemy ships, without exposing himself to fire from the shore batteries, and evolved an audacious plan to enable him to take on the two French vessels single-handed should they attempt to force the channel to the open sea: a hundred of his most stalwart men were to be sent to board one of the frigates, and he would then leave her in charge of the first lieutenant and proceed in pursuit of the second with *Bellerophon*.

Political developments in France had reached a point such that the information Hotham and Maitland could glean by contact with the Whites was more useful than the instructions coming from their own chiefs, which had to travel from London to Plymouth by courier whenever the telegraph was interrupted by bad weather, and then from Plymouth to Quiberon and the Basque Roads by small vessel or chasse-marée, thus often arriving after the news had become public.

So that while Lord Keith was writing jokingly to his wife from Plymouth on July 6: 'I have not got Bonny, yet, my dear, but a rumour ran that I had, and that he was at Windsor's Hotel, to which place all Plymouth and Dock repaired,' Hotham was already alerting Maitland from Quiberon: 'Having this morning received information that it is believed Napoleon Bonaparte has taken his road from Paris for Rochefort, to embark thence for the United States, I have to direct you will use your best endeavours to prevent him from making his escape in either of the frigates at Ile d'Aix. . . .'

And on the same day, put on his guard by the rumours circulating among the Royalists, Hotham informed Keith of his plans for capturing Bonaparte, without however taking into account his special interest in the Rochefort Roads – probably, so as to keep for himself all the credit for the operation when the time came;

> *Superb*, Quiberon Bay,
> July 6, 1815.

I am much obliged to your Lordship for your letters of the 27th and 2nd and for the intelligence they contained. Since I heard of Bonaparte's abdication I have been most anxious in adopting every measure I could devise to intercept him; and as the inactivity and weakness of the Royalists provided very little employment for many vessels of war here, I have only kept the two smallest with me since the commencement of hostilities; and I have even despatched both of them for the important object of intercepting the fugitive. I consider every part of the coast under my control from hence to the Basin of Arcachon inclusive well guarded, and a tolerably good outside line of ships too; but two more frigates could be well bestowed, if your Lordship could send them to me, one to join the *Bellerophon* and another for the Loire, where I have only two brigs, one close off and the other outside. . . .

Enclosure: Disposition of H.M. ships under the orders of Rear-Admiral the Hon. Sir Henry Hotham on July 6, 1815.

Superb : In Quiberon Bay.

Sheldrake : Stationed close to entrance of River Loire.

Opossum : Cruising at the distance of twenty leagues on a N.W. bearing from the entrance of the River Loire.

Cyrus : In the entrance of the Pertuis Breton.

Bellerophon, Myrmidon, Slaney : Off Chassiron Lighthouse.

Daphne : Off Maumusson Passage as close as weather will allow.

Phoebe, Larne : At entrance of River Gironde.

Endymion : Cruising at a distance of a night's sail from the entrance of the River Gironde.

Cephalus : Off La Teste, Arcachon.

The trap had been set: now all they had to do was wait for the Emperor to be driven back by Louis XVIII's myrmidons, until he had no choice but to fall into it.

✢   ✢   ✢

On July 7, Hotham passed on to Maitland the official reports from Plymouth, as drafted by Lord Keith on the 2nd in the light of an Admiralty dispatch of the 1st.

H.M.S. *Superb*,
Quiberon Bay,
July 7, 1815.

... the *Ferret* brought me information last evening, after the *Opossum* had left me, from Lord Keith, that Government received, on the night of the 30th, an application from the rulers of France, for a passport and safe-conduct for Bonaparte to America, which had been answered in the negative, and, therefore, directing an increase of vigilance to intercept him: but it remains quite uncertain where he will embark; and, although it would appear by the measures adopted at home, that it is expected he will sail from one of the northern ports, I am of opinion that he will go from one of the southern places, and I think the information I sent you yesterday by the *Opossum* is very likely to be correct; namely, that he had taken the road to Rochefort; and that he will probably embark in the frigates at Ile d'Aix; for which reason I am very anxious you should have force enough to stop them both, as the *Bellerophon* could only take one, if they separated, and that might not be the one he would be on board of.

I have no frigate to send you; if one should join me in time, I will send her to you, and I hope you will have *two* twenty-gun ships with you (...)

I depend on your using the best means that can be adopted to intercept the fugitive, on whose captivity the repose of Europe appears to depend. If he should be taken, he is to be brought to me in this bay, as I have orders for his disposal; he is to be removed from the ship in which he may be found, to one of His Majesty's ships.

VIII

NEGOTIATIONS WITH MAITLAND

✦✦✦

Mission of Savary and Las Cases – New plans for
escape – The Emperor on the Ile d'Aix – Visit from
King Joseph – The Roads blockaded – Napoleon
decides to go to England – Second mission to the
Bellerophon – The letter to the Prince Regent – Plans
to take Napoleon into custody.

✦✦✦

At daybreak on Monday, July 10, the officer of the watch informed
Maitland that a boat had put out from the French squadron and
seemed to be making for the open sea. His suspicions aroused, the
Englishman was making preparations to give chase to the small
vessel, when he saw the white flag at the mast-head. Savary and Las
Cases were bringing the captain of the *Bellerophon* a message which
was to take the drama a stage further.

The two emissaries were courteously received at the gangway by
the still young, lean, distinguished and cautious Maitland; as his
knowledge of French was poor, it took him some time to decipher
General Bertrand's letter:

The Emperor Napoleon, having abdicated from power and chosen the
United States of America as a retreat, has embarked on the two frigates
now lying in the Roads, for the purpose of proceeding to his destination.
He awaits the safe-conduct from the British Government, of which he has
been informed, and this leads me to send the present flag of truce to ask
you whether you have any knowledge of the above-mentioned safe-conduct, or if you think it may be the intention of the British Government to
impede our passage to the United States. I should be extremely obliged if
you would give me any information you may possess on this subject.

He had just finished reading this missive, when the *Falmouth*
arrived from Quiberon, with a very important dispatch from Admiral

Hotham, containing the secret orders sent from the Admiralty on July 1.

H.M.S. *Superb*,
Quiberon Bay,
July 8, 1815.

The Lords Commissioners of the Admiralty having every reason to believe that Napoleon Bonaparte meditates his escape, with his family, from France to America, you are hereby required and directed ... to keep the most vigilant look-out for the purpose of intercepting him; and to make the strictest search of any vessel you may fall in with; and if you should be so fortunate as to intercept him, you are to transfer him and his family to the ship you command, and there keeping him in careful custody, return to the nearest port in England (going into Torbay in preference to Plymouth) with all possible expedition; and on your arrival you are not to permit any communication whatever with the shore, except as herein after directed; and you will be held responsible for keeping the whole transaction a profound secret, until you receive their Lordships' further orders.

In case you should arrive at a port where there is a flag-officer, you are to send to acquaint him with the circumstances, strictly charging the officer sent on shore with your letter, not to divulge its contents: and if there should be no flag-officer at the port where you arrive, you are to send one letter express to the Secretary of the Admiralty, and another to Admiral Lord Keith, with strict injunctions of secrecy to each officer who may be the bearer of them.

The Admiralty's special precautions had not been in vain: their orders reached the captain whose duty it was to apply them, at the precise moment when the man sought by the Royal Navy between the Channel and Arcachon was about to present himself.

Napoleon's emissaries naïvely believed that they could guess the plans of an adversary pledged to military secrecy, and they accepted an invitation to breakfast with Maitland, who felt the need of a respite in which to reflect and prepare his plan of action. They at once started overwhelming him with questions, clearly revealing their anxieties:

We suggested the possibility of the Emperor's leaving on the frigates under a flag of truce, and were told that they would be attacked. We spoke of his travelling on a neutral ship, and were told that every neutral ship would be strictly searched, perhaps even taken to English ports, but he suggested that we might come to England, and affirmed that no ill-treatment need be feared there.[1]

[1] Las Cases: *Mémorial*, July 10, 1815.

Maitland's answers were reluctant; he was absorbed in concocting a plan by which he would gain possession of Bonaparte's person without running the risk of a naval engagement. He quickly saw that it was essential to temporise, at whatever cost, until he received special instructions from the Admiral, and also reinforcements. He therefore feigned astonishment and declared that he had heard no news except that Napoleon had been defeated at Waterloo.

Having received, in my orders, the strictest injunctions to secrecy (he wrote afterwards) and feeling that the force on the coast at my disposal was insufficient to guard the different ports and passages from which an escape might be effected, particularly should the plan be adopted of putting to sea in a small vessel, I wrote the following reply to the above communication; hoping, by that means, to induce Napoleon to remain for the Admiral's answer, which would give time for the arrival of reinforcements:[2]

> H.M.S. *Bellerophon*,
> off Rochefort,
> July 10, 1815.

Sir,

I have to acknowledge the receipt of your letter of yesterday's date, addressed to the Admiral commanding the English cruisers before Rochefort, acquainting me that the Emperor, having abdicated the throne of France and chosen the United States of America as an asylum, is now embarked on board the frigates, to proceed for that destination, and awaits a passport from the English Government; and requesting to know if I have any knowledge of such passport; or if I think it is the intention of the English Government to prevent the Emperor's voyage.

In reply, I have to acquaint you, that I cannot say what the intentions of my Government may be; but the two countries being at present in a state of war, it is impossible for me to permit any ship of war to put to sea from the port of Rochefort.

As to the proposal made by the Duc de Rovigo and Count Las Cases, of allowing the Emperor to proceed in a merchant vessel; it is out of my power – without the sanction of my commanding officer, Sir Henry Hotham, who is at present in Quiberon Bay, and to whom I have forwarded your dispatch – to allow any vessel, under whatever flag she may be, to pass with a personage of such consequence.

Savary and Las Cases spent two hours on board the *Bellerophon*, talking and asking questions without pause, in hopes of getting the

---

[2] He had been in possession of an order 'to prevent Bonaparte making his escape in either of the frigates at Ile d'Aix,' since July 7.

Englishman to disclose his plans, or let fall a few revealing words to the Captain of the *Falmouth*, who was present at the interview.

If the Emperor agreed to becoming an exile, they suggested, it was solely through feelings of humanity, for his party was still very formidable, especially in the south and centre of France; if he chose to protract the war, fortune might still turn in his favour and his enemies be caused a great deal of trouble. It was in the interests of England to allow him to proceed to America. Maitland replied:

Supposing the British Government should be induced to grant a passport for Bonaparte's going to America, what pledge could he give that he would not return, and put England, as well as all Europe, to the same expense of blood and treasure that has just been incurred?

Las Cases and Savary expostulated. The Emperor's influence over the French people was a thing of the past; feelings had changed towards him since the return from Elba and he could never regain the ascendancy he had once possessed. He preferred to retire into obscurity, to live forgotten and end his days in peace; moreover, if he were asked to return to the throne, he would firmly refuse.

'If that is the case,' suggested Maitland, rather casually, 'why not seek asylum in England?'

Savary objected that the climate was too damp and cold, it was too near France, and there would be a tendency to involve the Emperor in any possible developments in European politics; also that England had for too long considered him as their most inveterate enemy, as a monster without any human virtues. It was a conversation between deaf men.

To find out what Maitland was really thinking, one must look at his report to Admiral Hotham, written after the French had left: it shows the awkwardness of his position, and his inability to get out of it except by lying in the most cynical manner to Napoleon's envoys:

H.M.S. *Bellerophon*,
off Rochefort,
July 10, 1815.

I send back the *Falmouth* without a moment's loss of time with the accompanying despatches, which I received this morning by a schooner bearing a flag of truce from the hands of the Duc de Rovigo and Count de Las Cases, two of Bonaparte's most attached friends. I likewise send my answer which I have given to gain time, as I do not of course wish that Bonaparte should be aware there are such strict orders concerning him. The two people who brought the letter seem very anxious to convince me that the peace of Europe is concerned in Bonaparte being allowed to depart quietly, and that he will still be enabled to join the army in the centre and south of France and make some stand, and even ventured to throw out a hint that if I refused to give my sanction to the frigates passing that they might endeavour to force their way, to which I replied, 'as far as my power goes I shall do my best to prevent you;' I shall therefore keep as close in as possible to prevent the attempt being made, or if made to frustrate it. . . .

It appears to me from the anxiety of the bearers to get away that they are very hard pushed either by the Government at Paris, or from the approach of the armies. The Duc de Rovigo has again repeated, and wishes to impress me with the idea that Bonaparte's feelings are dictated by the sole desire of preventing any further trouble and warfare, as he says there is a considerable force in the south of France that look to him as their head, and that it is still in his power to put himself at their head and make resistance; he states that it is the Emperor's determination not to move till he has a passport, or a decision negative, when he will provide for himself as best he can. I could give him an answer at once, but think it better you should be acquainted with what is going forward, and at all events it puts beyond a doubt the part of France that requires to be particularly looked after.

Savary, the Duc de Rovigo, has again addressed me with a proposal that, should you agree to Bonaparte going in any way, either in a disarmed frigate or on board an English ship, or in any way, he will be ready to receive proposals at Ile d'Aix, as he thinks that might bring the thing sooner to a termination. All this I feel myself called upon to state, that these officers may not suppose I keep back anything from you, though I am aware the thing cannot be done. Excuse the confusion of this letter as the two Frenchmen are constantly addressing me with new proposals, which all tend to the same thing.[3]

This report, scribbled while Napoleon's envoys were being entertained by encouraging descriptions of the English climate, brings into harsh relief the duplicity of Maitland's behaviour, for in his account to the Admiral of the fugitive's different plans for escape, he was careful not to mention his unexpected proposal to seek asylum in England. The sailor was trying to make use of the famous

---

[3] Maitland did not include this vitally important report in his account of Bonaparte's surrender, no doubt because of the discreditable passages in it.

principle of Wait and See. The only policy enabling him to await the indispensable reinforcements, without committing himself, was to put the anxious Frenchmen off the scent by receiving them courteously, assuring them that he had no news of what was happening in Paris and London, and advising them to wait patiently at the Ile d'Aix for the arrival of a reply that was already known to him by heart, since it had been contained in his secret instructions. A stratagem of war, a procedure which was bound to achieve its end, but by what a means!

When they had come to the end of their arguments, the Frenchmen put to sea again and reached the *Saale* about two o'clock. At the same time Maitland, who was determined to leave nothing to chance and no card unplayed, and who had therefore followed the envoys' boat closely, openly dropped anchor in the Basque Roads in full view of the French frigates: from this position he could spy on their movements and forestall any enterprise.

❖   ❖   ❖

After the emissaries had returned, the rest of that day, July 10, was spent in long and futile discussions about the best course to choose. Bertrand, Las Cases, Gourgaud and Savary were in favour of asking for English hospitality; Montholon and Lallemand were for a return to the army. Napoleon defended himself against the latter by repeating:

'I do not want to be the cause of a single cannon-shot.'

Then it was the turn of Captain Ponée of the *Méduse*,[4] on which General de Montholon had embarked, to make a brave offer:

I will go ahead of the *Saale* under cover of darkness, take *Bellerophon* by surprise as she lies at anchor, grapple with her broadside on, and thus prevent her moving. The engagement might last two hours, and the *Méduse*, being a frigate of sixty guns while the *Bellerophon* has seventy-four, cannot fail to be sunk, but meanwhile the *Saale* could take advantage of the wind off shore that blows every evening, to get away, and the twenty-two gun corvette and advice-boat that made up the rest of the English flotilla would not be able to stop the *Saale*, a frigate of the first rank,

---

[4] Ponée, François (1775–1863). Entered the service in 1794 and had taken part in every campaign during the Directory, Consulate and Empire. The frigate *Méduse*, launched in 1810, was to achieve tragic fame in 1816 by sinking on the Arguin sandbank.

carrying twenty-four guns in batteries and carronades of thirty-six on the bridge.

This was logical reasoning, and Maitland himself was afterwards obliged to recognise that his forces would have been inadequate to prevent the French ships leaving in a body. Preparations for the operation were begun at once and the log of the *Saale* gives us an insight into this final attempt: 'From six o'clock until midnight a good breeze from NNE, fair weather. At half past nine decks were cleared for action and topsails made ready for hoisting. At half past ten the boat that had been sent to Le Chapus arrived alongside with the pilot from that place.' The *Méduse* and the *Saale*, reinforced by the *Épervier* might be lucky enough to surprise the enemy, provided that the secret of their preparations was safely kept.

Alas! on July 11, about noon, a small boat brought two 'respect-able-looking' countrymen to the *Bellerophon*, from the Ile d'Oleron, and they lost no time in telling their story:

A message had been sent from the Ile d'Aix early that morning, for a man who was considered the best pilot on the island for the Maumusson passage, being the only person that had ever taken a frigate through; that a large sum of money had been offered to him to pilot a vessel to sea from that passage, and that it certainly was Bonaparte's intention to escape from thence; either in the corvette, which had moved down some days before, or in a Danish brig, which was then lying at anchor near the en-trance.

Maitland decided to get under weigh immediately and take up his position, with the *Slaney*, between the lighthouses of Ré and Oléron, while the *Myrmidon* anchored in the Maumusson passage.

This manoeuvre was useless, for events were developing fast on board the *Saale*. The gazettes announced Louis XVIII's entry into Paris, and Philibert, who as senior captain was responsible for move-ments of ships in the roadstead, made a sudden change of front, although telling Bertrand that 'out of regard for the Emperor, he would not treat the suggestion made by Captain Ponée and the offi-cers of the *Méduse* as an act of rebellion, but he could not allow it to be spoken of further'. He took refuge behind secret orders received from the Minister for the Navy, dated June 27: 'All warships that may be encountered should be avoided. If forced to engage with them, the frigate on which Napoleon has not embarked will be sacrificed to hold back the enemy, and so give the one on which he is present some means of escaping.' As the other dispatches specified that 'the frigates will get under weigh if the position of the enemy cruisers makes it possible without danger to themselves,' it was clear that the plans of battle foreseen by the Minister were of a purely defensive order, and that the French were not to engage in any action deliberately.

This sudden change gave a new turn to the drama, and Napoleon very naturally ceased to feel at ease on board a ship whose captain might at any moment and without warning rally to Louis XVIII, or simply carry out the orders of the new Minister for the Navy. He therefore decided to send General Lallemand to Le Verdon, to sound Baudin as to the *Bayadère*'s chances, reconnoitring on the way to find out how dangerous the run from Fouras to the Gironde might be. The baggage would be disembarked from the *Saale* at four o'clock and taken to the Ile d'Aix.

It is clear, therefore, that he had abandoned all hope of using the two frigates, and his disembarkation at ten o'clock on the 12th had all the appearance of a farewell, watched with dismay by the crew. Ponée vividly conveys their confusion and resentment: 'Ah, why did he not come on board my ship instead of the *Saale*? I should have got him out, in spite of the blockade. In whose hands was he going to trust himself? Who could have given him such pernicious advice? That nation is all perfidy. Poor Napoleon, you are lost! A horrible presentiment tells me so.'

As Napoleon went down the gangway, the crew drawn up on deck shouted 'Long live the Emperor'. Captain Philibert had been a poor councillor and an unenthusiastic host, but Napoleon showed his royal generosity by giving him a pair of pistols. 'A king's bounty should always be magnificent.'

Maitland's labour was in vain therefore, when on that very same day, already being in control of the Pertuis d'Antioche and the Pertuis de Maumusson, he sent the *Cyrus* to block the last exit, the Pertuis Breton.

Napoleon was not going to fight for his liberty.

✳   ✳   ✳

It was with a certain satisfaction that he set foot on the tiny landing stage on the Ile d'Aix; he felt less of a prisoner here than on the frigate. He walked up the broad street through the little town to the commandant's house, a gloomy grey two-storey edifice, built on his own instructions a few years earlier.[5]

Napoleon occupied a modest room over the front door, but by taking a few steps on the balcony he could see the English squadron insolently tacking to and fro in spite of the 'calms' which had worried the maritime prefect. A walnut bed, mahogany armchairs, some of the typical rush-seated chairs of the Charente, a pedestal table, a fireplace of brown stone, these made up the decor of his last days in France; and to remind him of the passage of time – never before so precious – a small clock with columns.

While he rested upstairs on the rustic bed in its curtained alcove, alone and lulled by the murmur of the wind and surge of the sea, tongues were wagging down below.

Six young naval officers of the fourteenth regiment of marines,[6] were trying to persuade the Grand Marshal to agree to a crazy enterprise: Genty, Doret, Salis, Peltier, Châteauneuf and Montcousu offered to arm the *Zélie*, a chasse-marée or decked whaleboat, and reach the open sea with the Emperor on board; it would then only be necessary to speak to the first merchant vessel they met and get him conveyed to America. An improvised adventure, with nothing attractive about it except the courage, youth and devotion of its promoters. Napoleon wavered, did not at once reject the offer, gave orders for the fragile vessel to be chartered, and discussed the matter with Gourgaud, whose inexhaustible energy and unconditional fidelity he knew well:

His Majesty asked my advice: whether to leave on a little chasse-marée or the Danish brig anchored close to the island, or to surrender to the English. I replied that I dared not let him know my opinion, because so much depended on chance in any case. His Majesty insisted. I told him that in my view it was preferable to surrender to the English nation,

---

[5] In 1808. Sold by the municipality in 1925, and acquired by Baron Gourgaud, a descendant of the Emperor's aide-de-camp, the house was transformed into a museum and bequeathed to the State. Napoleon's room has been preserved as it was.

[6] They were punished by the marine prefect a few weeks later, for openly showing devotion to Napoleon. In 1840, Doret commanded the brig *Oreste*, and was present at the exhumation of the Emperor's body on St. Helena.

among whom he would find admirers, rather than escape on the chasse-marée. The boat would probably be taken, and then the position would be very different, for in that case the Emperor would be thrown into the Tower of London. Perhaps it would be better to try and force the passage with the two frigates, or else reach the *Bayadère*.

However, orders were given for the first stages of the young officers' plan to be carried out: some of the suite, the men only, were to crowd into the chasse-marée, with the baggage and arms, while the women remained on the Ile d'Aix. The *Zélie*, the humble barque destined to convey Caesar and his fortune, was prepared for the glorious and unexpected role that had fallen to her; the helmsman put on board compass, hour-glass, octant, maps, log-book and signals, as well as 'three mattresses and bedding;' the sail-maker his foresail, mizzen top gallant and thread; the master-at-arms, six pistols and 154 rifles; the ship's steward 240 litres of brandy, wine, firewood, cheese, beans and mustard, soup cubes and kegs of sorrel, candles and biscuits. A filibuster's outfit for the former master of the most splendid throne in Europe.

That evening the first white flags began timidly appearing on the walls and church-towers of La Rochelle, and the *Bellerophon* insolently penetrated the Basque Roads to greet them with a royal salvo, 'flying the Bourbon colours at her masthead'.

On the morning of the 13th, Napoleon was surprised to see his brother Joseph arriving; in his capacity as Grand Master of the Grand Lodge of France, he had taken refuge with a local freemason, whom he had asked to charter a ship for him at Bordeaux. According to some, the ex-king of Spain had come to persuade his brother to sail with him for America,[7] according to others he offered to pass himself off as the Emperor and give himself up to the English squadron, while Napoleon escaped on the Danish vessel. At all events, he was very much opposed to the plan of the Emperor's surrendering to the English, and more in favour of a return to the army.

Napoleon embraced his brother; though he had often quarrelled with Joseph or treated him with sarcasm, he was now making up for the frivolities and errors of his public life. Napoleon thanked him for an offer that was difficult to accept because it did not conform to

[7] Joseph reached his destination without difficulty, under the assumed identity of Monsieur Bouchard.

his slightly theatrical notions of his own grandeur, and made his brother concentrate on his own escape, and get to Bordeaux without a moment's delay.

Maitland, lying at anchor at three miles distance from the frigates, seemed to have guessed what was going on at Ile d'Aix, and grew impatient; to make sure of getting the credit for a capture for which others might be tempted to compete, he sent a report directly to Lord Keith:

> H.M.S. *Bellerophon*,
> At sea,
> July 13, 1815.

I send for your information the copy of a letter I received on the 10th inst. by the hands of the Duc de Rovigo and the Count Las Cases, together with my answer, both of which I have already transmitted to Sir Henry Hotham. Having since received information from the shore that it was the intention of Bonaparte to escape by the Maumusson Passage either in the corvette lying there or in a Danish brig, I have directed the *Daphne* and *Myrmidon* to anchor off that passage, the *Cyrus* is stationed off the Pertuis de Breton, while this ship and the *Nancy* are either at anchor in the roads or under way between the lighthouses. I trust therefore it will be impracticable for him to escape by either of the passages.

Maitland wrote confidently, and yet . . . General Lallemand, returning from the Gironde, walked straight into the interview between the Emperor and King Joseph. He was optimistic, for Baudin had assured him that he was ready to take the Emperor to the ends of the earth, either in the *Bayadère*, or in an American vessel offered him by the United States consul. The conversation grew animated, everyone gave his advice, expressed his doubts, and there was 'a great deal of mysterious palaver,' as Gourgaud described it.

As Joseph's successful voyage clearly proves, Napoleon's safety depended on his making the right choice, but it was necessary to act quickly and discreetly, and get rid of his clamorous little Court, for Baudin was not prepared to take them. Napoleon could not be persuaded, whether from fear of attempting the voyage from Fouras to Bordeaux under uncertain conditions, or from dislike of abandoning to the Bourbons those of his officers who had stuck with him to the end, and of openly opposing Beker, whose task it was to see that the fugitive did not again set foot on French soil.

At this crucial moment, without will of his own, pushed this way and that, and besieged by complaints and requests, he once again hoped that destiny would give him some sign, hesitated between one course and another and waited for the British to make the first move. He had forgotten that the fate of a battle is decided in an instant. . . .

Long hours were spent in conversation with members of his suite, as Gourgaud describes in his *Souvenirs*. Napoleon still talked about the United States, and said that history would not be able to reproach him for trying to preserve his liberty by going to America. Gourgaud told him that if he were captured by the English, he would be harshly treated.

He assured me that in that case he would show that he was master of his fate, he would kill himself. 'No,' I said to him, 'Your Majesty could not do that. At Mont-Saint-Jean, perhaps; but now it is impossible. A gambler kills himself. A great man faces adversity.' The Emperor interrupted me, saying that last night he had had the idea of surrendering to the English squadron, and writing when he arrived there: 'Like Themistocles, I do not want to take part in the destruction of my country, and I have come to ask you for asylum,' but that he could not make up his mind to it. At this moment a little bird flew in at the window, and I cried: 'It's a sign of good fortune!' I caught the bird in my hand and Napoleon said: 'There are quite enough unfortunates, let it go'. I obeyed and the Emperor went on: 'Let us read the omens!' The bird flew to the right, and I exclaimed: 'It is flying towards the English squadron, Sire!'

Then the Emperor went back to the subject of his conversation, and assured me that if he felt bored in the United States he could always jump into a carriage and drive for a thousand leagues, and that he did not believe anyone would suppose he would ever return to Europe. Then he talked of the Danish boat: 'Rubbish! It could well take five of us. So you shall come with me.'

After dinner, at about ten o'clock, Beker – who was in favour of departure, so that he could be rid of an awkward mission and return to the capital where there were posts going abegging, came and informed Napoleon that all was in readiness, Besson was only waiting for his passenger to say the word. No reply. The General withdrew, intimidated and in silence, and rejoined the group collected in the ground floor room and the garden. After what seemed to them all an interminable interval, the Grand Marshal ventured upstairs in his turn; it was nearly midnight, and before he had time to ask a single question, Napoleon said to him quickly, in a low voice and as if speaking to himself:

'It is always dangerous to trust to one's enemies, but better to take the risk of trusting to their honour than to be a lawful prisoner in their hands. Say that I will not embark and that I shall spend the night here.'[8]

The clock let fall twelve chimes; these were his last hours of his life as a free man. The choice had at last been made, and while he issued orders to Lallemand and Las Cases to go to the *Bellerophon* early next morning, he was already revolving in his mind suitable phrases with which to bring so great a reign to an end, and give his insensate gesture the flavour of one of Corneille's tragedies: 'I come, like Themistocles. . . .'

✤   ✤   ✤

At dawn on July 14, the officer of the watch on the *Bellerophon* reported that a French boat, flying a flag of truce, was making for the ship: Las Cases and Lallemand[9] had come to carry out their historic mission. Desiring to have a witness present, Maitland signalled for the captain of the *Slaney*, Captain Sartorius, to join him as soon as possible.

Las Cases opened the conversation by asking for a reply to the Grand Marshal's letter concerning safe-conducts, and Maitland said ingenuously that he had received no news from the Admiral, but was expecting him to arrive at any moment: not a muscle of his face betrayed his lie.

'If that was the only reason you had for sending off a flag of truce,' he said curtly, 'it was quite unnecessary, as I informed you when last here that the Admiral's answer, when it arrived, should be forwarded to the frigates by one of the *Bellerophon*'s boats; and I do not approve of frequent communications with an enemy by means of flags of truce.'

[8] According to Gourgaud, Napoleon was doubtful whether he would succeed in getting away: 'At eight o'clock the Duc de Rovigo returned; he reported that the officers who were to man the chasse-marée were beginning to be tired of waiting; they said it would be very difficult to get by once the British had got their ships under weigh.' The prospect of being captured in such a wretched boat must have disgusted Napoleon.

[9] By a curious coincidence, Lallemand had been taken prisoner by Maitland on the *Cameleon* during the Egyptian campaign.

He then ordered breakfast to be served, to give Captain Sartorius time to be rowed to the *Bellerophon*. The witness arrived and the meal was eaten, after which Las Cases again returned to the attack: the Emperor wished to avoid all bloodshed, he would proceed to America in any way sanctioned by the British Government, either on a French ship, a vessel carrying only half its guns, or even on a British warship.

'I have no authority to agree to any arrangements of that sort,' Maitland replied, 'nor do I believe my Government would consent to it; but I think I may venture to receive him into this ship, and convey him to England: if, however, he adopts that plan, I cannot enter into any promise as to the reception he may meet with, as, even in the case I have mentioned, I shall be acting on my own responsibility, and cannot be sure that it would meet with the approbation of the British Government.'

This, at least, is his own version of the conversation. Pressed by the French, who tried to extract some sort of moral guarantee from him, and consumed by a desire to lay hands on Bonaparte under cover of military secrecy, he let fall some words which were to be cruelly belied by the facts: 'He added', reported Las Cases, 'that in his private opinion (and several other captains who were present agreed with him), Napoleon would find all the respect and good treatment he could wish for in England; in that country, the sovereign and his ministers did not exercise the same arbitrary control as on the continent; that in generosity of feeling and liberality of opinions the English people were superior to the throne itself.'

Yet Maitland had known ever since July 8 that the passports were refused, and that his chief, Admiral Hotham, had orders for the disposal of the fugitive, who was to be brought to Quiberon Bay. . . . And Maitland went further still in his hypocritical encouragement: when Lallemand asked whether London would hand over to Louis XVIII any of Napoleon's companions who arrived with him on the *Bellerophon*, he said emphatically that such an idea was inconceivable, 'in view of the circumstances of the arrangement we had been speaking about'.

Then the conversation moved on to Lucien Bonaparte's enforced stay in England,[10] and the respect with which he was treated in

---

[10] Captured by a British cruiser in 1810, when on his way to the United States, Lucien Bonaparte had lived in a country house he had bought near Worcester, under the supervision of a single police inspector.

adversity at Thorngrove; this time, Maitland thought it best to be non-committal, and, although he knew perfectly well that Napoleon could not expect to enjoy the same sort of tranquillity in an English country-house, he repeated that he could not vouch for what sort of reception he would have in England; but, being still haunted by the problem of secrecy, he was careful not to mention the precautions decreed by the Admiralty for the isolation of the ex-sovereign as soon as he arrived on the English coast – measures that did not augur favourably for what was to follow.

As the two Frenchmen were about to leave the *Bellerophon*, Maitland casually asked Las Cases where the Emperor was at that moment.

'At Rochefort; I left him there yesterday evening.'

'The Emperor is at the Hotel in the Grand Place,' elaborated Lallemand, 'and is now so popular there that the inhabitants assemble every evening to get a glimpse of him and shout "Vive l'Empereur!"'

'Under all the circumstances,' added Las Cases just as he was leaving, 'I have little doubt that you will see the Emperor on board the *Bellerophon*.'

When he recorded this remark in his book, published in 1826, Maitland made the point that Napoleon must have determined on his step before the visit of Las Cases and Lallemand, because the letter to the Prince Regent, which was brought to him soon afterwards, was written on July 13. This assertion is open to doubt; it is true that the letter ends: 'Rochefort, July 13, 1815',[11] but it was written after the return of the envoys,[12] and it is therefore permissible to believe that since on July 13 and 14 Napoleon still had means of possible escape at his disposal, it was Maitland's encouragements that led him to choose the 'terrible hospitality of the *Bellerophon*,' and hand himself over to the generosity of the Prince Regent's ministers.

The two emissaries arrived back at the Ile d'Aix at eleven o'clock and were present at a final council, where everyone, according to Las Cases, 'was agreed to go on board the English ships'. The Grand

[11] The original is the property of the British Crown and is preserved at Windsor. It bears the date July 13, as can be seen from the accompanying reproduction, due to the courtesy of Her Majesty Queen Elizabeth, and this should settle the discussion there has been on this detail.

[12] Gourgaud: *Journal*, July 14, 1815.

Marshal, Savary and Las Cases were in favour of an aide-de-camp going ahead and taking the letter to the Prince Regent to England: they were labouring under a delusion as to their master's position! For form's sake, the different solutions that had been proposed were once more examined: the chasse-marées might have difficulty in getting out of the channels, and this left no alternative except a landing at Fouras and a return to the army, or English hospitality. This last plan aroused vain imaginings, with which Las Cases was already comforting himself: 'As soon as we go on board the *Bellerophon* we shall be on British soil; the English will be from that moment bound by the sacred rules of hospitality – held sacred even among barbarians; from that moment we shall be governed by the civil laws of that country; the English will not be so indifferent to their glory as to let slip the golden opportunity, but seize it eagerly.'

This recently created chamberlain did not know that if French politics had for the last ten years moved with an impetuosity betraying military influence, British diplomacy had been dictated by the figures of the national debt, and that London financiers would make Bonaparte pay with interest for the sacrifices the British had made to arm Europe.

There would be no return to the Ile d'Aix.

✤   ✤   ✤

While the Grand Marshal hurried away to give orders for embarking next day at dawn, Napoleon showed Gourgaud the draft of his letter to the Prince Regent, which Bertrand was to copy; Gourgaud exclaimed that it 'brought tears to his eyes'.

Your Royal Highness,
    Exposed to the factions which distract my country and to the enmity of the greatest powers of Europe, I have ended my political career, and I come, like Themistocles, to throw myself on the hospitality of the British people; I put myself under the protection of their laws, which I claim from Your Royal Highness as the most powerful, the most constant, and the most generous of my enemies.

Napoleon.
Rochefort, July 13, 1815.

Gourgaud was to go as ambassador, bearing this romantic appeal

9

from the vanquished to the conqueror, and Las Cases was to take a copy to Maitland with a letter from General Bertrand:

The Count de Las Cases has given an account to the Emperor of the conversation he had on board your ship this morning. His Majesty will proceed on board your ship with the ebb tide tomorrow morning, between four and five o'clock. I send you the Count de Las Cases, Councillor of State performing the function of Maréchal de Logis, with a list of persons making up his Majesty's suite.[13] If, as a result of the request you forwarded to him, the Admiral should send the safe-conduct for the United States, His Majesty will go there with pleasure; but in the absence of a safe-conduct he will willingly proceed to England as a private individual, there to enjoy the protection of the laws of your country.

His Majesty has dispatched General Baron Gourgaud to the Prince Regent with a letter, a copy of which I have the honour to enclose, requesting that you will forward it to the minister to whom you may send this officer, so that he may have the honour of delivering the letter with which he is charged to the Prince Regent.

The Grand Marshal
Comte Bertrand.

Las Cases and Gourgaud, accompanied by an usher, a page and a footman, arrived on board the British ship at about seven o'clock. Maitland, his suspicions aroused, said point-blank:

[13] List of persons comprising the Emperor's suite:

Generals: Lieutenant-General Count Bertrand, Grand Marshal; Lieutenant-General the Duc de Rovigo; Lieutenant-General Baron Lallemand, aide-de-camp; Brigadier-General Count de Montholon, aide-de-camp; Count de Las Cases, Councillor of State; General Gourgaud.

Ladies: Countess Bertrand; Countess de Montholon.

Children: Three children of Countess Bertrand, one child of Countess de Montholon.

Officers: Lieutenant-Colonel de Planat; Lieutenant-Colonel Resigny; Lieutenant-Colonel Schultz; Captain Autric; Captain Mesener; Captain Piontkowski; Lieutenant Rivière; Second-Lieutenant Sainte-Catherine; M. Maingault, surgeon to His Majesty; M. de Las Cases, page.

Service of the chamber: M. Marchand, head valet; M. Gillis, valet; M. Saint-Denis, valet; M. Noverraz, valet; M. Denis, page of the wardrobe.

Livery: M. Archambaud, Olivier, footman; M. Gaudron, footman; M. Gentilini, footman; M. Archambaud, Achille, footman; M. Joseph, footman; M. Le Charron, footman; M. Lisiaux, pantry man; M. Orsini, footman; M. Fumeau, footman; M. Santini, usher; M. Chauvin, usher; M. Rousseau, lamplighter.

Food service: M. Fontain, major-domo (or Totain); M. Cipriani, steward; M. Pierron, chef; M. La Fosse, cook; M. Le Page, cook.

Servants of persons accompanying His Majesty: Two Lady's-maids of Countess Bertrand; one Lady's maid of Countess de Montholon; one valet of the Duc de Rovigo; one valet of the Comte de Montholon; one footman of Count Bertrand.

'It is impossible you could have been at Rochefort, and returned, since you left me this morning.'

'It was not necessary,' explained Las Cases; 'I found the Emperor at the Ile d'Aix on my arrival there.'

After reading the letters, Maitland eagerly declared that he would receive the Emperor on board his ship, and that he would send General Gourgaud to England at once, in the *Slaney*. Was he to be authorised to go on shore with the appeal to the Prince Regent? Opinions differ concerning this important point. Maitland said afterwards that he had told Las Cases that Gourgaud 'would not be allowed to land until permission was received from London, or the sanction of the Admiral at the port he might arrive at obtained.' Gourgaud, for his part, maintained that: 'Captain Maitland and his two officers did not appear to doubt that I should be at once sent to London.' Somewhat vain, and eager to shine and cut a figure, the first aide-de-camp was quite infatuated with having a mission unprecedented in history, and put the special instructions dictating his conduct into his portfolio with an ambassadorial air:

My aide-de-camp Gourgaud will proceed to the British squadron with the Comte de Las Cases. He will leave in the advice-boat dispatched by the Commanding Officer of that squadron either to the Admiral or to London. He will try to obtain an audience of the Prince Regent and deliver my letter. If there appears to be no objection to granting me passports to go to the United States, that is what I would prefer; but I do not wish to go to any colony. Failing America, I prefer England to any other country. I will take the name of Colonel Muiron.[14] If I must go to England, I wish to live in a country house, about ten or twelve leagues from London, and I hope to arrive there in the strictest possible incognito. I should need a big enough house to accommodate all my suite. I desire to avoid London, and this will accord with the views of the British Government. If ministers wish to attach a British commissioner to me, they will take care that this gives no impression of servitude.

The corvette *Slaney* therefore prepared to convey Gourgaud to England, and the General was all impatience to deliver the letter from His Majesty the Emperor of the French to His Royal Highness the Prince Regent. Maitland avows that he profited by these last minutes to repeat his previous warnings:

14 Bonaparte's aide-de-camp, killed beside him at Arcole.

'Monsieur Las Cases, you will recollect that I am not authorised to stipulate as to the reception of Bonaparte in England, but that he must consider himself entirely at the disposal of His Royal Highness the Prince Regent.'

The Englishman has often been blamed for not having explained to the French that his orders to Captain Sartorius were that the letter to the Regent should simply be entrusted to the first lieutenant of the *Slaney*. This interpretation, greatly to the taste of Maitland's detractors, depends on a translator's error many times repeated: it was his own dispatch, a report to the Lords of the Admiralty written in haste, that Sartorius was to take to London, and either the Lords or the Admiral at the port of arrival were to decide what reception should be given to Gourgaud.

As briefly as possible, for time was short, the Captain of the *Bellerophon* described the circumstances of a surrender that he was beginning to think of as a capture made by himself:

The Count Las Cases and General Lallemand this day came on board His Majesty's ship under my command, with a proposal from Count Bertrand for me to receive on board Napoleon Bonaparte, for the purpose of throwing himself on the generosity of the Prince Regent. Conceiving myself authorised by their Lordships' secret order, I have acceded to the proposal, and he is to embark on board this ship tomorrow morning. That no misunderstanding might arise, I have explicitly and clearly explained to Count Las Cases that I have no authority whatever for granting terms of any sort, but that all I can do is to carry him and his suite to England, to be received in such a manner as His Royal Highness may deem expedient.

As soon as the optimistic Gourgaud had been transferred to the *Slaney*, Maitland began making arrangements to accommodate the fifty French who made up 'Boney's escort'; thirty-three would travel on board the *Bellerophon* and seventeen on the *Myrmidon*. Preparations continued in all haste until one o'clock in the morning. Maitland's second-in-command, Andrew Mott, was permanently on the alert. 'All was expectation and excitement', notes a witness of the night's events, Midshipman George Home. 'The first lieutenant was engaged seeing all the belaying pins get an extra polish, and that every rope was coiled down with more than usual care, while every hush from the shore, or speck on the water, was listened to and watched with intense anxiety, lest our prey should escape us.'

✤   ✤   ✤

Napoleon spent his last night in France in the commandant's house on the Ile d'Aix – a short night, for he had asked to be woken soon after midnight. The decision he had so blindly left to fate was now forced upon him, and any delay might expose him to his adversaries' schemes.

In Paris Talleyrand and Fouché were straining every nerve to hasten the capture of the 'Usurper,' vying with each other in their newly assumed royalism.

Talleyrand, now President of the Council and Minister for Foreign Affairs, had placed an expert in changing sides at the Admiralty, the Count de Jaucourt; a colonel under Louis XVI, deputy to the Legislative Assembly and member of the Tribunate, chamberlain to King Joseph, this noble weathercock later rallied to Louis-Philippe, and (in his nineties) to Louis Napoleon.

In 1815 he was merely an aristocrat, anxious that people should forget his behaviour during the Revolution and his functions with the 'Usurper's' family; anything could be expected of such a man, he nevertheless managed to surprise everyone.

Hardly was he installed in his ministry on July 10, than he sent secret instructions to Bonnefoux, with the idea of blockading the former sovereign in Rochefort Roads: 'You ought to have opposed any attempt at a landing on Napoleon's part . . . and any attempt at communicating with English ships. . . . I confirm the information that Napoleon is on board the *Saale*, Captain Philibert. I formally add to this that Napoleon must, on no pretext whatever, leave the frigate on which he has embarked.'

Eager to give 'the people of France a great moral lesson',[15] the Allies were preparing for a last effort. Even while they were occupied in looting the treasures of the Tuileries with bayonets fixed, billeting their troops under conditions that made the French pain-

---

[15] Wellington to Castlereagh, dispatch No. 997, September 23, 1815.

fully aware of the defeat of their armies,[16] levying ten millions towards the cost of the war, and occupying the provinces with more
than a million men, the conquerors' representatives did not lose
interest in Bonaparte's fate. On July 8, Castlereagh was careful to
emphasise to Lord Liverpool: 'I understand from the King this
evening, that he had given orders to Fouché to use every exertion to
arrest Bonaparte.'

Fouché did his utmost to avoid hostility from Louis XVIII's
followers. Having been the author of the earlier instructions, broad-
cast by Decrès, he had no difficulty at all in picking up the business
where he had left it, when the enemy's arrival had driven the Executive Commission from the Tuileries.

When Jaucourt took over from Decrès, he made a point of going
through the papers in company with John Croker, secretary to the
British Admiralty, who had come to Paris with Lord Castlereagh –
the latter was extremely annoyed that Fouché had not arrested
Bonaparte instead of letting him escape to the Ile d'Aix. Although
he had no legal authority, since he received orders from the Lords of
the Admiralty, Croker, under pressure from Castlereagh, sent a dispatch on the same day to Admiral Hotham, cruising off Quiberon,
which was to be entrusted to the officer charged by Jaucourt with the
task of apprehending Bonaparte – Captain de Rigny. After describing
the position of French ships in the Basque Roads, as given him
by the French Minister, Croker set forth a detailed plan of capture:

I understand also, from the French Minister of Marine, that the British
squadron in that neighbourhood consists of two or three ships of the line
and two or three frigates; and as in some communications I had with Lord
Keith on the subject before I left England, his Lordship assured me that
his attention had been directed to Rochefort, I cannot doubt that, except
under some very extraordinary circumstances, the escape of Bonaparte's
squadron, or of any vessel from the Charente is impossible; but as it is for
obvious reasons of very great importance that the question with regard to
this person should be brought to a decision as speedily as possible, Lord
Castlereagh wishes you to consult confidentially with the officer of His
Most Christian Majesty, who is the bearer of this letter, and to afford him

[16] Each Prussian soldier's bed had to possess one pillow, a mattress, a blanket and two
linen sheets; his ration must consist of two pounds of bread, a pound of meat, a bottle of
wine, butter, rice, brandy and tobacco. Each householder must take not less than ten
soldiers. Hatred has never been more exacting.

your most cordial assistance in all practicable measures he may be disposed to recommend for the capture of Bonaparte.

The plan which has struck his Lordship and the French Minister as being most likely to succeed, and will be suggested to the French officer is as follows: If it be ascertained that Bonaparte is certainly embarked in Aix-roads, it may be concluded that he is, as he thinks, sure of the governor and garrison of the forts which protect the anchorage; and as these forts are very considerable, I entertain little hope that you could think yourself justified in expecting to reduce them, or capture Bonaparte while lying under their full and active protection. . . .

It is therefore expedient that before you proceed to attack the ships, you should send a flag of truce to the governor of the Ile d'Aix, to say that 'by the King of France's express commands you are about to seize the person of the common enemy; that you have no hostile intentions against the ships or subjects of His Most Christian Majesty, but on the contrary look upon them as allies so long as they do not oppose the King's authority; that you do not mean to capture or injure the French ships, or to interfere with them beyond the mere seizure of Bonaparte's person, except so far as their own opposition may make it necessary'. . . . And you may add, 'that the French Government has assured you that the King will consider the death of any British sailor employed in the execution of his commands as a murder, of which the governor of the garrison from which that shot may proceed will be held guilty.' This notice on your part will be accompanied by an order from the King to the same effect; and as soon after they shall have been delivered to the governor as may be possible, it seems expedient that you should commence the attack, as it would be desirable not to give the influence of Bonaparte's remonstrance time to operate on that officer's mind. . . . If, however, you should find it impracticable with any prospect of success to attack the ships, or if having attacked them you should not find it expedient to continue the engagement, you will of course continue the blockade with the greatest rigour; and if you should require any increase of force, you may either draw something from the neighbourhood of Brest, or write to Lord Keith by one of your own cruisers.

If Bonaparte or the governor of the fort, or commander of the squadron for him, should propose to surrender on terms, Lord Castlereagh is of opinion that you should reply that you are not authorised to enter into any engagement of that nature; and that your orders are to seize the persons of Bonaparte and his family, and to hold them for the disposal of the allied Powers unconditionally. . . .

Such then were the Allies' true intentions, dictated as usual by His Britannic Majesty's ministers. In spite of Croker's anxiety as to how the Lords of the Admiralty would receive his plan,[17] it is easy to guess that neither the London Cabinet, nor Louis XVIII's Government would have deplored a naval engagement, and the disappearance of both the frigate and its troublesome passenger beneath the waves.

This fine plan failed as a result of a few hours delay, for on the morning of July 15, when Napoleon was preparing to go to the *Bellerophon*, Captain de Rigny was still several leagues from Rochefort. As for Bonnefoux, called upon to play a leading part in the capture in his capacity as maritime prefect, whatever repugnance he might feel for playing the policeman, he had to reckon with the zeal of the new prefect of the department, the Baron Richard, a former member of the Convention, regicide and friend of Fouché, who was anxious to expunge his compromising past and give proofs of loyalty to the rightful King. On receipt of the instructions brought by Richard, Bonnefoux could only fall back on the caprices of the weather, ironically enough, to save him from a degrading complicity in the capture of his former sovereign. In so far as it was preferable to be a captive on board the *Bellerophon* rather than in the King of France's prison, the Emperor owed his safety to the accidents of the tides, cleverly exploited by Bonnefoux.

The maritime prefect did not in fact arrive on board the *Saale* until two in the morning, having waited for the ebb-tide before he took his seat in his smart launch at Rochefort; he knew perfectly well that Napoleon was at the Ile d'Aix and that this delay would give him time to take to the sea. He communicated his instructions to Philibert and sent a copy to Beker on the Ile d'Aix, giving him to understand that after this two hours delay he could no longer be responsible for the Emperor's safe-keeping. Although he did not yet know the terms of the letter from the new Minister of Marine, which Rigny was bringing along with Croker's, he had guessed at its drift. Jaucourt's envoy had only to set foot on the *Saale* for the Emperor's fate to be sealed by the French themselves.[18]

❖　　❖　　❖

Bonnefoux's warning became known on the Ile d'Aix just when Napoleon had finished dressing, and Marchand was helping him

---

[17] See Appendix 2.

[18] See Appendix 1. Instructions from the Minister of Marine to the captain of the *Saale*.

into his legendary attire – the green colonel's uniform with red lapels and the little hat with its tricolour cockade.

Between two and three o'clock in the morning all the members of his suite except the generals who were to escort him had taken their places in the launches plying between the jetty and the brig *Épervier*, which was to convey the Emperor to his new destiny under a flag of truce. With apparent indifference, Napoleon descended the wooden ladder and came out into full daylight, somewhat as he used to appear in an encampment in the middle of the night, booted and gloved, to make a reconnaisance. But this time no rolling drums announced His Majesty, the Emperor and King; he was Napoleon Bonaparte, posing for an Epinal engraving.

The silent population of the Ile d'Aix peered through the light of dawn, searching for the familiar figure; the frail boat bobbed on the waves, the oarsmen pulled together, it was three o'clock in the morning.

The crew of the *Épervier* shouted 'Long live the Emperor', while her captain, Jourdan de la Passadière, stood saluting at the gangway; Napoleon walked along the ranks and spoke to the officers. Then General Beker came forward, showing it is true greater emotion than the situation called for, and asked whether the Emperor would like to be escorted as far as the *Bellerophon*.

'Don't do anything of the kind. We must think of France; I am going on board of my own free will. If you came with me, they would be sure to say that you handed me over to the English. I do not want to leave France under the weight of such an accusation.'

He preferred to arrive on board the British ship without the representative of the former Executive Commission at his heels, the better to emphasise the freedom of his choice. Beker was not unmoved by the nobility of this speech, and he could not conceal his tears when Napoleon held out his hand to him.

'Embrace me, General; thank you for all the trouble you have taken; I regret that I did not get to know you sooner, I would have attached you to me personally.'

'Goodbye, Sire, be happier than we are.'[19]

[19] Human nature being as it is, Beker afterwards solicited the Grand Cross of the Legion of Honour from Louis XVIII. He was a peer of France and a Chevalier of Saint Louis under Charles X. Louis-Philippe at last bestowed the coveted decoration on him. It had been merely a matter of survival!

On board the *Épervier*, Napoleon was just as much at ease as if he had been going to take part in a naval review; he chatted to the captain, and asked him what were the chances of forcing the British blockade and what sort of hospitality his enemies would offer him. Jourdan was frankness itself: according to him the Emperor should have tried to get through, and was wrong to trust Maitland.

'It is too late. They expect me; I am going.'

Then he rejoined his officers and dropped on to a seat next to Madame de Montholon. Since he left Malmaison, this man who used to talk dogmatically and in a loud voice, demolishing frontiers with a word, had expressed himself only in monotonous phrases, as if to break an awkward silence. Now he passed his hand over the lapel of his uniform and asked the Countess:

'Is it blue or green?'

'Green, Sire.'

He gazed at the cloth in silence and listened to the sound of the brig labouring through the waves. The sun was rising, feebly lighting up the coast and accentuating the pallor of those anxious faces. So this was defeat: what an experience and what a lesson for a conqueror, who although of humble origin, had developed certain ideas of a sovereign's grandeur and imperial dignity, and was now reduced by repudiation, treason and inertia to an outlaw voyaging into exile in a cockle-shell! Such may have been his thoughts, while the peaceful, swelling bulk of the *Bellerophon* stood against the pale morning sky; but it was surely a dramatic moment for his legend. 'No boat had been charged with such a destiny since that which carried Caesar.'

He asked for some coffee and a cup was served him on the capstan; then he paced the bridge, inquiring about the wind, the ship's progress, how much water she drew; what guns she carried, almost as if he were unaware that every tack brought him closer to the end of his liberty.

'Where was she built?'

'At Bayonne, Sire.'

'Is the dam at Bayonne finished yet?'

'No, Sire.'

'What a lot of things were ordered but never carried out!'

Perched on a chest, he surveyed the horizon through his field-glasses, and caught sight of the tricolour still flying on the shore and the island of Oléron. The wind was from the west and the *Épervier* made slow progress; at about six o'clock a ship flying the British Admiral's flag was observed in the distance.

On board the *Bellerophon*, where excitement was rising and each man was swelling with importance, Napoleon's approach produced as much agitation as if the decks were being cleared for action. Maitland had been scrutinising the ocean, and fiddling nervously with his spy-glass; he suddenly stifled an oath. While the *Épervier* was battling against wind and tide, a ship silhouetted on the horizon was approaching with a favourable breeze. The *Superb*, flying the standard of Rear-Admiral Sir Henry Hotham, might well arrive in time to claim the lion's share.

Midshipman George Home, who had just left the watch, renounced sleep rather than miss the spectacle.[20] 'Captain Maitland . . . gave immediate orders to hoist out the barge, and dispatched her under the command of the First lieutenant to the French brig, being apprehensive that if the Admiral arrived before the brig got out, that Napoleon would deliver himself up to the Admiral instead of us, and thus have lost us so much honour.'

The English boat was commanded by Andrew Mott, 'the best upper-deck officer in the Navy'; as he did not understand a word of French, the Countess Bertrand acted as interpreter when he arrived on the deck of the French vessel. Napoleon asked him how long the voyage from the Basque Roads to the English coast would take.

'Eight days.'

There was a silence, then Napoleon turned to the ladies:

'Well, mesdames, do you feel able to reach the English ship?'

He thanked the captain and crew of the *Épervier* and was the last to descend into Mott's barge, cheered by the sailors on the brig; his gaze drifted among those deeply moved faces, and then over the ship, the order for whose laying down he had probably signed; absentmindedly he plunged his hand into some fresh water and sprinkled the hull several times. A farewell or a benediction? No-one will ever know, nor what thoughts filled his mind as he staked his all and gave himself up to a mere captain in the Royal Navy.

Someone thought they heard him murmur: 'All my life I have sacrificed everything – tranquillity, advantages, happiness – to my destiny. I am a man condemned to live.'

[20] George Home: *Memoirs of an aristocrat.*

IX

HOSPITALITY ON THE *BELLEROPHON*

✦✦

Maitland's welcome – Admiral Hotham – Goodbye to
France – Life on board – Arrival in England – Security
measures.

✦✦

Midshipman Home was all eyes and ears.

A general's guard of marines was ordered aft on the quarter-deck, and
the boatswain stood, whistle in hand, ready to do the honours of the side.
The lieutenants stood grouped first on the quarter-deck, and we more
humble middys behind them, while the Captain, evidently in much
anxiety, kept trudging backwards and forwards between the gangway and
his own cabin, sometimes peeping out at one of the quarter-deck ports to
see if the barge was drawing near.... A young midshipman ... walked
very demurely up to Manning, the boatswain, who was standing all importance at the gangway, and after comically eying his squat figure and
bronzed countenance, gently laid hold of his whiskers. ...

'Manning,' says he most sentimentally, 'this is the proudest day of your
life; you are this day to do the honours of the side to the greatest man the
world ever produced or ever will produce.'

Here the boatswain eyed him with proud delight.

'And along with the great Napoleon, the name of Manning the boatswain of the *Bellerophon* will go down to the latest posterity; and as a
relict of that great man, permit me, my dear Manning, to preserve a lock
of your hair.'

Here he made an infernal tug at the boatswain's immense whisker, and
fairly carried away a part of it, making his way through the crowd and down
below with the speed of an arrow.

The barge was now alongside and Maitland leaned over and asked
the first lieutenant anxiously: 'Have you got him?'

Mott answered in the affirmative, as he came up the side four steps
at a time. He was followed by Savary, and then Bertrand, who bowed
and said, falling back a pace: 'The Emperor is in the boat.'

Napoleon climbed slowly, panting a little; all the English followed him with their eyes. 'And now came the little great man himself, wrapped up in his grey overcoat buttoned to the chin, three-cocked hat and Hussar boots, without any sword, I suppose as emblematical of his changed condition.'[1] As the colours had not been hoisted the guard received him without honours; only the piercing sound of Manning's whistle was heard, and then Maitland saw Napoleon come forward, raise his hat and say in a confident tone:

'I am come to throw myself on the protection of your Prince and Laws.'

Instead of having him arrested on the spot and locked into a well-guarded cabin, in accordance with his orders, which would have revealed British intentions towards their prisoner, Maitland bowed and offered to show his guest the cabin on the poop set aside for him. As he went, Napoleon saluted the officers drawn up and smiled at them; with all the enthusiasm of eighteen, Home noted in his diary: 'Now have I a tale for futurity.'

'This is a handsome cabin,' said Napoleon pleasantly, as he looked round.

'Such as it is, Sir, it is at your service while you remain on board the ship I command.'

Noticing a portrait on the wall Napoleon asked: 'Who is that young lady?'

'My wife.'

'Ah, she is very young and very pretty.'

He had resumed his royal manner and his self-possession now that he was free of the torments that had preceded his final decision; once again he was the leader who wanted to see everything and know everything. Questions followed one another: where was Maitland born? Where had he served? Could Napoleon meet the officers, hear about their conditions of service, and inspect the ship? To this last request, Maitland objected that it was still very early, and cleaning was only done after breakfast. A quarter of an hour later Napoleon repeated his request, and Maitland did the honours; the orderly and well-kept appearance of everything made a great impression, but it was the fine bearing of the sailors that surprised the Emperor most.

[1] The Emperor carried his sword beneath his overcoat, unlike English officers who wore their weapon over it.

They were surely a different class of people from the French; and that
he thought it was owing to them we were always victorious at sea. I answered, 'I must beg leave to differ with you: I do not wish to take from the
merit of our men; but my own opinion is, that perhaps we owe our advantage to the superior experience of the officers; and I believe the French
seamen, if taken as much pains with, would look as well as ours.' . . . 'I
believe you are right,' said he . . .'Your laws are either more severe or
better administered than ours; there are many instances of French officers
having conducted themselves ill in battle, without my being able to punish
them as they deserved.'

There followed a long conversation about the artillery, in the
course of which the Emperor asked about the weight of iron carried
on every deck, disapproved of the mixture of different calibres and
praised the English system of practice firing with powder and shot,
finally putting a question that his eager desire for enlightenment had
not yet resolved:

He asked me 'if I thought two frigates, with four-and-twenty pounders
on their main decks, were a match for a seventy-four gun ship; and whether
it was my opinion, if he had attempted to force a passage in the ships at
Ile d'Aix, it would have been attended with success.' I replied, 'that the
fire of a two-deck ship was so much more compact, and carried such an
immense weight of iron in proportion to that of a frigate, and there was so
much difficulty in bringing two or three ships to act with effect at the same
time upon one, that I scarcely considered three frigates a match for one
line-of-battle ship; – that with respect to forcing a passage past the *Bellerophon*, it must have depended greatly on accident, but the chances were
much against it; as the frigates would have to beat out against the wind for
three or four leagues, through a narrow passage, exposed to the fire of a
seventy-four gun ship, which, from being to windward, would have had
the power of taking the position most advantageous for herself.'

As a whole, the French were enchanted by Maitland's courtesy
and pleasant manners. Bertrand quickly wrote a reassuring note for
Beker, who was about to leave Aix for Paris, and gave it to the captain of the *Épervier*: 'We have arrived on board the English ship; we
can congratulate ourselves without reserve on the welcome we have
received. . . . I have sent you a copy of the Emperor's letter to the
Prince Regent; I do not need to advise you not to communicate it to
anyone for at least a fortnight. You will realise how undesirable it

would be for it to be known before the English papers have published it.'[2]

Unfortunately the Grand Marshal, like Gourgaud, could not distinguish between hospitality and captivity, and took the Emperor's capture by the English for a diplomatic success, of which the chancelleries of Europe should be the first to be informed.

In the Royal Navy, nine o'clock is breakfast time: Napoleon did not enjoy the cold meat served him with tea and coffee, and Maitland thoughtfully gave orders for his own cook to hand over his oven for the Emperor's service, so that hot dishes in the French style could be prepared for him. Napoleon continued to ask questions during the meal, smiling apologetically.

'I must now learn to conform myself to English customs, as I shall probably pass the rest of my life in England.'

At half past ten the *Superb* dropped anchor a few cable-lengths away; Maitland at once went to greet his chief and gave an account of recent events.

'Tell him that I wish to see him,' Napoleon enjoined him.

'I trust I have done right,' said Maitland to Rear-Admiral Sir Henry Hotham, 'and that the Government will approve of my conduct, as I considered it of much importance to prevent Bonaparte's escape to America, and to get possession of his person.'

'Getting hold of him on any terms would have been of the greatest consequence; but as you have entered into no conditions whatever, there cannot be a doubt that you will obtain the approbation of His Majesty's Government. . . . How do you feel as to keeping him? Would you like to part with him?'

'Certainly not,' Maitland said quickly . . . 'but if he desires to move into another ship, I shall certainly not object.'

When Maitland returned to the *Bellerophon* and announced that the Admiral would visit the Emperor that afternoon, Napoleon at once sent the Grand Marshal to make the first visit, according to

---

[2] Beker at once gave an account of his mission to the Minister for War: 'Convinced of the impossibility of leaving for the United States on one of the warships, and scorning any lesser means of getting a passage to America, His Majesty has come to the noble decision of writing to His Royal Highness the Prince Regent of England to ask him for hospitality. As a result of this decision, the Emperor has gone on board the British ship *Bellerophon*, Captain Maitland, who as a result of orders received from his Government has given His Majesty a welcome suitable to the high position he has occupied among the sovereigns of Europe.'

protocol. Pleasing illusion or insane chimera? The reality did not disappoint him: the Admiral arrived, accompanied by his flag-captain and his secretary, and Napoleon, who delighted in such official ceremonial, received them genially and carried on a desultory conversation, pacing to and fro in his cabin and entirely at his ease. He enjoyed showing off his travelling library, resumed his questions about naval discipline, and then, enchanted by what he took for the prelude to the welcome he would get in England, invited everyone to dinner at five o'clock.

The Admiral remained bare-headed both in the cabin and on deck, and seemed pleased to answer all his questions; Maitland and his officers followed his example and now took the slightest excuse to uncover, while Napoleon once more became the sovereign, serene and thoughtful, his lively grey eyes observing every movement, and sometimes expressing his satisfaction with a pleasant smile.

Dinner, prepared by the Emperor's kitchen staff, was served on the imperial silver which had arrived that morning; Napoleon walked first into the dining-saloon, placed Sir Henry on his right, Countess Bertrand on his left and Maitland opposite; two of the *Bellerophon* officers occupied the ends of the table. 'Bonaparte viewing himself as a Royal personage,' admitted Maitland . . . 'which under the circumstances I considered it would have been both ungracious and uncalled for in me to have disputed.' What a good-natured fellow! The misunderstanding was carefully fostered and by letting the prisoner 'play the Emperor', Hotham and Maitland, both of whom had Draconian instructions in their pockets, must be held largely responsible for what now became a traffic in lies. During the meal, Napoleon led the conversation, just as though he were at the Tuileries:

'Have you any property in Scotland?' he asked Maitland.

'No, I am a younger brother, and they do not bestow much on people of that description in Scotland.'

'Is your elder brother a Lord?'

'No, Lord Lauderdale is the head of our family.'[3]

[3] Maitland, James, Earl of Lauderdale (1759–1839). Scottish representative peer and admirer of the French Revolution; created Baron Lauderdale in the peerage of Great Britain after Pitt's death, he was a minister in Fox's Cabinet and ambassador extraordinary to France for the peace conference. He proposed a motion against Napoleon's exile on St. Helena.

After dinner coffee was served in the cabin, where everyone gathered for lively conversation; to satisfy the curiosity of the English, Marchand the valet shewed off his master's camp-bed and its ingenious mechanism. The French praised the attentiveness of the crew: sofas had been rigged up out of flags for the comfort of the ladies, and nets fitted over the portholes for the children's safety. 'The first lieutenant, withal not a man of the melting mood, seemed to breathe the air of a court, at least the air of the court of Napoleon, for his was a court of warriors, and nothing remained undone that could soothe the feelings of the illustrious fugitives. By illustrious, I do not mean their rank, I mean their great deeds, which alone render men illustrious; and theirs had filled the whole earth with their fame.'[4]

After such a warm welcome, Napoleon's arrival in England might well have turned into a triumph; but the Government relied on the exuberance of the young and the extremism of the Liberals being counteracted by the determined hostility of tradesmen, ruined by fifteen years of war, and of officers like Hotham and Maitland who had tirelessly scoured the seas to save Great Britain from sharing the fate of Carthage.

At half past seven, Napoleon took his leave of these warders who were playing the part of guests so admirably, and after accepting an invitation to breakfast with the Admiral next day, retired for the night with the feeling that the impression he had made on the sailors augured well for his meeting with the Prince Regent. With what an amused smile he would have watched Midshipman Home scribbling in his journal: 'When Admiral Hotham and the officers of the *Bellerophon* uncovered in the presence of Napoleon, they treated him with the respect due to the man himself, to his innate greatness, which did not lie in the crown of France or the iron crown of Italy, but the actual superiority of the man to the rest of his species.'[5]

If he had been in the Admiral's cabin he might have experienced different feelings: placidly dictating to his secretary, Hotham summed up the situation for Lord Keith's benefit:

I have the honour to acquaint your Lordship that on my arrival here this day, in consequence of information from Captain Maitland on the

---

[4] George Home: *op. cit.*
[5] George Home: *op. cit.*

13th inst. of Napoleon Bonaparte having enquired if he would be permitted to pass H.M. ships in the French frigates at the Ile d'Aix on his way to America, I found that he had embarked with his suite this morning on board the *Bellerophon*, having obtained Captain Maitland's consent to receive him for conveyance to England; and I beg leave to report to your Lordship that I have ordered that ship and the *Myrmidon* to proceed with him and the persons described in the accompanying list, composing his suite, to Torbay, agreeable to your Lordship's recommendation of that anchorage in preference to Plymouth; and in compliance with the directions of the Lords Commissioners of the Admiralty a copy of this letter will be conveyed, on the ships' arrival, to their Lordships' secretary containing the original letter from the Count de Bertrand to Captain Maitland of yesterday's date.

Hotham thought it advisable to supplement this official dispatch with a private letter, written in a freer and more cynical style:

I heartily congratulate your Lordship on Bonaparte being safe in England on any terms, as he will not be able to do any more mischief, and as I presume H.M. Government will be glad that he is not left at liberty in any other country. . . . The White Flag flies everywhere in sight from this anchorage and it is expected the ships of war at the Ile d'Aix will hoist it tomorrow. As soon as I see the French ships require no further watching and I can leave anything here to meet any vessel coming to join me I shall return to Quiberon Bay. Captain Maitland having, before my arrival, consented to convey Bonaparte to England, and actually embarked him and his suite, little has been left me to do but to expedite the voyage, to report the circumstances to your Lordship and to express my hope that the measure will be approved of.

The French continued to misunderstand the situation throughout July 16.

Before being conveyed to the *Superb* for breakfast, Napoleon enjoyed inspecting the marines on board the *Bellerophon*, who were instructed to present arms; he examined their weapons and accoutrements and embarked on a criticism of the British form of charge. Everyone was interested, except Maitland, who afterwards complained that he saw that preparations were afoot on the flag-ship to treat 'Boney' as if he were the Prince Regent. He at once sent an officer on board the *Superb*, who returned with Sir Henry Hotham's confirmation that he would receive Bonaparte with manned yards but without a salute from the guns. As the barge put out from the *Bellero-*

phon and made for the Admiral's ship the yards of the *Superb* were in fact manned by sailors in their blue and white uniforms, and the marines were drawn up by the gangway to receive 'the wonderful stranger'.

The French were delighted, and Napoleon did not conceal his satisfaction; he teased Las Cases, who had buttoned himself into a smart naval captain's uniform.[6]

'What, Las Cases, are you a military man? I have never till now seen you in uniform.'

'Please your Majesty, before the Revolution I was a lieutenant in the navy; and as I think a uniform carries more consideration with it in a foreign country, I have adopted it.'

His reception on board the *Superb* was ostentatious and respectful. The Grand Marshal slowly climbed the gangway ladder and announced: 'The Emperor!' The Admiral was standing on the quarter-deck, in front of the guard lined up presenting arms; after greeting them, he led his guests to his cabin, introduced his officers to them and took them round his ship. Napoleon asked his usual questions, but this time he seemed particularly interested in the clothing and victualling of the seamen.

'I believe it happens with you, as it does with us, that the purser is something of a rogue!' he remarked.

Everyone laughed. But in spite of this amiable atmosphere he hardly touched his breakfast, and Maitland, who missed nothing, recorded with some emotion that Colonel Planat was silently weeping and seemed 'greatly distressed at the situation of his master'. As for Napoleon, he was aware of possible danger from the Ile d'Aix, where emissaries from Paris had perhaps already arrived. He was longing to be off, and he breathed more freely after he got back to the *Bellerophon* shortly after midday, and she at once got under weigh. While the crew were busy round the capstan, and setting the sails, he remained on the poop the better to watch their manoeuvres. Followed by the *Myrmidon*, the *Bellerophon* glided slowly through the Pertuis d'Antioche towards the open sea. Without a word, without a gesture,

[6] Las Cases was also wearing the ribbon of the Legion of Honour. When Gourgaud heard this he flew into a rage: 'I hear that Las Cases went in the Emperor's boat to board the *Bellerophon*; and that he asked him to make him a Chevalier of the Legion of Honour, so as to cut more of a figure on his arrival in England.'

the Emperor watched the flat wooded coasts of the islands of Ré and Oléron, and the headlands of Chassiron and Baleines gradually fade into the distance. At the last moment a boat from the Ile d'Aix brought him a parting present from Captain Philibert: three or four sheep and some vegetables.

It was not only goodbye to France, it was goodbye to liberty. Did he realise it? Deceived by the flattering reception his enemies had given him, he naively stopped behaving as a refugee, and let himself be carried away by the grandeur of his downfall, like that of one of Plutarch's heroes; he was no longer Napoleon, but already 'a legendary figure composed of the fancies of poets, soldiers' talk, and popular tradition'.[7]

✤   ✤   ✤

'The English took so much trouble to please us that we hoped for an equally good reception in England,' wrote Marchand, Napoleon's valet, and the voyage from the Basque roads to Torbay, which lasted seven days, certainly did nothing to disabuse them. During the whole week, Napoleon received respectful attentions from Maitland and his crew. In the large cabin in the poop he went on behaving as a sovereign, received whom he wished in the company of one or other of his generals, and even instituted a semblance of protocol: the room outside the cabin was used as a dining-room and servants' room, and at night an aide-de-camp kept watch at the door of the imperial apartment.

Maitland was often invited to his own table, now exclusively under the control of Napoleon's catering staff; so was Las Cases, who as a naval officer was able to provide information about the ship's progress, winds, currents and rules of navigation. The *Bellerophon*'s doctor, a smiling, polite and obliging young Irishman called Barry O'Meara, was always ready to join in conversations on the quarter-deck.

'Where did you study your profession?' Napoleon asked.

'In Dublin and London.'

'Which of the two is the best school of physic?'

'Dublin for anatomy and London for surgery.'

---

[7] Chateaubriand: *Mémoires d'outre-tombe.*

'You say Dublin is the best school of anatomy because you are an Irishman.'

As O'Meara was in daily attendance on Planat, who had fallen ill, Napoleon sent for him and asked him about illnesses and the remedies used to cure them in Great Britain; the Irishman was not without ambition, and was pleased to find himself, 'placed by peculiar circumstances arising from my profession, near the person of the most extraordinary man perhaps of my age'.[8]

In the evenings Napoleon would suggest a game of vingt-et-un, from which Maitland begged to be excused, as he always left his money at home with his wife; one evening the midshipmen gave a theatrical performance, dressed up for the occasion like musical comedy actresses.[9]

The gaiety reigning on board the *Bellerophon* on that first day, when she was no longer in sight of the Ile d'Aix, was truly surprising. Dinner was served just as the ship was rounding Chassiron point, and the French coast was dissolving into the mists of dusk. Napoleon was in an excellent humour, joking about his dealings with Sir Sidney Smith;[10] then patting Maitland on the head he exclaimed: 'If it had not been for you English, I should have been Emperor of the East; but wherever there is water to float a ship, we are sure to find you in our way.'

There was only one really sad moment: it was on the morning of the 23rd, when it was announced that they had just passed Ushant:

I had come on deck at four in the morning, to take the morning watch, wrote Midshipman Home, and the washing of decks had just begun, when, to my astonishment, I saw the Emperor come out of the cabin at that early hour, and make for the poop ladder. . . . From the wetness of the decks he was in danger of falling at every step, and I immediately stepped up to him hat in hand, and tendered him my arm, which he laid hold of at once, smiling, and pointing to the poop saying in broken English 'the

[8] Barry O'Meara: *Napoleon in exile.*

[9] 'We performed the comedy of the *Poor Gentleman* before Bonaparte and suite, and I acted the part of Corporal Foss. It went off very well, our scenery was excellent.' Midshipman E. Graebke.

[10] Smith, Sir William Sidney (1764-1840), had fought against the French in Syria and Egypt with the rank of commodore. When he challenged Bonaparte to meet him in single combat, he received the reply: 'If Marlborough were to appear for that purpose I should be at his service, but I have other duties to fulfil besides fighting a duel with an English commodore.'

poop, the poop'; he ascended the poop-ladder leaning on my arm; and having gained the deck, he quitted his hold and mounted upon a gun-slide, nodding and smiling thanks for my attention and pointing to the land he said, 'Ushant? Cape Ushant?' I replied 'Yes, Sire,' and withdrew. He then took out a pocket-glass and applied it to his eye, looking eagerly at the land. In this position he remained from five in the morning to nearly midday, without paying any attention to what was passing around him, or speaking to one of his suite, who had been standing behind him for several hours.

Whenever they met another ship, the French hurried on deck; alas! they were all English, keeping a watch on the coast, and Maitland was jubilant at the thought that his passengers, who were still reckoning what the chances had been of forcing their way out of the Basque Roads and gaining the open sea, must be silenced by seeing the powerful blockade Lord Keith had established. He always replied to questions on this subject categorically: it was impossible to avoid being caught in the Royal Navy's net, but when he came to write his account of these great events in 1826, he frankly admitted that 'as it afterwards appeared . . . the *Endymion* having gone into the Gironde, the *Liffey* having sprung her bowsprit and returned to England, and the others from various causes having quitted the station . . . had he passed the squadron off Rochefort, there can be little doubt he would have made his voyage in safety to America'.

✤   ✤   ✤

The voyage seemed interminable to the French, who were not used to such restricted quarters, nor to the hubbub made by the sailors, and the sudden changes of mood of the Atlantic; the Emperor was only moderately inconvenienced by this, but Las Cases's face was sometimes pale above his becoming captain's uniform.

Maitland's joy and pride were barely concealed under a mask of frigid courtesy.

'Well, I have got him!' he triumphantly announced to the captain of an English ship which hove to for a short conversation.

'Got him! Got whom?'

'Why, Bonaparte; the man that has been keeping Europe in a ferment these last twenty years.'

And in the privacy of the cabin he had occupied since giving his own to Napoleon, he spent hours polishing reports which he believed would gain him universal approval, and recognition from the Admiralty and the Prince Regent's ministers. On July 18 he explained to Lord Keith:

After the first communication was made to me by Count Bertrand . ., that Bonaparte was at Ile d'Aix, and actually embarked on board the frigates for the purpose of proceeding to the United States of America, my duty became peculiarly harassing and anxious, owing to the numerous reports that were daily brought from all quarters, of his intention to escape in vessels of various descriptions and from different situations on the coast, of which the limited means I possessed, together with the length of time requisite to communicate with Sir Henry Hotham at Quiberon Bay, rendered the success at least possible and even probable. . . .

A flag of truce was sent out, for the ostensible reason of enquiring whether I had received an answer to the former, but I soon ascertained the real one to be a proposal from Bonaparte to embark for England in this ship.

Taking into consideration all the circumstances of the probability of the escape being effected, if the trial was made either in the frigates, or clandestinely in a small vessel (as, had this ship been disabled in action, there was no other with me that could produce any effect on a frigate) . . . and looking upon it as of greatest importance to get possession of the person of Bonaparte, I was induced without hesitation to accede to the proposal as far as taking him on board and proceeding with him to England: but at the same time stating in the most clear and positive terms, that I had no authority to make any sort of stipulation as to the reception he was to meet with. I am happy to say that the measures I have adopted have met with the approbation of Sir Henry Hotham, and will, I trust and hope, receive that of your Lordship as well as of his Majesty's Government.

One may smile at this dispatch, revealing as it does the astuteness of an officer eager to receive the reward deserved by his daring, as well as anxiety that, in case of disapproval, his direct superior should bear a large share of the responsibility.

At dusk on the 23rd, the outline of the English coast became visible on the horizon. Maitland hurried to inform Napoleon who was just getting into bed. Putting the grey overcoat that had seen so many victories over his dressing-gown, the Emperor went out on deck and gazed at the erratic shapes of the cliffs. Now, at the end of his career, he was at last approaching – but in slippers – the land he had so often dreamed of treading underfoot as a conqueror.

At dawn on the 24th, the *Bellerophon* was tacking off Dartmouth, and Napoleon, with Bertrand at his heels, paced the deck from four in the morning until they dropped anchor off Torbay. An officer sent by Lord Keith came on board and was closeted in Maitland's cabin. Events now began to move quickly, while Napoleon admired the coast, the reddish cliffs and the luxuriant semi-tropical vegetation of Devonshire.

'What a beautiful country! It very much resembles the bay of Porto Ferrajo in Elba.' But he was to receive a very different welcome from that given him by the people of Elba.

Maitland read Lord Keith's orders: there was a sinister precision in their baldness:

Let him and his want for nothing; and send to me for anything Brixham cannot furnish; I will send it you by a small vessel. You may say to Napoleon that I am under the greatest personal obligations to him for his attention to my nephew, who was taken and brought before him at Belle Alliance, and who must have died, if he had not ordered a surgeon to dress him immediately and sent him to a hut. I am glad it fell into your hands at this time, because a Frenchman had been sent from Paris on the mission, a Monsieur Drigni.

When Gourgaud rejoined the *Bellerophon* and described his lack of success there was general consternation, for the French had been quite taken in by their reception by Maitland and the Admiral and were already delighted by English hospitality, even going so far as to believe that the Captain would enthusiastically accept a gold snuff-box in remembrance of his illustrious guest, and that the Prince Regent would offer the Emperor the blue ribbon of the Order of the Garter. . . .

Then, as the hostile intentions of the Government were clearly shown in the stern measures for isolating the ship, the English looked glum and suddenly changed their attitude. 'The officers' reserve defied all our efforts. . . . We could have imagined ourselves on one of the Venetian galleys of the Council of Ten, the air of mystery seemed so impenetrable and mouths became so tightly shut. Captain Maitland's worried frown was the only clue to the news he had received in the Torbay roads.'[11]

At last it was borne in upon this handful of exiles that their testing time was at hand, and that the Emperor would soon be regretting that he had not fallen to a bullet at Waterloo.

[11] Montholon: *Récits de la captivité.*

X

LONDON DELIBERATES

✢✢✢

The Regent and his ministers – News of Bonaparte's
capture – Plans for his deportation – The opposition
and public curiosity – Lawyers intervene – Bonaparte
is to go to St. Helena – The 'little island' of St. Helena –
Interview with Lord Keith.

✢✢✢

Since June 19, London had been living in a state of euphoric delight
at the Duke of Wellington's victory, first heard of and exploited by
Rothschild's bank. Never had a military victory been more necessary
to the moral health and the economy of any nation. 'After twenty
years of war, Great Britain had emerged the strongest, richest and
most powerful country in the world. . . . But the war and the Continental System had aggravated the confusions and social disasters
of rapid industrial changes. In 1815 Great Britain seemed to be on
the edge of bankruptcy and social revolution.'[1]

To disguise the desolating spectacle of poverty and hunger, to
obliterate the memory of the bloody repression the working classes
had been subjected to, and of the millions of pounds the Napoleonic
wars had cost, the London Cabinet meant to make the most of the
victory so tenaciously won, thus glorifying their own policy and presenting the Tory movement as the symbol of a new era. Bonaparte
himself only played a small part in these grandiose projects; the
correct attitude to adopt towards an enemy reduced to impotence
must simply be a traditionally British one: discreet and quick, but
apparently fulfilling the requirements of legality and generosity.

As the Government of a constitutional monarchy, Lord Liverpool's Cabinet could only legislate with the agreement of both
houses and the sovereign's endorsement. So unexpected a measure

[1] J. H. Plumb: *England in the 18th century.*

as Bonaparte's detention would necessarily be affected by public opinion; from the day of Waterloo to that of the Emperor's arrival off Torbay – a period of a little over a month – the subject of all thought, writing and discussion concerned the troublesome problem: What was to be done with 'Boney'?

But the views of the man in the street were to have little effect on official decisions. There was no debate in the Commons, except to approve measures that were already being executed, and when the voice of the opposition was at last heard, Napoleon was already on his way to the rock of St. Helena. The three protagonists in this drama, the Prince Regent, Lord Liverpool and Lord Bathurst had precipitated the march of events.

George, Prince of Wales, and Regent since his father had been shut up at Windsor after several attacks of madness, was an indolent, pompous and perfumed buffoon, a debauchee who frequented the most disreputable companions, but who enjoyed royal display and was an enthusiastic amateur of architecture, painting and music. Despised by his ministers, and hated by the humble inhabitants of the capital, Prinny (for short) was a daily target for pamphleteers and caricaturists. 'A libertine,' wrote Leigh Hunt, 'over head and ears in debt and disgrace, a despiser of domestic ties, the companion of gamblers and demireps, a man who has just closed half a century without one single claim on the gratitude of his country or the respect of posterity.'

Although a stubborn adversary of the Tories, he had to put up with a Conservative ministry presided over by Lord Liverpool, who was careful not to ask the Prince's advice over this thorny and urgent matter. Besides, how much would the Prince's intervention have counted with ministers and members of parliament who thought of George III's eldest son as a 'drunkard', 'a spendthrift', 'an adulterer', 'a soulless sot', and 'a traitor'? When the letter Napoleon had entrusted to Gourgaud finally reached its destination, Prinny only said with a laugh: 'Upon my word, a very proper letter: much more so I must say than any I ever received from Louis XVIII.' That was because Napoleon had addressed him as *Altesse Royale*, whereas the Bourbon had gone no further than *Monseigneur*.

To English historians, Lord Liverpool, whom his contemporaries thought of as a wit and a gifted orator, is 'one of those statesmen who failed to impress his personality on the public, and he figures in the pages of history as the most insipid of English Prime Ministers'.[2] He had reigned at Downing Street ever since the assassination of Perceval in 1812;[3] this patient but ambitious man had negotiated the Treaty of Amiens and borne the burden of the continental wars in the most difficult ministerial departments, the Foreign Office and Home Office. And, faithful to his reputation of inflexible severity, he was naturally not tempted to show clemency towards the man who had kept him on the alert for fifteen years.

Having been present at the taking of the Bastille as a young man, both revolutionaries and imperialists were objects of his persistent hatred: 'it was quite enough that they were French, and had helped overthrow thrones.' He was to make Bonaparte pay dearly for the exhausting efforts of former Prime Ministers to bolster up European resistance to the dangerous ideology originating on the banks of the Seine.

As for Lord Bathurst, Secretary for War and the Colonies since 1812, his hatred of Bonaparte and scorn for France had been aggravated by a period spent at the Board of Trade, trying to reorganise an economy disabled by the Napoleonic wars.

On July 7, when Napoleon's plans were still unknown, Lord Liverpool sent a note to the head of the Foreign Office then in Paris, leaving no doubts as to his Cabinet's intentions:

If we take him, we shall keep him on board of ship till the opinion of the Allies has been taken. The most easy course would be to deliver him up to the King of France, but then we must be quite certain that he would be tried and have no chance of escape.

A week later he returned to the charge:

If . . . the King of France does not feel sufficiently strong to bring him to justice as a rebel, we are ready to take upon ourselves the custody of his person on the part of the Allied Powers; and, indeed, we should think it better that he should be consigned to us than to any other member of the Confederacy.

---

[2] R. Fulford: *George the Fourth*.
[3] Perceval, Spencer (1762–1812). Chancellor of the Exchequer (1807) and Prime Minister (1809), he was assassinated in the lobby of the House of Commons. The death of this mediocre statesman was no great tragedy for the English.

At that date the noble Lord therefore had not the slightest doubt what would be the outcome of the manhunt so zealously and cunningly organised by the navy. His correspondence with Lord Keith at Plymouth (through Lord Melville), and with Lord Castlereagh in Paris, had kept him well posted from day to day concerning a strategy which would leave 'Boney' no choice.

On July 14, the Admiralty, represented by Croker who prided himself on his knowledge of literature, had sent the following warning to Lord Keith:

The opinion here seems to be that Bonaparte is not at Rochefort but either with the army or at Paris. Perhaps rather he is lurking about some part of the coast from whence he will endeavour to steal away in some small vessel. If the White Flag should be flying at Rochefort I suppose our ships will anchor in the roads, but with every precaution it will be exceedingly difficult, if not impossible, to stop him if he embarks like Hamlet 'naked and alone'. Ministers are very anxious about getting him.

And on the same day Keith wrote to the First Lord of the Admiralty:

Very late last night letters came from Sir Henry Hotham which I sent after the mail. . . . I am of the opinion Napoleon will not be able to sail on the two frigates at the Ile d'Aix, but I am fearful of the corvette in the Maumusson Passage – there are land winds every night at this season. He may also conceal himself about Blaye in the Gironde and then wait for an opportunity of getting away in a small vessel, although the river is generally well watched.

Next day, Lord Melville, who was daily receiving at the Admiralty bulletins from Paris, where Wellington was acting as viceroy, wrote to Keith on the part of the Government:

It appears by the letters which we have received from Paris during the last two or three days that Bonaparte was still at Rochefort. Today we have letters from Lord Castlereagh of the 12th which state that three vessels, the *Saale* and *Meduse* (which I believe are of the same class as our 38-gun frigates) and an *aviso*, had been placed by the Provisional Government at the disposal of Bonaparte, and they seemed to think that at the date of their last accounts that he was actually on board the *Saale* in Aix Roads or in the Charente. . . . Lord Castlereagh was endeavouring through the intervention of Louis XVIII's government to get our ships introduced into Aix Roads without molestation from the batteries. If that measure has been accomplished and the *Saale* is still there with him on board, the business will soon be settled.

Two days later, Captain de Rigny's mission having been formulated in Paris,[4] Lord Melville confided Croker's audacious plan[5] to Lord Keith, but suggested a subtler manoeuvre than Castlereagh's. 'The officer who may be fortunate enough to secure Bonaparte on board his ship (is) not to proceed with him to England immediately, but to retain him on the French coast until the officer receives a further communication from Lord Castlereagh.' Such had been the instructions of the British Foreign Secretary, whose intention had been simply to hand the 'Usurper' over to Louis XVIII.

Fearing a change in public feeling, or that the troops in the west of France might rally to the Emperor, Lord Melville preferred to see the ship with Bonaparte and his suite on board 'anchor in Basque Roads, or in some other safe anchorage, from whence she could proceed to England at any time without hindrance, and without the French authorities in the neighbourhood being able to prevent it if they should be so inclined. I take it for granted also that Lord Castlereagh meant to confine his request to the seizure of Bonaparte under the mission of the Capitaine de Rigny, but that if he was captured at sea, or under any other circumstances than those described in Mr. Croker's letter, the captain of the British ship should act of course in conformity to the instructions he had received from the Admiralty and your Lordship'.

These tactics, which left the English free to dispose of the Emperor's person, would enable the London Cabinet to claim the merit of his capture and decide on the conditions of his detention.

News travelled fast, and on July 15, when forwarding Sir Henry Hotham's precious letter[6] to Lord Melville, Lord Keith could assure him:

We have got somewhat like information about the fugitives. The wind has been strong and adverse of late, so that there are hopes; I wish Maitland had sent the ambassadors[7] to Hotham for his answer and a message

[4] See page 124.
[5] See page 124.
[6] See page 135.
[7] Savary and Las Cases.

to Napoleon today, having no authority to answer from himself. Perhaps they will not sail on the national ships without safe-conduct from us.

The trap was closing, for flight by way of Brest was absolutely impossible, if we are to believe the captain of the *Chatham*, who sent a triumphant report on the interior situation, on July 20:

A flag of truce is just arrived with an officer charged by the commandant at Brest and the French Admiral with letters addressed to the Commander of the British Squadron, informing me that Brest and its dependencies have submitted to their lawful sovereign, and I have the pleasure of descrying the French flag now flying on the island of Malin as it does on all the coast of the Department of Finisterre. I shall stand in to the Black Rocks and to St. Andrew's Point, hoist the Royal Flag of France and fire a Royal Salute.

✢ ✢ ✢

News sent by couriers or telegraph travelled faster than dispatches entrusted to cutters plying between Quiberon and Plymouth. On July 21 the First Lord of the Admiralty sent instructions as to what should be done with Napoleon to the Commander-in-Chief at Plymouth. If he touched at Plymouth 'he should remain in the Sound in a line-of-battle ship and the most positive orders should be given to prevent any person whatever, except the officers and men who form the complement of that ship, from going on board. . . . I do not want of course to put any restraint on your Lordship or on Sir John Duckworth[8] in case either of you should think it necessary to go on board, but you will probably agree with me in opinion that any such visit had better if possible be avoided'.

It is clear that the Admiralty was very much afraid that Maitland's action might not receive the complete approval of the Government, and that false moves on the part of the Plymouth admirals might follow. The Cabinet must therefore keep the prisoner in absolute isolation, while remaining free to prepare and give orders for their plans for his custody.

When Lord Keith finally sent ministers the triumphant news, they were already making arrangements for Bonaparte's detention. It was

[8] Port Admiral, Plymouth.

not in fact until the 22nd that the Commander-in-Chief of the Channel Fleet was able to announce: 'Captain Sartorius of H.M. ship *Slaney* has this moment landed with the enclosed dispatch from Captain Maitland of the *Bellerophon*, by which it appears that Bonaparte proposed on the 14th inst. to embark on board the *Bellerophon* and throw himself on the generosity of H.R.H. the Prince Regent, and that he had acceded thereto.'

Delighted by the prospect of taking part in so historic an encounter, Lord Keith ended his letter by informing the Lords that he would go in person to Torbay and await instructions.

While the arms of the semaphore were busily at work and couriers were galloping between Plymouth and London, the Prime Minister had already made his choice and given its final shape to an affair that might well set on foot an inconvenient campaign of protest in Great Britain.

On July 20 he had written to the Foreign Secretary:

I have this moment received your letters of the 17 instant, with the intelligence of the surrender of Bonaparte, of which I wish you joy. When your letter was written, you had evidently not received mine of the 15th, which will explain to you the sentiments of Government on the subject of his detention.

We are all decidedly of opinion that it would not answer to confine him in this country. Very nice legal questions might arise upon the subject, which would be particularly embarrassing. But, independent of these considerations, you know enough of feelings of people in this country not to doubt he would become an object of curiosity immediately, and possibly of compassion, in the course of a few months: and the circumstance of his being here, or indeed anywhere in Europe, would contribute to keep up a certain degree of ferment in France.

Since I wrote to you last, Lord Melville and myself have conversed with Mr. Barrow[9] on the subject, and he decidedly recommends St. Helena as the place in the world the best calculated for the confinement of such a person. There is a very fine citadel there, in which he might reside. The situation is particularly healthy. There is only one place in the circuit of the island where ships can anchor, and we have the power of excluding neutral ships altogether, if we should think it necessary. At such a distance and in such a place, all intrigue would be impossible; and, being

[9] John Barrow, Second Secretary of the Admiralty, and colleague of J. W. Croker.

withdrawn so far from the European world, he would very soon be forgotten.

We are very much disinclined to the appointment of Commissaries on the part of the other powers; such an arrangement might be unobjectionable for a few months, but when several persons of this description get together in a place in which they had nothing to do, they would very soon be tired; they would be very likely to quarrel amongst themselves; and the existence of any disputes amongst them might seriously embarrass the safe custody of the prisoner.

The head of the Government had lost no time, and now that Bonaparte was a prisoner at Plymouth, he was eager to start putting his plan into operation before the opposition had time to act. Two hazards preoccupied him: Bonaparte's popularity in certain quarters, and the possibility of the former sovereign's having recourse to the protection of British law, by devious ways.

The reaction of the man in the street was certainly not the least threatening of these dangers. Midshipman Home was on the boat which took the first lieutenant of the *Bellerophon* ashore with dispatches from Maitland, on the morning after they had anchored off Torbay; he was set upon by twenty young ladies, who stuffed him with tea and cakes, and tormented him with questions. They challenged him to say whether Napoleon was a normal man, whether he had not been covered in blood when he came aboard, and whether they could possibly see him. The midshipman was so carried away by youthful enthusiasm that he suddenly became the first evangelist in the campaign feared by the Government. Not only was the Emperor a man like others, he said, but he was well-dressed and young; there was no more blood on his famous uniform than on the pretty white frocks of his charming questioners, and if the ladies once saw him at the gangway of the *Bellerophon*, they would fall in love with him.

The foolish girls insisted on piling into the cutter and asking to be rowed round the ship, now rolling heavily in the Channel swell; they had to be put on dry land again by the strong arms of sailors.

But the infatuation of the girls of Torbay was less alarming to Lord Liverpool than the wrath of the Liberal aristocracy, and the malicious gossip circulating in high society, now that the season was in full swing. Behind this agitation, he guessed that the powerful organisation of the Whig party was at work, dominated by the Duke of Sussex, Grand Master of the English Freemasons, Lord Holland,[10] and Hobhouse[11] – whose heroes were Byron and Napoleon, and who 'found his eyes somewhat moistened at the sight of the world's wonder' – and inspired by that demigod of the young, the poet who had been boiling with indignation ever since the news of Waterloo, and who was to exclaim as he trod the battlefield:

'Stop – for thy tread is on an Empire's dust.'

Now that his downfall had turned Napoleon into a romantic hero, everything concerning his fate aroused echoes that reverberated through Holland House and the fashionable drawing-rooms. On his return to England, Hobhouse noted: 'Find Bonaparte's surrender to the *Bellerophon* had made ten times the sensation here it has in Paris. . . . The curiosity to see him here is unabated.'

The excitement in Plymouth, though largely curiosity, might in the end have raised those 'judicial problems' so dreaded by the Prime Minister, the first of which was the legal status of this inconvenient guest.

Was he to be treated, as he himself had suggested, like the Athenian statesman who took refuge with Artaxerxes and was offered three royal cities? This thought amused his lordship. If Bonaparte was a prisoner of war, could he be treated as a captive sovereign, like Jean de Bon,[12] in spite of his abdication in 1814? And how could his detention on one of His Britannic Majesty's ships be put on a legal footing? Of course the Government was in a good position to prove that Bonaparte had come on board of his own accord, without any written undertaking on Maitland's part. Although he did not fall into the hands of the Royal Navy sword in hand, it suited Cabinet ministers best to pass him off as an ordinary prisoner of war, in spite of the danger that he might have to be liberated when the peace treaty was signed. As Wellington had violently opposed handing him over at once to Louis XVIII, only two satisfactory ways of disposing of him remained, once his status had been defined: internment in

---

[10] Holland, Henry Richard Vassall Fox, Lord (1773–1840), nephew of Charles James Fox and leader of the Whig Party. His wife, the famous hostess of Holland House, gave him constant support in his efforts on behalf of Napoleon when a prisoner at St. Helena.

[11] Hobhouse, John Cam, Lord Broughton (1786–1869). Writer and politician, intimate friend of Byron.

[12] Died in the Tower of London in 1364.

Great Britain – and this ministers refused to consider, even in a dungeon in the Tower of London – or else deportation to a distant colony.

Liverpool decided to get the best legal advice in the country: Lord Eldon, the Lord Chancellor, the highest legal authority in England, and his brother Sir William Scott,[13] were entrusted with the task of giving a semblance of legality to an iniquitous action. They worked diligently, in company with Lord Ellenborough, the Lord Chief Justice, Sir William Grand, Master of the Rolls, the Attorney General and the Solicitor-General.

According to Ellenborough, a state of war could exist between a power and a single individual. Peace had been concluded with France, but not with Napoleon; he could therefore be considered as an enemy and confined as such.

According to William Scott, a greater expert in international law than his brother, Bonaparte must be regarded as a prisoner of war, since he was only responsible to France for his illegal actions; peace with France *ipso facto* implied peace with the subjects of France.

As a result of his reflections and the opinions he had heard, Lord Eldon prepared a memorandum which may be summarized thus:

The state of war between France and England authorised Bonaparte's detention as a prisoner of war, especially as, according to Captain Maitland, no undertakings had been entered into with him.

Bonaparte was no longer a French subject since his abdication and accession to the throne of the island of Elba. It was therefore possible to consider him as having been defeated in a legitimate war fought *against himself alone*, and to declare him a prisoner of war.

An Act of Indemnity protected ministers from proceedings in the British courts, but afforded them none in international law, since Napoleon was not a British subject.

European policy and the safety of the world jointly authorised Bonaparte's detention *sine die*, since this was the only way to prevent future trouble on the part of an individual who could be regarded as an adventurer, one of those men who 'do not feel bound by any treaty'.

The result of this investigation was to authorise Lord Liverpool to treat Napoleon as a 'prisoner of war', notwithstanding the secular

[13] Sir William Scott (1745–1836). M.P. for Oxford University, and judge of the High Court of Admiralty. Created Baron Stowell, 1821.

traditions of a country that had always welcomed refugees, including tyrants who had been driven from their thrones, and in spite of an important section of public opinion. Like Mary Queen of Scots, who had also been placed under the protection of another sovereign – who was her cousin – and experienced nothing but humiliations and fortresses, Napoleon was to be subjected to the harshness of the State's revenge.

The jurists' conclusion left him no practical means of appealing to the law. England had carried the cult of individual liberty and respect towards the person to the highest degree, and (ever since 1679) had set great store by the Habeas Corpus Act as a defence against violation of these principles. A writ based on *habeas corpus subjiciendum* could rapidly be translated, by means of the judge's summing-up, into another obliging the plaintiff to produce the physical person of his prisoner, and show reason for his incarceration, together with dates and facts.

Napoleon's suite were aware of the existence of these legal dispositions, probably thanks to Las Cases who prided himself on his knowledge of English customs, but they did not realise how little help they gave in time of war, when the judge's gown had for once to give way to arms. Through the agency of Lady Clavering, a friend of Las Cases living in London, they quickly sought the advice of a famous lawyer, Sir Samuel Romilly.[14]

✢   ✢   ✢

Like the members of the London Cabinet, the party on the *Bellerophon* wanted things to happen quickly, but for quite different reasons. London had a lead of several days, for Lord Bathurst had been on the job since July 21: through his staff and from travellers, he collected together all existing documents about the island of St. Helena, and opened negotiations with the East India Company to transfer the rock to the Crown for the period of Bonaparte's detention. On the 24th, the day the *Bellerophon* arrived at Torbay, the

---

[14] Sir Samuel Romilly (1757–1818). Descended from Huguenots, established in England after the revocation of the Edict of Nantes; an eminent advocate, friend of Fox and Mirabeau, Attorney-General and M.P. On Fox's death he entered the opposition where he distinguished himself by his eloquence. He committed suicide after the death of his wife in 1818.

Minister for War and the Colonies had already selected Sir Hudson Lowe[15] to occupy the function of Governor and Commander-in-Chief of this fragment of land lost in the Atlantic ocean. On the 25th, the Directors of the Company met at India House, that proud edifice symbolising British power beyond the sea, and put their signatures to the following handwritten document:

Napoleon Bonaparte having surrendered himself to the Government of this country, His Majesty's ministers, deeply sensible of the high importance of effectually securing the person of a man whose conduct has proved so fatal to the happiness of the world, and judging that the island of St. Helena is eminently fitted to answer that purpose, have proposed to us that he shall be placed there. . . . As the East India Company hold the principle of rendering their means and faculties, on all practical occasions, conducive to the national interests and objects, we have not thought ourselves at liberty to decline a compliance with the proposal thus made to us in so remarkable a case, although it involved some consequences which we cannot contemplate without pain.

For the Ministers of the King, being responsible to the nation and the other powers of Europe for the safe custody of Bonaparte, they deem it necessary that such custody should be committed to the care of a General Officer of the King's Service.

So, while Maitland was pacing the deck of his ship, pointing out the beauties of the bay and its surroundings to his guests, who had now become his prisoners, the business had been practically settled by the Cabinet, sentence without judgment passed by Liverpool, Bathurst and Castlereagh, and the gaoler chosen.

When Gourgaud arrived back on the *Bellerophon* from the *Slaney*, with the precious letter to the Prince Regent still pathetically shut away inside his portfolio, he brought with him a few newspapers, collected during his short stay in the roadstead; they already contained articles echoing rumours that Bonaparte was to go to the Tower of London, Dumbarton Castle,[16] Fort George,[17] or, better still, the island of St. Helena.

Faced with such threats as these, the man who had trusted to

---

[15] Sir Hudson Lowe (1679–1844). Former Commander of the Corsican Rangers, a regiment of Corsican deserters to the British army. His post at St. Helena earned him a place in history, but he played a part that even some of his own compatriots reproached him for.

[16] An old fortress on the Clyde, reputedly impregnable.

[17] A Scottish fortress, built after the Jacobite rising of 1745.

British generosity had nothing to count on except an agitation provoked by the opposition, or the activities of lawyers, although communications with the latter were subjected to the same strict control as was exercised by Maitland over all contacts with the shore. As for the good-natured populace, the authorities did not seem to be troubled by them: 'crowds of boats and spectators', Las Cases noted. The sea was covered with boats, and the Emperor was amused by them; he greeted the throngs in their best clothes, showed himself on deck or at a porthole, and occasionally raised his hat to a particularly well-dressed lady. The sailors of the *Bellerophon* had invented a system for keeping inquisitive sightseers informed: they scribbled announcements on large placards to the effect that Bonaparte was 'lunching', 'in his cabin', or 'about to go up on deck'. All this had something of the air of a fair or a circus, with the crowd delightedly waiting for the lion-tamer to arrive and the wild beast to wake up.

But did this popular enthusiasm really mean anything? 'From the enormous rush that was made from every part of the country to Plymouth Sound, to get a single glance of the hero of Marengo and Lodi Bridge, he must have conceived that he was as much admired by the English as by his own beloved French.'[18] The weather was delightful and orchestras played French airs to get the Ogre to show himself. How could this goodnatured behaviour be reconciled with the appalling news that was being spread by the gazettes?

Escaping from his excited companions, Napoleon often paced the deck, morose and despondent, but still forming plans to make his protests carry as far as the banks of the Thames.

✤   ✤   ✤

St. Helena. Did those sonorous syllables waken old memories? And as he listened to the shouts of the crowd did the Emperor think of a young penniless officer, studying a geography book at Auxonne, and quickly scribbling in his notebook: 'British possessions in America, Asia and Africa: in Africa, Cabo Corso in Guinea, a fairly strong fortress. Nearby is Fort Royal, defended by sixteen guns. St. Helena, a little island. . . .' His pen had stopped after this ingenuous

[18] George Home: *op. cit.*

and laconic description of the rock which was to be the tomb of an Emperor of the French.[19]

Later on, in 1804, he wrote to Decrès from Mainz:

There are three expeditions we must make. . . . To take St. Helena and establish a squadron there for several months. For this, 1200 to 1500 men will be needed. The expedition will send 200 men to the aid of Senegal, retake Goree, and requisition and burn all British establishments along the African coast. . . . In this way immense harm can be done to the English in the course of three or four months. The squadron will be reinforced by all the ships we have in Mauritius; and when it seems advisable to withdraw, the colony will be left with provisions for eight or nine months.

Eight ships, fifteen hundred men, six pieces of ordnance and a thousand muskets were to break down the island's resistance, which would only have been slight. The squadron was to sail in November, but on October 2 Napoleon was still complaining of the slowness of the preparations, and suddenly decided to suspend them and give all his attention to an attack on Surinam.

There was more talk of the rock in 1805, when the Emperor asked the Minister for the Navy to make ready a winter expedition. The Minister suggested the direction of the Cape of Good Hope and this idea was approved by the master of the Tuileries.

The expedition to St. Helena seems to me perfect. . . . The admiral must be given instructions allowing scope, and leaving him free to proceed to the Cape or St. Helena, so long as his ships definitely all join up and arrive at Martinique . . . to return afterwards to St. Helena. If the squadron does not return to St. Helena until four months after leaving it, it should find no more enemies there. These erratic and incalculable exploits will do the enemy considerable harm. . . . I intend Monsieur Jerome to command one of the ships on this expedition.

Jerome Bonaparte, commanding the *Vétéran*, was not destined to see that ocean prison rising surprisingly from the horizon, wrapped in clouds. Chance (which is also the god of the sea), the English and the winds decided otherwise, and Admiral Willaumez's ships never saw the island, either from far or near.

Such recollections as these were not of a sort to relax the nerves

---

[19] A facsimile of these notes will be found in the collection entitled *Napoléon et L'Empire* (Hachette).

of the man who had once threatened England's furthest possessions, and who was now brooding over his humiliation. But absolute power is a bad school; it had often deceived him by presenting the world in false colours, and individuals under the guise of courtesy and submission. Accustomed to obsequious attentions from courtiers and dependants, Napoleon clung rather naively to outward signs. When Lord Keith sent him an amiable message in a letter to Maitland dated July 24,[20] he at once began building castles in the air, and almost believed he had found an ally, whereas in reality the old Admiral was jubilantly confiding to his daughter:

Bony is in Torbay with fifty-three men and women; five are generals, but I am obliged to prohibit all intercourse with the ship, as all Plymouth would have been off to gape at him. . . . There has been a most ridiculous altercation between Gen. Browne and Duckworth about which was to keep Bonaparte. . . . To this I replied: 'He is in my care; I am responsible, and shall give neither of you any trouble till the Government send orders.' . . . Napoleon seems in good spirits and converses with the officers.

Orders were on the way, and on the 25th Lord Keith broke the seals of a letter from Lord Melville, which at last revealed the truth:

I am much obliged to you for remembering me in directing Capt. Sartorius to come to Wimbledon; he arrived there between three and four this morning and we have since had a Cabinet on the business. I am afraid that the result will not come in the shape of an official letter from Lord Bathurst in time to send off by post; but I can state for your private information that in all probability the ex-emperor will be sent to some foreign colony, and in the meantime he will not be allowed to land or to have any communication whatever with the shore, and we shall not apprise him immediately of his future destination. With a view to his personal accommodation, we must diminish the number of his suite in the *Bellerophon*, but they also must be kept in strict seclusion. Sir John Duckworth and you will be able to judge whether if there is any influx of small boats getting round the ship from curiosity, it may not be necessary to have guard boats to keep everything at a distance. . . . I suppose he will usually walk on the quarter-deck only, where he will not be easily seen and gazed at from the water. We once thought of allowing him to remain in Torbay, but as he may be here some weeks, and that anchorage is not very eligible at all times, and as moreover the strict surveillance which we require may be

[20] 'I beg to present my respects to Napoleon, and if I can render him any civility I will consider it my duty, as well as in gratitude for Captain Elphinstone's report of the attention he received from him on the field of battle.'

under your eye or Sir J. Duckworth's. . . . I thought it on the whole better and more secure to trust to Plymouth Sound. . . . The aide-de-camp in the *Slaney*[21] will be sent back to the *Bellerophon*, there to remain, and he will be told that he must send this and all letters through you. . . . I am afraid that we shall find Bonaparte and his suite troublesome guests while they remain here; but we have no cause to grumble on the whole – very much the reverse.

Lord Melville was rubbing his hands: the defeated Bonaparte was to go to a distant colony and would be left no means of claiming justice from the country in which he had sought asylum. It was a short-sighted view! As one of His Britannic Majesty's ministers, he lightly engaged his country, and thus exposed it to the judgment of History, which is the conscience of nations.

✢ ✢ ✢

On July 26, Maitland received orders by courier from the Admiralty to proceed to Plymouth Sound, under escort of the two frigates *Myrmidon* and *Slaney*. Ignorant of the reason for this move, the French gradually gave way to uneasiness. 'Every face seemed to be studying us with gloomy interest,' complained Las Cases; 'the most sinister rumours had reached the ship.'

All that morning the *Bellerophon* beat against adverse winds, and no sooner had she dropped anchor in the magnificent roadstead of Plymouth than she was surrounded by a battle array: two frigates the *Liffey* and *Eurotas* anchored beside her, and launched armed longboats to discourage inquisitive spectators. While Maitland was preparing to pay the customary visit to his chief, Napoleon gave him a message for Lord Keith, inviting him to come and see him on board ship.

However great may have been his curiosity, the Commander-in-Chief of the Channel Fleet refused the invitation, in the absence of definite orders from the Admiralty, and confined himself to repeating his previous orders to Maitland.

'I am extremely anxious to see the Admiral,' Napoleon grumbled, when Maitland reported on the result of his mission; 'and therefore beg he will not stand on ceremony; I shall be satisfied to be treated

[21] General Gourgaud.

as a private person, until the British Government has determined in what light I am to be considered.'

Lord Keith, who was champing with impatience to meet the man he described as 'the reptile' face to face, was anxious all the same not to upset his superiors by making the first move. He explained to his daughter:

I wrote Lady K. to Exeter that she may not go to Torbay upon the chance of the influence of the name to get on board the *Bellerophon*. I also refused Mrs. Maitland permission to go, and Govt. has approved of it. I did not like to go myself, first because I did not know how to address him, secondly because my visit might have been construed into insult or curiosity; therefore I left it to the Great Man to determine these weighty points. Yet I am not without curiosity. . . . I have not failed to thank the ci-devant Emperor on account of James, and am answered he recollects the circumstance and feels the obligation of my early notice of his kindness on the occasion.

If Lord Keith was still hesitating whether to keep his distance from Bonaparte, a note from the Admiralty, dated July 25, was enough to make him even more prudent:

It would appear that the yards were manned when Bonaparte visited the *Superb* (which was an unnecessary visit), that he insists upon being treated with royal respect, that he invites Captain Maitland and other officers to dine with him, and in short that if we do not interfere the same follies in this respect are likely to be committed as were exhibited last year by some officer in the Mediterranean. . . .[22]

I think we shall send Bonaparte to St. Helena, and that Sir George Cockburn's appointment as Commander-in-Chief on the Cape Station, which was suspended, will now go forward, and that he will convey this prisoner to St. Helena and remain there for some time. We must take it under the King's military authority, to which the Court of Directors (of the East India Company) I believe will not object. If Bonaparte or his suite are desirous of writing letters, they must be sent through you open, or addressed to some member of the Government. You had better transmit them all to the Admiralty, unless there is anything very confidential which you may prefer sending direct to me.

This letter contained an enclosure designed as a guide for the

---

[22] Probably Campbell, the British Commissioner on Elba, who was at Leghorn at the time when Napoleon embarked for his return to France.

conduct of all British subjects called upon to meet the Emperor: it established the exile's status until 1821:

On conversing with the officer who came to England in the *Bellerophon* with the dispatches from Sir Henry Hotham and Captain Maitland, I think it would appear that Bonaparte had been allowed to assume a great deal more state, and even authority, and had been treated with more submissiveness than belongs to his station as a prisoner of war, or to his rank as a General Officer, which is all that can be allowed him in this country. No British officer would treat his prisoner with inhumanity, and the recollection of that station which Bonaparte has so long held in Europe would naturally, and almost involuntarily, lead an officer to abstain from any line of conduct that could be construed into insult, and therefore to go rather beyond than to fall short of due respect; but such indulgent feelings must be restrained within proper bounds.

Lord Keith hastened to admonish Maitland, at the same time doing his utmost to justify his subordinate's behaviour in the eyes of the Admiralty, and cursing the indiscretions committed by members of the 'reptile's' suite.

I have seen Capt. Maitland who says that when he went on board Sir H. Hotham in Basque Roads, on his return he found the table covered with the plate of Bonaparte. He assumes the company (?) and invites officers to dine with him. No-one sits down covered in his presence. Capt. Maitland sups in the master's cabin. . . . I was much hurt at having the substance of his letter to the Prince Regent repeated word by word two days ago at Plymouth, but find it was the son of the Count (Las Cases) who copied the letter and kept one for himself, but which he let one of the midshipmen translate into English and showed to the Comte de Bertrand, who said it was well done. I am very happy that this is thus explained, because it might have been supposed that it had got out of my house, which I knew to be impossible.

On July 27 Maitland at last received the mark of satisfaction from the Admiralty he was waiting for. The Lords asked the Secretary to 'signify their approval' to the Captain of the *Bellerophon* for the way he had received Napoleon Bonaparte and conducted the negotiations preceding his embarkation in Aix Roads. It was therefore with a lighter heart that he went to see Admiral Lord Keith that day, and even agreed to take charge of the letter from the Emperor to the Prince Regent. Lord Keith, too, was in excellent spirits. 'I shall now have no difficulty whatever having received full instructions as to the manner in which he is to be treated: he is to be considered as a General Officer.'[23]

Melville's private letter had been more explicit than the ministerial decision, for it mentioned St. Helena, but the old sea-dog was careful not to reveal what he knew. A meeting was arranged for the following day, the Admiral himself fixing the hour of his audience.

Meanwhile, Maitland had the task of transferring the imperial suite to the frigates, with the exception of four or five persons and their families, and of keeping a close watch for any sudden move on Napoleon's part, since the rumours current in Plymouth that he was to be deported to St. Helena might drive him to some act of desperation.

Maitland bowed to fate; he was the first to suffer from these harsh orders, for he had to be content with looking at his young wife from afar, as she circled despondently round the *Bellerophon* in a hired boat. In vain Napoleon took off his hat to the lady and invited her to come up and visit him; it was all to no purpose.

'That is very hard . . . Lord Keith is a little too severe; is he not, Madam?'

Then he turned to Maitland smiling: 'I assure you her portrait is not flattering; she is handsomer than it is.'

At night an even stricter watch was kept; sentinels were doubled and boats were constantly on the move. The Emperor was locked up just as securely in the ship where he had sought asylum as in a dungeon in the Tower of London: he was in fact a prisoner of war.

In his office, Lord Keith was putting the last words to two dispatches to Lord Melville, before preparing to visit the 'reptile'.

I am honoured by your Lordship's letter of the 25th and shall carefully attend to the suggestions therein mentioned, and that part relating to a future destination shall remain a profound secret with me. I have the honour to enclose the letter to the Prince Regent[24], which had been withheld by the French general but who is now on board the *Bellerophon*.

Then, from the same pen, came one of those private notes sometimes written by those who think themselves politically important and who have disguised their thoughts in their official missives:

I am infinitely obliged by your private letter concerning the rank and way in which Napoleon is to be considered, for I felt awkward as he had

[23] See Appendix 3.
[24] Endorsed by Lord Melville: 'Transmitted to Lord Bathurst, July 26.'

sent repeatedly desiring me to see him, and this morning he asked Capt.
Maitland to inform me that he from this moment considered himself as
an individual and expected no honour or public attention beyond that of
a prisoner of war;[25] that many ways of escape had been pointed out and
recommended to him, but which he declined! That the army on the Loire
had sent to invite him to the command of it as a General of France, and
that the garrison of Rochelle, Ile d'Aix etc. had offered to take him to that
army, but that he had declined so that he might throw himself upon the
humanity of England. He read in the papers that he was to be sent to St.
Helena, which idea was dreadful. He would prefer death. He would be
content to be put in the Tower or any place of confinement in England,
but above all to be permitted to live in private in any part of the kingdom
within a limited space. But it strikes me, if he has got the idea of St. Helena
and has heard he may by means of money attempt an escape, I conjure
Capt. Maitland to be on guard night and day.

When the Admiral went on board the *Bellerophon* at about eleven
o'clock on the 28th, he was very much on his guard. For the Emperor, this was his first meeting with someone of high rank, and he
had high hopes of it. Had not Lord Keith asked Maitland to satisfy
his passengers' wishes, and thank Napoleon for the care his nephew
had received after Waterloo? Besides which, his naval career was in
his favour and justified expectations that the conversation would be
interesting.

Alas, his visitor turned out to be a stiff, embarrassed and sus-
picious sailor, who took refuge behind the political neutrality of the
senior service.

'I am no more,' Napoleon kept on saying, 'and can disturb nobody.
Cannot I live in England?'

Could he have asked less of a generous enemy? The Emperor was
too well versed in Plutarch to realise the pride his downfall inspired
in a British aristocrat, the bitterness aroused in a sailor who was also
a politician by the danger his country had lived through in the last
twenty years, the resentment that devotion to the Crown and respect
for the sacred principles of inequality by birth provoked towards this
pale disturbing little general who had threatened the regime and upset thrones.

'I have seen General Bonaparte,' Lord Keith wrote that same
evening. 'He sent three times to desire I would come to him. . . .

[25] Napoleon never considered himself as a prisoner of war.

We talked on many subjects – of Toulon, Egypt, East Indies etc. I saw Madame Bertrand, a Dillon – speaks English perfectly. Madame Montaleaux (i.e. Montholon) also is good looking, but not a good figure. . . . He looks like a man in perfect health, thick calves, thin ankles, clear eyes and a thin mouth – like as possible the picture.'

In fact he received an unfavourable impression, because Countess Bertrand, who was distinctly overwrought, assailed him with questions as he left; she entreated him to oppose the departure of the Grand Marshal and he at once detected something mean-spirited among Napoleon's anxious, noisy and indiscreet companions, and thus something reassuring to the English in Bonaparte's absolute isolation. Surrounded by this crowd of boasters and silly women, the great Emperor could hardly be contemplating any drastic exploit.

The truth was even worse, if we are to believe Gourgaud's ruthless eye or the comments of the officers of the *Bellerophon*. While Bertrand continued to carry out his functions as a displaced Grand Marshal in minute detail, his wife was plotting to get out of taking part in this new Odyssey. Irish by birth, and related to the best London society, she was counting on the fifteen thousand or so pounds sterling her husband had deposited in the bank to secure her a comfortable home and a fashionable existence in England. Montholon was already intriguing for advancement, and his pretty wife was making herself pleasant and looking about for conquests. Las Cases was cooped up with his son, copying out the first pages of his *Mémorial*, while Gourgaud ground his teeth with rage at the sight of all these last-minute followers stealing the Emperor's affection from him: herein lay the potential ingredients of the drama of St. Helena. Only Savary and Lallemand, who knew they would be doomed if they went back to France, kept cool-headed enough to try and get the best possible conditions from the English.

Fatigue, uncertainty, and the rain beating sadly down on the slippery deck of the *Bellerophon*, increased their boredom and aggravated their anxiety. July 29 ended in the blackest despair. Maitland brought gazettes from the town which confirmed that St. Helena would be the place of exile, and while the men scarcely concealed their dismay, Madame Bertrand behaved in the most unbridled fashion, and implored the English to cross the name of her husband, the Grand Marshal of the Empire, off the list.

'The Emperor is a monster of egotism,' she cried, 'and would see women and children perish without feeling a thing.' That evening, she had a nervous attack and rolled on the floor.

The 30th was a Sunday, an English Sunday, and the crowds of visitors surpassed all anticipation: nearly a thousand boats, each containing eight people, circled tirelessly round the old ship, now become a floating prison. Napoleon remained shut in his cabin for some time, reading a life of Washington and a translation of Ossian's poems,[26] until the moment when Maitland came to announce the arrival of Lord Keith, accompanied by one of the under-secretaries of State. 'Although Lord Keith had acquainted me that Bonaparte was to go to St. Helena, he had at the same time desired me not to communicate this information, and I was therefore obliged to evade his interrogatories as best I could.'[27]

As the denouement of this sordid drama approached, the atmosphere grew more and more oppressive, and the English officers stole covert glances at the man pacing restlessly to and fro.

Bonaparte is a fine-looking man, wrote Midshipman Graebke to his mother, inclined to corpulency, is five feet six inches in height, his hair turning grey and a little bald in the crown of the head, no whiskers, complexion French yellow, eyes grey, Roman nose, good mouth and chin, neck short, big belly, arms stout, small white hands and shows a good leg. He wears a cocked hat somewhat like our old-fashioned three cornered ones, with the tricolour cockade in it, plain green coat, cape red and cuffs the same, plain gold epaulets, and a large star on the left breast, white waistcoat and breeches and white silk stockings, thin shoes and buckles. Eats but two meals in the day, breakfast and dinner, and these are sumptuous: fish, flesh and fowl, wines, fruit, various French dishes etc., etc. He breakfasts about eleven and dines at six, is about half an hour at each, when he generally comes on deck or goes into the after-cabin to study. We do not know what's to be done with him yet.

---

[26] This was one of Napoleon's bedside books.
[27] Maitland: *op. cit.*

XI

THE LAST BATTLE

✦✦

The mission of Lord Keith and Sir Henry Bunbury –
Napoleon's protest – Thoughts of suicide – The Paris
Convention of August 2 – Intervention of Capell
Lofft – Procedure – Napoleon protests again – Arrival
of the *Northumberland*.

✦✦

Lord Keith and the Cabinet representative arrived at ten o'clock on
July 31. Major-General Sir Henry Bunbury, Permanent Under-
Secretary of State for War, could have dealt directly with the Emperor, but by an extraordinary refinement of contempt, the message
he brought – deciding the fate of the man who had put himself under
the protection of the British flag – was addressed to Lord Keith and
had been issued by the office of the First Lord of the Admiralty.
By refraining from sending a notification to the prisoner in person,
and already treating him as a convict who could only be addressed
through his gaoler, the Cabinet inaugurated a series of vexations and
mean acts of persecution through which they hoped to reduce him
to subjection.

Napoleon was alone in his cabin; after a few polite preliminaries,
Lord Keith introduced Sir Henry Bunbury and handed the Emperor a copy of the letter from Lord Melville dated July 28. The
Major-General has left a report of this scene and the dialogue that
followed, which is worth quoting almost in extenso:

(Bonaparte) inquired if it was in French; and on being told that it was
in English, he observed that it would be useless to him and that it would
be necessary to translate it. Upon this Lord Keith began to read the paper
aloud in French, but Bonaparte appeared not to hear distinctly, or not to
comprehend; and after a line or two had been read, he took the paper from
Lord Keith's hands and proposed to me that I should translate. I believe

he meant that I should make a written translation, but I preferred reading it aloud in French.

Napoleon listened attentively to the whole without interrupting me and appeared as if he had been previously aware of what was to be communicated to him. At the conclusion Lord Keith asked Bonaparte if he wished to have a written translation made. but he answered No; that he comprehended the substance perfectly, that the translation had been sufficiently good. He received the paper and laid it upon the table, and after a pause he began by declaring his solemn protest against this proceeding of the British Government; that they had not the right to dispose of him in that manner; and he appealed to the British people and to the laws of the country. Bonaparte asked what was the tribunal, or if there was not a tribunal, where he might prefer his appeal against the illegality and injustice of the decision taken by the British Government. '*I am come here voluntarily*,' said he, '*to place myself in the home of your nation*[1] and to claim the rights of hospitality. I am not even a prisoner of war. If I were a prisoner of war you would be bound to treat me *according to the laws of your people*; but I came to this country a passenger on board one of your ships of war, after a previous negotiation with its commander. If he had told me I was to be a prisoner, I should not have come. I asked him if he was willing to receive me and my suite on board and carry me to England. *Admiral* Maitland answered that he would, and after telling me that he had received the special orders of his Government concerning me. *So he set a trap for me.* In coming on board a British ship of war, I confided myself to the hospitality of the British nation as much as if I had entered one of their towns – *a ship, a village, it's all the same. As for the island of St. Helena, it is my death warrant.* I protest against being sent thither, and I protest against being imprisoned in a fortress in this country. I demand to be received as an English citizen. I know, indeed, that I cannot be admitted to the rights of an Englishman at first. Some years are requisite to entitle one to be domiciliated. Well, let the Prince Regent place me during that time under any surveillance he may think proper. Let me be put in a country house in the centre of the island, thirty leagues from the sea. Place a commissioner about me to examine my correspondence and report my actions; and if the Prince Regent should require my parole, perhaps I would give it. There I might have a certain degree of personal liberty and could enjoy the liberty of literature. In St. Helena I should not live three months: with my habits and constitution it would be immediate death. I am used to ride twenty leagues a day. What am I to do on this little rock at the end of the world? The climate is too hot for me. No I will not go to St. Helena; Botany Bay is better than St. Helena. If your Government wishes to put me to death, they may kill me here. It is not worth while to send me to St. Helena. I

---

[1] Passages in italics are in French in Bunbury's account, published in the *Keith Papers*.

prefer death to St. Helena, and what good is my death to you? I can do you no harm. I am no longer a sovereign, I am a simple individual. Besides, times and affairs are altered. What danger could result from my living as a private person in the heart of England under surveillance, and restricted in any way the Government might imagine necessary?'

Bonaparte returned frequently to the circumstances under which he had come on board the *Bellerophon*, insisted that he had been perfectly free in his choice, and that he had preferred confiding to the hospitality and generosity of the British people rather than take any other course. 'Why should I not have gone to my father-in-law, or to the Emperor of Russia who is my personal friend? We have become enemies because he wanted to annex Poland to his dominions – and my popularity among the Poles was in his way; but otherwise he was my friend and would not have treated me in this manner. If your Government acts thus, it will disgrace itself in the eyes of Europe; and even your own people will disapprove and blame its conduct. Besides, you do not know, perhaps, what a feeling my death will create both in France and Italy, and how greatly the character of England will suffer if my blood rests here. There is a high opinion of the justice and honour of England. If you kill me, your reputation will be lost in France and Italy, and it will cost the loss of many Englishmen. There never has been a similar instance in the history of the world; and what was there to force me to the step I took? The tricolour flag was still flying in Bordeaux, at Nantes, at Rochefort; the army has not submitted at this hour, I could have joined them; or, if I had chosen to remain in France, what could have prevented my remaining concealed for years among a people who were all attached to me? But I preferred to settle as a private individual in England.'

Bonaparte reverted again to his negotiations with Captain Maitland, the assurance that he should be carried to England, the honours and attentions shown him by Captain Maitland and Admiral Hotham. 'And after all, has this been a snare laid for me? If you now kill me it will be an eternal disgrace to the Prince Regent, to your Government, and to the nation. *It would be an act of unparalleled cowardice. I have offered the Prince Regent the finest episode in his history.* I am his enemy and I place myself at his discretion. I have made war upon you for twenty years, and I do you the highest honour, and give you the greatest proof of my confidence, by placing myself voluntarily in the hands of my most inveterate enemies. Remember what I have been, and how I stood among the sovereigns of Europe. This courted my affection; that gave me his daughter; all sought my friendship. I was an Emperor, acknowledged so by all the Powers of Europe except Great Britain; and she had acknowledged and treated with me as Chief Consul of France.' Then, turning to the table and laying his finger on the paper, 'And', said he, 'your Government have not the right to style me General Bonaparte. I am First Consul, and I ought to be treated as such if treated with at all. When I was at Elba I was as much a sovereign as when I was on the throne of France. I was as much a sovereign in Elba as the King was in France. We had each our flags. I had my flag', he repeated. 'We had each our ships, our troops. To be sure,' said he smiling, 'mine were on a small scale. I had 600 soldiers, and he had 200,000; *all the same I made war on him; I beat him, I drove him out of the country, and off the throne.* But there was nothing in all this to alter my position or to deprive me of my rank as one of the sovereigns of Europe.'

Napoleon spoke with little or no interruption from Lord Keith or myself. He sometimes paused, as for a reply. I could only say that I was little more than the bearer of the dispatches to Lord Keith; that I was not authorised to enter into discussions; and that I could only undertake to hear General Bonaparte's representations and communicate them to the King's Ministers. I observed that I felt convinced that the chief motive which had made the Government fix upon St. Helena was that its local situation admitted of his enjoying there a greater degree of indulgence than could be admitted in any part of Great Britain. Bonaparte immediately said, '*No, no, I will not go to St. Helena; you would not go there – you, Sir, nor you, my Lord.*' He then renewed his protest against being imprisoned or sent to St. Helena. '*I will not leave here. I will not go to St. Helena. I am no Hercules, but you will not be able to take me there. I prefer death here.* You found me free; send me back again. Replace me in the state you found me. and which I quitted only under the impression your Admiral was to land me in England. If your Government will not do this, and will not permit me to reside here, let me go to the United States. But I appeal to your laws, and I throw myself on their protection to prevent my being sent to St. Helena or being shut up in a fortress.'

Bonaparte inquired when the *Northumberland* was likely to arrive and to be ready to sail, and he pressed the Admiral to take no step towards removing him from the *Bellerophon* before the Government should have been informed of what had passed on this occasion, and should have signified their final decision. He added that, as to going on board the *Northumberland*, he could not do it. '*I will not go – I will not leave here.*'

Lord Keith appeared to think that even if the *Northumberland* should arrive, this delay might be granted. As he addressed me, I answered that I could give no opinion on this point, and that it rested with his Lordship to decide.

Bonaparte urged me to acquaint His Majesty's Government without the least delay of what had passed. I told him I should dispatch a written report immediately; and that I should remain myself at Plymouth until the next day, in case he should have anything further to state. Lord Keith asked Napoleon if he wished to put his answer in writing. He said, '*No, this gentleman understands French well, he will draw up a report, he occupies an important post and must be an honourable man; he will communicate the reply I have given to the Government.'*

After some pause, Bonaparte began again. He went over the same grounds, dwelling particularly on his having been free to come or not, and having decided to come here, from understanding that Captain Maitland, acting according to the orders of his Government, would undertake to bring him in safely; upon the illegality of sentencing him to death or imprisonment; and his desire to appeal formally to the laws, and the people of England; upon the disgrace which would attach to the nation, and particularly to the Government. He repeated his desire to live in England as a private citizen under any restrictions and with a Commissioner to watch him 'who would also be of great use to me for the first year or two, in showing me what I ought to do'; and he added, 'I will give my word of honour that I will not hold any correspondence with France, and that I will not engage in any political affairs whatever.' Finally, he repeated his fixed determination not to go to St. Helena.

We made our bows and retired.[2] In a few minutes Bonaparte sent for Lord Keith again. I did not return with his Lordship, who remained a very short time.

When the Admiral returned to the cabin, he found Napoleon a beaten man, conscious of the uselessness of flying into one of the furious rages that once petrified his interlocutors, and apparently calm.

'What is your advice?' he asked.

'I am an officer and have discharged my duty.'

'Is there any tribunal to which I can apply?'

'I am no lawyer, but I believe none. I am satisfied there is every disposition on the part of the British Government to render your situation as comfortable as is consistent with prudence.'

'How so? St. Helena?'

'Sir, it is surely preferable to being confined in a smaller space in England, or being sent to France, or perhaps to Russia.'

'Russia! God preserve me!'

When the Englishman had left, Napoleon sent for Bertrand and dictated a protest, designed to go over the heads of the envoys to

---

[2] Bunbury left an excellent portrait of the Emperor. See Appendix 4.

the men who were politically responsible; it was an able letter, couched in terms of bitter seriousness:

My Lord, I have read with attention the extract of the letter which you sent me.

I have given you my views in detail. I am not a prisoner of war, but I am the guest of England. I came to this country on the warship *Bellerophon*, after informing the Captain of the letter written by me to the Prince Regent and obtaining his assurance that he had orders to receive me on board and convey me to England with my suite, if I presented myself for this purpose. Admiral Hotham subsequently repeated the same things. From the moment that I was freely received on board the *Bellerophon* I was under the protection of the laws of your country.

I would rather die than go to St. Helena, or be shut up in some fortress. I desire to live in the interior of England, a free man, protected by and subject to the law, and bound by any undertakings or measures that may be thought necessary; I do not wish to engage in any correspondence with France, nor interfere in any political matters. Since my abdication, my intention has always been to make my home in one of two countries – the United States or England.

I believe that you, my Lord, and the Under-Secretary of State, will faithfully report all the arguments into which I have entered in order to prove to you the rights of my position. It is in the honour of the Prince Regent, and the protection of your country's laws, that I have put my trust, and I still continue to do so.[3]

Maitland had been sent for to see that this letter should be forwarded without losing any time, and Napoleon gave free rein to his indignation in his presence. He delivered himself of a violent monologue, in the jerky, passionate tones that always impressed his hearers; his apparently disconnected sentences seemed to follow his train of thought with difficulty.

The idea of being sent to St. Helena is a perfect horror to me. To be placed for life on an island within the Tropics, at an immense distance from any land . . . it is worse than Tamerlane's iron cage. I would prefer being delivered up to the Bourbons. Among other insults – but that is a mere bagatelle, a very secondary consideration – they style me General! They have no right to call me General; they may as well call me Archbishop, for I was head of the church as well as the army. If they do not acknowledge me as Emperor, they ought as First Consul; they have sent ambassadors to me as such, and your King in his letters styled me brother.

---

[3] The original belongs to Mr. William M. Spencer.

Had they confined me in the Tower of London or one of the fortresses in England (though not what I had hoped from the generosity of the English people) I should not have so much cause of complaint; but to banish me to an island within the Tropics! They might as well have signed my death-warrant at once.

In spite of the rage that possessed him, he appeared at his usual hour for a walk on the deck of the *Bellerophon*, considerably to the surprise of Maitland, who thought he was prostrated in his cabin. At dinner he even seemed to be in specially good form, but when retiring for the night he suddenly gave orders to Marchand to take some cases of silver, jewels and other valuables to the Grand Marshal.

Withdrawing behind the bed-curtains, he began to undress, asking his valet to read him the life of Cato out of the volume of Plutarch lying open on the table. Alarmed by the reddish light filtering through the curtains, and also by the silence, the young man remembered the poison his master had carried in his waistcoat pocket ever since Malmaison, and unconsciously slowed the rhythm of his delivery.

'Read', a calm voice enjoined him.

The story of the death of Cato finished, the curtains were drawn, and the Emperor appeared in his dressing-gown. What had been happening? Had Napoleon thought of dying like the Stoic of Utica, after reading from his favourite book, or had he found encouragement to stand up to his enemies in this example from antiquity? Perhaps this self-communion, before taking an irreparable step, had given him a glimpse of what the final stage at St. Helena would add to his legend.

If he succeeded in preserving an appearance of dignified calm in that hour of humiliation the English considered to be the complement of victory,[4] it was not the same with his companions. Countess Bertrand, weeping bitterly, declared and wrote, both in French and English, that her husband would not be so heartless as to sacrifice his family to his duty; on July 31 she pretended to be mad, and tried

---

[4] One has only to turn the pages of albums of caricatures of the period to be convinced of this spiteful determination to humiliate a conquered enemy. *A rare acquisition for the Royal Menagerie* shows the Emperor dressed as a clown and shut into a parrot's cage. A Fury is threatening him with scissors and shrieking: 'I'll dock Head and dock Tail Him . . . I'll cut off his ears . . . I'll cut off his . . . I'll make a singing Bird of him.' This was on July 28, 1815.

to throw herself into the sea after forcing the Emperor's door and making a frantic scene.

'But, Madame, I am not forcing Bertrand to go with me. He is entirely free.'

Gourgaud, violent as ever, dreamed of setting fire to the gunpowder and perishing sword in hand while exterminating a few Englishmen. Taking Montholon and Lallemand with him, he hurried off to see Maitland and try one last transparent stratagem:

'You may depend upon it, the Emperor never will go to St. Helena; he will sooner put himself to death.'

'Has he ever said he will put himself to death?' asked the Captain suspiciously.

'No, but he has said he will not go, which amounts to the same thing; and were he to consent himself, here are three of us who are determined to prevent him.'

Maitland pacified the three agitated men, and sent them away, advising them to consider the consequences well, before they ventured on a measure of that kind.

Next Savary and Lallemand, who had been excluded from the voyage to St. Helena by a ministerial decision, laid siege to the Captain of the *Bellerophon*, reminding him of his promise that they would not be sent back to France – a promise that they declared had decided them to come on board ship.

'It was certainly not my intention to go to St. Helena,' said Savary. 'I took this decision out of sense of duty to my large family. I gather from the news from France that I am summoned to appear before a military tribunal. Were I to be allowed a fair and impartial trial I should have nothing to fear, but at present, when faction runs so high, I should inevitably be sacrificed to the fury of party.'

Lallemand adopted the same attitude and announced his intention of taking refuge in the United States or Denmark, urging that his case be put to Generals Slade and Long, with whom he had negotiated an exchange of prisoners in 1812.

Maitland wrote to his superiors on their behalf, emphasising that his honour was involved:

Savary and Lallemand believe that it is the intention of His Majesty's Government to deliver them up to the King of France. Far be it from me to assume such an idea, but I hope your Lordship will make allowance for the feelings of an officer who has nothing so dear to him as his honour, and who could not bear that a stain should be affixed to a name he has ever endeavoured to bear unblemished. These two men, Savary and Lallemand (what their characters or conduct in their own country may be I know not), threw themselves under the protection of the British flag; that protection was granted them with the sanction of my name. It is true no conditions were stipulated for; but I acted in the full confidence that their lives would be held sacred, or they should never have set foot in the ship I command without being made acquainted that it was for the purpose of delivering them over to the laws of their country.

Did the Captain of the *Bellerophon* realise that his words could equally well be applied to Napoleon himself? Or did he wish to take advantage of the case of Savary and Lallemand to remind his superior officers that so arbitrary a measure as sending back fugitives to France would ever stain the name of Maitland and the reputation of the British Navy?

From August 1 to 3, their isolation weighed heavily on the passengers in quarantine on the great ship. While Maitland carried out his duties with tight lips and a furrowed brow, Napoleon stayed in his cabin, sometimes conversing with Las Cases.

'After all, is it absolutely certain that I shall go to St. Helena? Is anyone really dependent on his fellow men if he doesn't want to be?'

He seemed distrait and at a loss.

Sometimes I feel a desire to leave you, and it would not be difficult; it is only a question of working on one's feelings a little, and I would quickly have escaped from you, it would all be over and you could go back to your families. Especially as I have absolutely no inner principles to bother me; I am one of those who believe that the torments of the next world have only been invented to supplement the insufficient attractions we are led to expect. God would never have designed such a counter-weight to his infinite goodness, certainly not for actions of this sort. And what does it amount to, after all? Wanting to come to Him a little sooner.

Las Cases was shocked, protested, and spoke of the philosophical way the ancients accepted misfortune; then he held out hopes of some always possible change in the situation.

'But what can we do in that desolate place?' insisted Napoleon.

'We will live on the past, Sire; there is plenty there to satisfy us. Do we not enjoy the lives of Caesar and Alexander? Better still, you will re-read your own writings, Sire.'

'Very well, we will write our memoirs! Yes, one must work; work is Time's scythe. After all one must fulfil one's destiny; that is my chief doctrine.'

Count de Las Cases, in his retiring, docile and discreetly flattering way, was already trying to score over his companions, by preserving the pliant moderation of a courtier only anxious to please, in the midst of their quarrels and extreme behaviour. For in the anguish of departure, the hatred and scheming that were to poison their stay at St. Helena were already fermenting.

Maitland felt sorry for Madame Bertrand; her nervous attack had left her fuming with rage at her own personal downfall, and she was retailing infamous scandals to the English. It was Savary who had fastened the lantern to the Duc d'Enghien's chest at the time of the sinister execution in the moat at Vincennes. Nor did she any longer control her abuse of the Emperor himself.

'If his ends are served, he does not care what becomes of other people. . . . He deserves nothing at our hands; and indeed there is not one of his people who would not most gladly quit him.'

But when she pretended to throw herself into the sea in her despair, hoping to make the Grand Marshal give way and consent to stay in England and lead the life of a rich exile, Savary cried out with cruel delight to Bertrand, who was trying to restrain his wife: 'Let her go – why don't you let her go!'

She took deep offence at this remark and revenged herself by exclaiming to all and sundry that her husband was no gentleman, and inciting him to quarrel with Gourgaud, who had made the English laugh by describing how the great Fanny Bertrand had tried to seduce the attractive Montholon.

In spite of these incidents, Napoleon did not change his mind: the Grand Marshal must go with him, for his status as chief officer of the Crown would shed a little lustre on a makeshift establishment.

With the same pen that copied the sentences evoking the fate of Themistocles, addressed to the Prince Regent, Bertrand now wrote out the names of those who were to be called upon to share the exile of a master not all of them had served at the Tuileries. There would be the Montholons, Las Cases and his son, and Gourgaud, who – with the Bertrands – would make up a suitable Court. Servants would be numerous: Marchand, Saint-Denis, Noverraz, Cipriani,

Pierron, Lepage, the two Archambault brothers, Rousseau, Gentilini and Santini. But Maingault, the doctor, who suffered dreadfully from sea-sickness, refused the post offered him; he was to be replaced by the surgeon from the *Bellerophon*, Barry O'Meara, who had impressed everyone favourably; he spoke Italian and had taken part in the Egyptian campaign; as he was an Irishman it was to be hoped that he would not accept all the views of the English without a murmur.

Even when the list had been drawn up, Napoleon put off the moment of sending it to Maitland; he still hoped against hope for a conciliatory message from the British Cabinet.

While Lord Keith and Maitland were standing by at Plymouth, the members of the Cabinet endeavoured to give their decision the seal of legality. The agreement concerning the Emperor's custody was communicated to the ambassadors of the Allied Powers in London by Lord Castlereagh on July 28, and signed in Paris on August 2 by the representatives of Great Britain, Russia, Austria and Prussia:

Napoleon Bonaparte being in the power of the Allied sovereigns, their Majesties the King of the United Kingdom of Great Britain and Ireland, the Emperor of Austria, the Emperor of Russia, and the King of Prussia, have agreed, in virtue of the stipulations of the Treaty of the 25th of March, 1815, upon the measures most proper to render all enterprise impossible, on his part, against the repose of Europe.

Article 1. Napoleon Bonaparte is considered by the Powers who have signed the Treaty of the 25th of March last as their prisoner.

Article 2. His custody is especially entrusted to the British Government. The choice of the place, and of the measures which can best secure the object of the present stipulation, is reserved to his Britannic Majesty.

Article 3. The Imperial Courts of Austria and of Russia, and the Royal Court of Prussia, are to appoint Commissioners to proceed to and abide at the place which the Government of his Britannic Majesty shall have assigned for the residence of Napoleon Bonaparte, and who, without being responsible for his custody, will assure themselves of his presence.

Article 4. His Most Christian Majesty is to be invited, in the name of the four above-mentioned Courts, to send in the like manner a French Commissioner to the place of detention of Napoleon Bonaparte. . . .

Thus given a free hand, the Prince Regent's ministers could proceed to carry out the sentence. But they had to wait for the arrival of the *Northumberland*, on her way home from the East Indies in a pitiable condition, and needing overhauling and repainting before she set off for St. Helena. Since paint dries less quickly than the ink of treaties, the Sea Lords could not promise miracles to satisfy the political Lords. The sailors obstinately insisted on a delay of four or five days for the ship's toilet, and the Prime Minister was suddenly confronted by fresh difficulties.

Firstly the crowds, who were collecting in increasing numbers: 'I am miserable with all the idle people in England coming to see this man,' wrote Keith to his daughter. 'Not a bed in all the town . . . you may guess my trouble and anxiety. I wish him at the – or anywhere but here.' The curiosity of the first days had given place to a sort of excitement, which might either be savage triumph or sympathy; the visitors wore red carnations in their buttonholes and burst into cheers when Napoleon appeared. 'Las Cases has high hopes of the wearers of carnations,' Gourgaud noted. These cheerful nautical festivities sometimes degenerated into disorder.

But the telegraph suddenly went into action between London and the great sea-port, for a new danger had just been noticed. Melville wrote warningly to Keith:

We cannot allow of any alteration in our instructions respecting the disposal of Bonaparte. He must therefore submit, and I hope that he will not compel Sir George Cockburn or Captain Maitland to resort to measures of personal compulsion. I shall be sorry if all his attendants refuse to accompany him; but if they shall, there is no help for it – he must still go. I should particularly wish that the surgeon should go with him. . . but as Lord Bathurst's instructions do not admit of any expectation being held out that any of Bonaparte's attendants will be allowed to quit the island during his life, the surgeon now with him ought not to be indulged with that hope.

You will receive what is perhaps, and most probably, unnecessary – I mean official instruction *on no account* to permit Bonaparte to come on shore. In some of the newspapers a notion is held out that he may be brought out of the ship by a writ of *habeas corpus*. . . . If we were to receive any intimation of such proceeding going forward here, we should order the *Bellerophon* to sea, and to cruise off the Start or elsewhere, on some assigned rendezvous to meet the *Northumberland*. We may possibly have to apply to Parliament for their sanction to what we are doing respecting Bonaparte and the safe custody of his person, but we must do our duty in the meantime.

Whatever the expense incurred in the maintenance of the party in the *Bellerophon* and *Liffey* will be defrayed on application of the captains. It is an extraordinary case, and we must pay in consequence.

Once the danger had been defined, the decision followed, and next day the Admiralty sent off a dispatch:

As it appears that considerable inconvenience is occasioned by the continuance of General Bonaparte in Plymouth Sound, I have to signify to your Lordship the commands of the Lords Commissioners of the Admiralty that you do immediately, on the receipt of this letter, order Admiral Sir B. Hallowell in the *Tonnant* to take the *Bellerophon* under his command, together with any frigate you may please to appropriate to this source; and putting to sea with all possible expedition, proceed to cruise with the three ships (the *Bellerophon* having the General and his suite on board) off the Start, or other such rendezvous as your Lordship may think proper, until they shall be joined by Sir George Cockburn in the *Northumberland*; when General Bonaparte and the persons who are to accompany him to St. Helena are to be transported to the latter ship, which is to proceed immediately afterwards in execution of their Lordships' former orders. . . .

My Lords reckon confidently on the zeal and vigilance of Sir Benjamin Hallowell to keep the *Bellerophon* in sight, and to prevent any communication with them whatever; and when the General and those who accompany him shall be safely on board the *Northumberland*, and that ship has proceeded on her voyage, he is to return with the ships to Plymouth Sound, the remaining part of Bonaparte's suite continuing on board the *Bellerophon* for further orders. . . .

It has been stated to their Lordships that some persons of the General's suite on board the *Bellerophon* have used violent and threatening language. Your Lordship will therefore, if you judge it necessary, take measures for removing such persons from the *Bellerophon* to the *Tonnant*. In the event of General Bonaparte or any of his suite escaping to the shore – which, however, it may be hoped is impossible – your Lordship will take the most active measures in securing them and sending them back on board the ship. It seems hardly necessary to observe to your Lordship that the most profound secrecy should be observed on the subject of the proceedings directed in this letter, which indeed need be communicated only to Sir Benjamin Hallowell and Sir George Cockburn.

Lord Keith was quite determined to be the sole official witness of these great events; deliberately setting aside Admiral Sir Benjamin Hallowell, whom he detested, he prepared to carry out the orders received in person, reporting briefly to London: 'I have decided on embarking in the *Tonnant* and proceeding off the Start with that ship, the *Bellerophon* and *Eurotas*, for the purpose of meeting the *Northumberland* and more effectually executing their Lordships' directions respecting General Bonaparte.' At the same time he wrote curtly to Maitland: 'You are to acquaint General Bonaparte that I have this morning received the final directions of H.M. Government respecting him; and as not the slightest alteration is to be made in the arrangements already communicated to him, you are to request him to furnish you, for my information, with the names of the persons whom he wishes to accompany him to St. Helena. I am in hourly expectation of meeting Sir George Cockburn in the *Northumberland* and any further delay will therefore be inconvenient.'

He wrote to his daughter in a more relaxed style: 'Bony is to have 15 with him, but I believe not half the number will go with him, indeed no one but Bertrand has offered. . . . He was hot, agitated and verbose, and repetitive in the extreme.' I am worried to death with idle folk coming, even from Glasgow, to see him; there is no nation as foolish as we are.'

On the morning of August 4, Maitland therefore received orders to get under weigh and keep along the shore as far as Start Point. Finding these instructions as surprising as his passenger did, he hurried off to the Admiral in hopes of some crumbs of information. 'A Habeas Corpus has been taken out for the purpose of bringing Bonaparte on shore,' said Lord Keith. 'A lawyer is on his way down to serve it.' Without losing any time, the *Bellerophon* weighed anchor and set the sails, followed soon afterwards by the *Eurotas*, the *Express* and the *Nimble*, as well as the *Tonnant*, flying the flag of the Commander-in-Chief of the Channel Fleet.

✤   ✤   ✤

On July 28, realising that his fate lay in the balance, Napoleon dictated to Las Cases a 'document to be used as a foundation for lawyers to discuss and defend his true political situation'. Means were found of getting it to the shore.[5] This memorandum may have

[5] Las Cases: *Mémorial*, July 28, 1815.

been sent either to Sir Samuel Romilly, or to Capell Lofft.[6] If it was the great Romilly, he was discreet and surrounded his actions with a veil of secrecy, as he did a few days later his efforts on behalf of Savary. Whether Lofft did or did not receive the memorandum, he was carried away by his almost proverbial enthusiasm, and at once wrote an open letter to the Morning Chronicle:

The intelligence that the great Napoleon will not be permitted to land, and is to be sent perhaps to St. Helena, is almost overwhelming me, though long accustomed to suffer much, and to expect everything!

I know not that the Emperor can be regarded as a prisoner of war. From a view of all the circumstances that affect his person, and situation, and of his coming thither, I am of opinion that he cannot. But if he could, it is not, nor has been for two centuries, the custom of Britain thus to treat her prisoners.

Could we try him? I know not by what right either we, or any, or all of the Confederates could. Can we without trial take his life? This were far worse than to kill a prisoner recently taken in battle.

Can we then exercise such a power over the personal and inherent dignity and honour, far dearer than life, of such a Personage, and send him to lonely imprisonment in a deserted far distant land?

Bonaparte with the concurrence of the Admiralty is within the limits of British local allegiance. He is temporarily considered as a private, though not a natural born subject, and as such within the limits of the Habeas Corpus Act our second Magna Charta, that no subject being an inhabitant or resident of England etc. shall be sent prisoner into Scotland or to places beyond the sea. All persons within the Realm of England, which includes the adjoining seas, are temporary subjects if aliens, or permanent if natural born.

Though not on the British soil he is within the protection of British law. If at Plymouth, he is in a British county. An Habeas Corpus if issued, must be obeyed: and no doubt would be willingly obeyed by the Captain of the *Bellerophon*. It would be issuable, being vacation, by the Chancellor, the Chief Justice of England, or other of the judges at their house or chambers, immediately, founded on an affidavit. And if all communication with the *Bellerophon* is shut out, which might enable Napoleon himself to make the application, the imprisonment of any individual within the limits of the English law and constitution concerns the dignity, the liberty and the

---

[6] Lofft, Capell, (1751–1824). He belonged to the most advanced section of the Whig Party. A passionate idealist, he took part in all liberal campaigns, fought for the abolition of slavery and reform of the severe penal code. He had openly declared that 'Napoleon could always count on his support'.

rights of every Englishman: and constitutes fault or error in respect to this all protective law which being remedial must be most liberally construed.

I am of opinion that deportation, or transportation, or relegation, cannot legally exist in this country, except when the law expressly provides it on trial and sentence.

It cannot be expected that many authorities should be quoted in such a peculiar case: neither is it necessary, as it differs from the common cases of every day, chiefly in the greatness of the Person who is the object. . . .

The task Capell Lofft had undertaken was no sinecure, since any procedure leading to the issue of a writ of Habeas Corpus had small chance of being crowned with success. Ministers considered that the former sovereign of the French had not been 'received' on board the *Bellerophon*, but captured as a prisoner of war.

There was a subtler plan, however, that might prove more fruitful: this consisted in summoning Napoleon to appear in court, as a witness in current legal proceedings. Once he was on the mainland, he would have time and means to demand the protection of those laws that safeguard all citizens against arbitrary detention – and the three months before the opening of the next judicial session might well provide some surprises.

Admiral Cochrane,[7] formerly Commander-in-Chief of the North American station, had brought a case for libel against a West Indian lawyer called Mackenrot, who had accused him of negligence in failing to attack the French squadron under Admiral Willaumez in 1806. Cochrane argued that the ships were in a bad state, and Mackenrot intended to call Napoleon as a witness for the defence, and to enlighten the magistrates concerning the imperial fleet. A *subpoena*[8] could speedily be made out and delivered to Napoleon, or his guardian Lord Keith, who would be unable to refuse it, on pain of the grave offence of contempt of court. The immediate result would be that the witness would have to be disembarked and his departure for exile postponed.

The scenario was somewhat crude and transparent, it is true, and the actors, Cochrane and his adversary Mackenrot, were a peculiar couple; as for the production, which involved choosing the ex-

---

[7] Cochrane, Sir Alexander (1758–1832), uncle of another and more famous admiral, Thomas, Lord Cochrane.

[8] A subpoena can only be served on a person who resides in England and is at liberty.

Emperor of the French as a witness in a libel case in which a British admiral and the ex-King of Westphalia[9] were implicated, it was not in the best of taste, but some legal experts thought it had a chance of success.

The Cabinet could find no solution except removing the *Bellerophon* to a distance and running away from the lawyer in charge of the menacing document. Hardly had Maitland weighed anchor when a strange general post began; the lawyer, who turned out to be Mackenrot himself, pursued Lord Keith, who escaped out of the back door of his house, was rowed to the *Tonnant*, climbed in at the larboard gangway, and out at the starboard, and took refuge on another ship. The frustrated Mackenrot went back to Plymouth and wrote a furious letter, which the Admiral would not be able to ignore:

King's Arms Tavern
Plymouth Docks
August 4, 1815.

My Lord,
   I arrived this morning from London with a writ issued by the Court of the King's Bench to subpoena Napoleon Bonaparte as a witness in a trial impending in that Court.

   I was extremely anxious of waiting on your Lordship, most humbly to solicit your permission to serve such a process on your said prisoner, but unfortunately could not obtain any admittance into your presence, neither at your own house, nor at the two offices, nor on board H.M.S. *Tonnant*, where your Lordship was said to be.

   I humbly entreat your Lordship to consider that an evasion to give due facility to the execution of any process would amount to a high contempt against that honourable Court from whence it issued and that under the continuance of such circumstances I shall be under the painful necessity of making my return accordingly. Leaving the issue to your Lordship's discretion, I shall remain here until tomorrow night. And to remove all doubts from your mind I beg leave to enclose a copy of the writ for your perusal, having exhibited the original to Sir Thomas Duckworth as likewise to your secretary and have the honour to subscribe myself with greatest respect.

Enclosure. The Writ.

George the Third by the Grace of God of the United Kingdom of Great Britain and Ireland King, Defender of the Faith, to Napoleon Bonaparte,

---

[9] King Jerome was called as a witness because he commanded a French ship in Willaumez's squadron.

Admiral Willaumez and Jerome Bonaparte greeting; We command you and every one of you that all other things set aside and ceasing every excuse, that you and every one of you be and appear, in your proper persons before our right trusty and well beloved Edward, Lord Ellenborough, our Chief Justice assigned to that plea in our court before us on Friday the tenth of November by nine of the clock in the forenoon of the same day, to testify to the truth according to your knowledge in a certain action now in our Court depending between Sir Alexander Forrester Cochrane, Knight, plaintiff, and Anthony Mackenrot, defendant . . . at the aforesaid day by a jury of the country between the parties aforesaid to the plea aforesaid to be tried; and that you nor any of you shall in no wise omit under penalty of every of you of £100. Witness Edward, Lord Ellenborough of Westminster the fourteenth day of June in the fifty-fifth year of our reign.

Lord Keith, who knew more about the sea than about procedure, at once sent Maitland a letter revealing genuine uneasiness: 'I have been chased all day by a lawyer with a Habeas Corpus: he is landed at Cawsand, and may come off in a sailing-boat during the night; of course, keep all sorts of boats off, as I will do the like in whatever ship I may be in.'

He had had a narrow escape: the *Bellerophon*, impeded by wind and currents, had to be towed by shallops to get out of Plymouth Sound, and was urgently pursued by a boat in which a man in black was gesticulating and brandishing a roll of papers. The obstinacy of a little colonial lawyer had been within an ace of frustrating the entire machinery of government.

On August 5, when Maitland's ship was rolling in the grey Channel waves, Napoleon sent to Lord Keith on the *Tonnant* his famous protest, in which Chateaubriand descried 'harmonies of immensity'.

I hereby solemnly protest, in the face of Heaven and of man, against the violence done me, and against the violation of my most sacred rights, in forcibly disposing of my person and my liberty. I came voluntarily on board of the *Bellerophon*; I am not a prisoner, I am the guest of England. I came on board even at the instigation of the Captain, who told me he had orders from the Government to receive me and my suite, and conduct me to England, if agreeable to me. I presented myself with good faith to put myself under the protection of the English laws. As soon as I was on board the *Bellerophon*, I was under the shelter of the British people.

If the Government, in giving orders to the Captain of the *Bellerophon* to receive me as well as my suite, only intended to lay a snare for me, it has forfeited its honour and disgraced its flag.

If this act be consummated, the English will in vain boast to Europe of their integrity, their laws and their liberty. *British good faith will be lost in the hospitality of the Bellerophon.*

I appeal to History; it will say that an enemy, who for twenty years waged war against the English people, came voluntarily, in his misfortunes, to seek an asylum under their laws. What more brilliant proof could he give of his esteem and his confidence? But what return did England make for so much magnanimity? They feigned to stretch forth a friendly hand to that enemy; and when he had delivered himself up in good faith, they sacrificed him.

On board the *Bellerophon*
August 4, 1815.[10]

Keith sent this document to Melville, together with moderately logical comments intended to whitewash Maitland; he took the opportunity to express his misgivings over his responsibility for thwarting Mackenrot, but without renouncing the part he was playing in this scurvy manoeuvre:

I am not sure it would be convenient for me to land at Plymouth before Bonaparte is delivered to Sir George Cockburn. Admitting he was on the ship under Hallowell's flag, that officer being under my orders, I would be considered liable to the court. . . . I send a formal protest from General Bonaparte against all proceedings on the part of the Government, but he mistakes one point. Capt. Maitland, in common with all the other captains, had orders to take them and detain his person, but no one foresaw that Capt. Maitland was to take him, nor could it be foreseen that to avoid a greater evil, he, Bonaparte, was to fly on board any one particular ship. Had the General been on board of an American ship and found a British ship coming fast upon them and got into a boat and come to the British ship, could that have been considered voluntary surrender or capture?

---

[10] It is interesting to note that the original of this letter, a facsimile of which is here reproduced for the first time, is dated as above (and not in the formula that delighted Chateaubriand and was given by Las Cases: 'On board the *Bellerophon*, at sea). An erasure indicates that the letter was meant to be sent earlier – the word 'July' has been replaced by 'August'. This was the Emperor's final shot and he had kept it in reserve for the last moment.

XII

H.M.S. *NORTHUMBERLAND*

✠✠✠

Arrival of Sir George Cockburn – Lord Bathurst's
regulations – Interview between Napoleon and Admiral
Cockburn – Fresh protest by the Emperor – Embarkation on the *Northumberland* – Lord Keith's last letter.

✠✠✠

At about nine o'clock on the morning of August 9, the masts of the
Northumberland were sighted to the East: she was escorted by two
frigates, with the future garrison of St. Helena on board.

The two groups of ships, Keith's and Cockburn's, were visibly
approaching one another from opposite directions, and at noon they
dropped anchor together to the west of Berry Head. The empty
horizon, the low sky and stormy sea, made an appropriate decor to
this furtive operation, sheltered from indiscreet observers so that
the admirals could carry out their inglorious mission with less embarrassment.

Maitland went on board the *Tonnant* to report to his chief, with a
feeling of relief because 'Bonaparte had at last made up his mind to
move from the *Bellerophon* without force being used;' he
told Lord Keith that Count Bertrand wished for an interview with
him in order to arrange the affairs of those of the French who were to
share their master's fate. Lord Keith handed Maitland instructions
concerning the arms of the vanquished soldiers: 'All arms of every
description are to be taken from the Frenchmen of all ranks on board
the ship you command; and they are to be carefully packed up and
kept in your charge while they remain on board the *Bellerophon*, and
afterwards in that of the captain of the ship to which they may be
removed.'

To disarm the hero of Marengo, a Grand Marshal and generals

such as Gourgaud, who had fought on every European battlefield, must have seemed a difficult and extremely embarrassing undertaking to this obscure ship's captain. He therefore did not mention the matter to General Bertrand, while escorting him to see Lord Keith, who had meanwhile been joined by Cockburn.

Harassed, but amiable and restrained as usual, the Grand Marshal had to put up with the arrogance and intransigence of these two men, who showed so little concern for formalities.

Count Bertrand commenced the conversation by inquiring into the intentions of the Government with regard to Generals Savary and Lallemand; but on being explicitly informed that there were no orders respecting them, and that the exception against them remained in full force, he gave the names of the persons whom it was proposed should accompany Bonaparte to St. Helena. He was then desired to prepare a list of the said persons in writing; and as he requested in the name of Bonaparte that Count de Las Cases might be permitted in the capacity of Secretary instead of the Surgeon, who was unwilling to accompany him and whom he did not wish to take against his inclination, Sir George Cockburn and myself were of opinion that this was a concession of which H.M. Government would not disapprove, and we therefore acceded to it; but to a most pressing solicitation that a person named Piontkowski, who was formerly a captain in the Polish service but had accompanied Bonaparte to Elba, and had there as well as since served as a private, might be allowed to go as a domestic, we considered it right to give a most decided and positive refusal, and as permission was also requested for the Surgeon of the *Bellerophon* to attend him on account of his speaking the Italian language, the Count was informed that that could only be taken into consideration upon a special application being received in writing, especially as the number of persons allowed by the Government would be complete without a Surgeon, from the Count de Las Cases being permitted to go as Secretary.

Sir George Cockburn then delivered to Count Bertrand an extract of such parts of his Instructions as he considered it right to be communicated to Bonaparte; and it was arranged that the Count should explain them, and report when the General would be willing to receive the visit he had solicited by Captain Maitland.[1]

The instructions that were designed to convert St. Helena into the safest prison in the world, and the Emperor into the best guarded prisoner in history, had been drawn up in the same spirit as the measures that isolated Napoleon and his party from the rest of the

[1] Keith Papers.

world on the *Bellerophon*. They were addressed to the Lords of the
the Admiralty, and for Cockburn's use; the latter only communicated
to Bertrand those paragraphs he thought suitable to be revealed. The
whole is the masterly creation of a mind better fitted to govern a
penitentiary than a ministerial department. In spite of the vague
promises contained in the preamble, the instructions destroyed the
prisoner's last hope.

Downing Street,
July 30, 1815.

My Lords, I wish your Lordships to have the goodness to communicate
to Rear-Admiral Sir George Cockburn a copy of the following memorial
which is to serve him by way of instruction to direct his conduct while
General Bonaparte remains under his care.

The Prince Regent, in confiding to English officers a mission of such
importance, feels that it is unnecessary to express to them his earnest desire that no greater personal restraint may be employed than what shall be
found necessary faithfully to perform the duties of which the Admiral, as
well as the Governor of St. Helena, must never lose sight, namely the
perfect secure detention of the person of General Bonaparte. Everything
which without opposing the grand object can be granted as an indulgence
will, his Royal Highness is convinced, be allowed the General. The Prince
Regent depends further on the well-known zeal and resolute character of
Sir George Cockburn that he will not suffer himself to be misled, or im-
prudently to deviate from the performance of his duty.

Bathurst.

Memorial. – When General Bonaparte leaves the *Bellerophon* to go on
board the *Northumberland* it will be the properest moment for Admiral
Cockburn to have the effects examined which the General may have
brought with him.

The Admiral will allow all the baggage, wine and provisions which the
General may have brought with him to be taken on board the *Northumberland*.

Among the baggage, his table service is to be understood as included,
unless it be so considerable as to seem rather an article to be converted
into ready money than for real use.

His money, diamonds, and his valuable effects (consequently bills of
exchange also), of whatever kind they may be, must be delivered up. The
Admiral will declare to the General that the British Government by no
means intend to confiscate his property, but merely to take upon itself the
administration of his effects, to hinder him from using them as a means to
promote his flight.

The examination shall be made in the presence of a person named by the General; the inventory of effects to be retained shall be signed by this person, as well as by the Rear-Admiral, and by the person whom he shall appoint to draw up the inventory. The interest on the principal (according as his property is more or less considerable) shall be applied to his support, and in this respect the principal arrangements to be left to him. For this reason he can from time to time signify his wishes to the Admiral until the arrival of the new Governor of St. Helena, and afterwards to the latter; and if no objection is to be made to his proposal, the Admiral or the Governor can give the necessary orders, and the disbursement will be made paid by bills on H.M. treasury. In case of death he can dispose of his property by a last will, and be assured that the contents of his testament shall be fairly executed.

As an attempt might be made to cause a part of his property to pass for the property of persons of his suite, it must be signified that the property of his attendants is subject to the same regulations.

The disposal of the troops intended to guard him must be left to the Governor. If the General is allowed to go out of bounds where the sentinels are placed, one orderly man at least must accompany the officer.

When the ships arrive, and as long as they remain in sight, the General must be confined to the limits where the sentinels are placed. During this time all communication with the inhabitants is forbidden. His companions in St. Helena are subject during this time to the same rules and must remain with him. . . .

It must be signified to the General that if he attempts to make any attempt to fly he will be put under close confinement; and it must be notified to his attendants that if it should be found that they are plotting to prepare the General's flight, they shall be separated from him, and, likewise put under close confinement.

All letters addressed to the General or to persons in his suite must be delivered to the Admiral or the Governor, who will read them before he suffers them to be delivered to those to whom they are addressed. Letters written by the General or his suite are subject to the same rule. No letter that does not come to St. Helena through the Secretary of State must be communicated to the General or his suite if it is written by a person not living on the island. All their letters, addressed to persons not living on the island, must go under cover of the Secretary of State.

It will be clearly expressed to the General that the Governor and the Admiral have precise orders to inform H.M. Government of all the wishes and representations which he may desire to address to it; in this respect they need not use any precaution. But the paper on which such request or representation is written must be communicated to them open, that they may both read it, and when they send it accompany it with such observations as they may judge necessary. . . .

When the Admiral arrives at St. Helena, the Governor will upon his representation adopt such measures for sending immediately to England, the Cape of Good Hope, or the East Indies such officers or persons in the military corps at St. Helena as the Admiral, either because they are foreigners, or on account of their character or their disposition, shall think it advisable to dismiss from the military service at St. Helena. If there are strangers in the island whose residence in the country shall seem to be with a view of becoming instrumental in the flight of General Bonaparte, he must take measures to remove them.

The whole coast of the island, and all the ships and boats that visit it, are placed under the surveillance of the Admiral. . . . The Admiral will adopt the most vigorous measures to watch over the arrival and departure of every ship, and prevent all communications with the coast, except such as he shall allow. Orders will be issued to prevent, after a certain necessary interval, any foreign or mercantile vessel from going in future to St. Helena.

If the General should be seized with a serious illness, the Admiral and the Governor will each name a physician who enjoys their confidence; they will give them strict orders to give in every day a report on the state of his health.

In case of his death the Admiral will give orders to convey his body to England.

Given at the War Office, July 30, 1815.

This piece of prose reveals the red-tapist attention to detail so characteristic of Lord Bathurst, son and grandson of lawyers, the man of whom Lord Rosebery justly wrote that he 'filled the most dazzling office with the most complete obscurity'. Had they been addressed to a man of good family – but would he have accepted the post? – these instructions would have been theoretically valuable; for officers of Cockburn and Lowe's stamp they were accepted as clauses in the regulations. They were drawn up by a handful of only moderately popular ministers; but they summoned the entire British nation to appear before the tribunal of history.

'It was not your Sir Hudson,' exclaimed Heine to the powerful England of the young Queen Victoria, 'but you who were the Sicilian *sbirro* hired by perjured kings to avenge in secret on the man of the people what the people once inflicted on one of them. And he was your guest, and he had thrown himself on your hospitality.'

It had been agreed with Bertrand that Lord Keith and Sir George Cockburn should come on board the *Bellerophon* in the course of the evening, for the prisoner to be introduced to his guardian. What could be hoped for from such play-acting?

Cockburn[2] was heart and soul a sailor, ruddy faced, incisive of speech; he had fought under Nelson and taken part in the cruel War of Independence. Victorious at Baltimore, he entered Washington, where he ruthlessly set fire to the American Government's stores. A resolute man, built all of one piece, he gained in these operations a reputation for inflexible determination. Little used to worldly life, or the subtleties of the Court, he did not bother about civilities, as Lord Keith sometimes did, but showed in this first interview how he intended to deal with the fallen tyrant.

'How do you do, General Bonaparte?' he asked in a loud voice when he found himself in the Emperor's presence.

Lord Keith, who had prudently brought his secretary, James Meek, with him – his only witness, since Sir George Cockburn was about to leave the country – was able to record in detail this painful interview, in which Napoleon was accompanied by no other Frenchman:

After the customary civilities upon entering the after cabin (where the General had remained since leaving Plymouth Sound on the fourth inst. without coming on deck or making his appearance at table), Bonaparte commenced the conversation by protesting against the measures adopted with regard to him by the British Government, repeating in detail, and almost *verbatim*, the language and reasoning contained in his protest. . . .

I then observed that his protest had been forwarded to the Government the moment that it had been received; and that as myself and Sir George Cockburn were officers in the execution of a duty prescribed to us by our superiors, we could only listen to the remarks he had made, but were not authorised to answer them. The General replied that that he was perfectly aware of, but as we were the only persons permitted to approach him, he owed it to himself and to the world to protest before us, and he did it in the most earnest manner, against the measures pursued by our Government with regard to him – adding that he trusted a faithful report would be made of all that he had said.

---

[2] Rear-Admiral Sir George Cockburn (1772–1853) had gained his first promotion in the wars against the French Republic, and like Keith had taken part in the siege of Toulon. From 1803 to 1808 he served in the East and West Indies; rear-admiral in 1812, he fought in the campaign against the United States. After the episode at St. Helena, he was a member of Parliament, then First Lord of the Admiralty from 1824 to 1846. He thus had time to be present at the return of the body to France in 1840, and the birth of the imperial legend.

I then asked General Bonaparte if he had read the extract of Sir George Cockburn's Instructions which that officer had delivered to Count Bertrand for his information. He replied that he had not; that the Count had not yet finished the translation; but that it was a matter of no consequence whatever, as the British Government appeared to have taken its course of proceedings with respect to him, and seemed resolved on pursuing that course even to his death.

Sir George Cockburn then enquired at what time he would be ready to remove to the *Northumberland*, and he replied any hour he pleased after breakfast, which was generally at about ten o'clock. Some unimportant conversation then ensued as to St. Helena, the extent of Sir George Cockburn's command, and presently afterwards I withdrew.

On board the *Bellerophon*, the French made the most of their last night by trying to abstract their most precious possessions from their luggage before it was ignominiously subjected to examination. Two hundred and fifty thousand francs in gold were sewn into belts and entrusted to members of the suite, together with some diamonds and important papers. Only eighty thousand francs were left in the trunks, to be seized and afterwards given to Sir Hudson Lowe, to pay for extra expenses at St. Helena.

At eight o'clock next morning, August 7, Las Cases went to see Lord Keith, taking a new protest that Napoleon had just signed:

When leaving Plymouth, I sent you my protest concerning the line of conduct which has been adopted towards me. Yesterday, when you did me the honour of coming to see me with Admiral Cockburn, I reiterated this protest.

However, it appears that without knowing the results of these complaints you insist upon my leaving the *Bellerophon*, and boarding the vessel destined to take me to the place of my exile. I am sending Count de Las Cases to you, with a request that you give him, firstly, the deed signed by the authorities who, without prior investigation and without hearing the Captain of the *Bellerophon* nor any of those who received me, have arbitrarily decided that I am a prisoner of war; in opposition to the evidence, since it is well known that I came of my own free will and in good faith, as is proved by my letter to the Prince Regent, which the Captain examined before receiving me.

I beg you, my Lord, also to hand him the decree which, having declared me a prisoner, directs that contrary to the laws of the country and of hospitality I should be taken from the *Bellerophon* and exiled two thousand leagues away, on a rock lost in mid ocean, and in the heat of the Tropics

It is obviously a death sentence on someone who will hardly be able to stand a temperature of such burning heat so suddenly.

My Lord, I have claimed and am again claiming the protection of your laws, and particularly of Habeas Corpus. I am now under your flag, in your roadsteads, with the Captain's offer and promise, and I can only be removed, deprived of my liberty and led into exile in accordance with your laws and their formalities.

Finally, I also request you, my Lord, to hand me the decree signed by those who, without any form or motive except their own decision, want to deprive me of my property, though of little value, and impose upon me and the members of my suite hardships that would be shocking to any sensitive man and surprising to those who are acquainted with and practice the law.

I require these documents in order to enable me to claim in due form the protection of your laws against these decrees, and also to appeal formally to both sovereigns and peoples against this extraordinary affair. You have expressed to me on several occasions, my Lord, the pain it gives you to carry out these orders; I could not therefore wish for a better interpreter to bring their hastiness, severity and injustice to notice.

Bellerophon, August 7, 1815.

The argument of this letter rested principally on the fact that Maitland had known of the letter to the Prince Regent before agreeing to take the Emperor on board. In authorising him to set foot on the *Bellerophon*, under very different conditions from those made to Themistocles, the English sailor's behaviour had been flagrantly unscrupulous, but the strict and secret orders he had received authorised him to proceed with the capture, at whatever cost, even that of honour.

It seems that the French were still hoping that Mackenrot's activities might lead to an intervention from the legal authorities. Las Cases did, in fact, back up the Emperor's efforts to gain time. Lord Keith simply objected that the mooring-ground off Berry Head was unsafe and that it was necessary to weigh anchor as soon as possible.

Las Cases then broached the main object of his mission: 'I asked whether it was probable that they would go so far as to deprive the Emperor of his sword.' The Englishman proved more conciliatory on this point, and decided of his own accord that the great man's weapon should be respected, 'but that Napoleon would be the only one, and the others would be disarmed'. The order to disarm all the Frenchmen having in fact emanated from Keith himself, he decided after some reflection to send Maitland a note specifying: 'When the General quits the ship, it is not intended to take his sword from him, but to let him wear it, but not the others. Pistols, guns, etc., must, *as in all instances*, be removed for the safety of the ship, but the arms are carefully to be kept, and restored at a proper occasion.'

As can be seen from his *Mémorial* for August 7, Las Cases tried to pursue his argument with Lord Keith, who showed that he was impatient to bring it to an end. The departure of the inconvenient 'reptile' would allow him to leave the Navy at last and return to his beloved Purbrook; he did not care much for those so often repeated and often read speeches.

After Las Cases left the *Northumberland*, Keith made haste to report his conversation to Maitland, and asked him to send him in writing any comments inspired by the Frenchman's remarks. The reply sent by the Captain of the *Bellerophon*, so important a keystone in the French defence, did not reach the Admiral until next day, when the *Northumberland* was already tacking her way out of the Channel.[3]

✤   ✤   ✤

Sir George Cockburn, rear-admiral and knight of the honourable Order of the Bath, had no objection to converting himself into a customs officer, and inspecting the Emperor's luggage in company with a representative from Lord Bathurst's ministry. However, piqued by the refusal of the Grand Marshal and the other officers of Napoleon's suite to be present, he soon retired and left the task to his subordinate, attentively watched by the faithful Marchand who had collected together, in the cabin next the Emperor's, trunks full of silver, Sèvres porcelain, linen and toilet articles. The English 'seemed astonished how little luggage there was for them to examine; probably measuring the Emperor's fortune by the heights of his glory, they expected to find piles of riches, where instead only a few odds and ends, hardly worth showing, were spread out'.[4] They seized the box containing four thousand napoleons, and entrusted it to Mait-

[3] See Appendix 7.
[4] Marchant: *Mémoires.*

land, with instructions to deliver it to the Admiralty.[5] In the confusion of the embarkation at Ile d'Aix, the two calashes with coats of arms, which would have been invaluable at Longwood if only to raise the tone of the Household, had been left at Rochefort, together with a great many cases (one containing the coronation robes) which fell into the hands of unscrupulous persons and were sold on the quiet.

At eleven o'clock, Cockburn signalled to Keith that the inspection was over. Keith noted:

I then went on board the *Bellerophon*, but found that the General was engaged with Count Bertrand. It was some time before I saw him, when he repeated his former protestations, and added 'I do not voluntarily go either from this ship or from England; it is you, Admiral, who take me.' To this I replied, 'I hope, Sir, that you will not reduce an officer like me to do so disagreeable an act as to use force towards your person.' He answered, 'Oh no, you shall order me.' I replied, 'I shall attend you at your convenience in my barge, and I beg not to hurry you.' He thanked me, and said he wished to speak to Bertrand, I then retired, and sent that officer into the after cabin.

Nothing now remained for Napoleon to do except make arrangements for those from whom he had to part: it was heart-breaking to witness their very genuine distress. The Emperor whom they adored – a generous master to his servants – was about to go into exile, leaving them behind as political refugees, to be prosecuted in France or left without resources in England. Napoleon ordered a sum of money in gold to be given to each; Savary received the contents of the belt in his charge, Lallemand the cargo of the Danish vessel at Ile d'Aix, and each of the servants pocketed a year's wages. Keith's account continues:

It was nearly two hours after this period before General Bonaparte finished his letters, conversations, and giving audience to the officers to take leave, some of whom shed tears while he appeared to bear it well. . . . He then came out of the cabin and said 'I am at your orders.'

Before leaving the *Bellerophon*, which was about half past one o'clock, he thanked Captain Maitland for the attention he had received from him. He then turned to the officers and did the same and added 'to all your

---

[5] This sum of eighty thousand francs was handed over to Sir Hudson Lowe on September 14, 1815.

crew', bowing at the same time to the ship's company.[6] He was received on the quarter-deck with a Guard in the manner usual for a General Officer,[7] and went into the barge alongside, into which I also sent all those of his suite whom he chose to name – Count Bertrand and his wife, General Montholon and his wife, General Gourgaud and Count de Las Cases,[8] and then followed myself, which induced him to observe 'Do you take the trouble of going in the boat? – I am obliged to you Admiral.' In the boat he appeared to be in perfect good humour, talking of Egypt, St. Helena, of my former name being Elphinstone, and many other subjects, and joking with the ladies about being sea-sick.

Upon arriving on board the *Northumberland* he was received by Rear-Admiral Sir George Cockburn on the gangway, and by a Guard in the manner above mentioned. I accompanied him to look at the accommodation provided for him, with which he appeared to be well satisfied, saying, 'The apartments are convenient, and you see I carry with me my little green bed', pointing to a small tent bed. Immediately afterwards I took my leave and withdrew.

Before leaving, Lord Keith had given Bertrand his reply to the Emperor's letter, brought by Las Cases to the *Tonnant* that morning. While siding wholeheartedly with Maitland, he could not help giving a last-minute lecture on citizenship to that 'rascal' Bonaparte:

I have received by the Count de Las Cases the letter which you have done me the honour to address to me, and I beg to assure you that I lost no time in forwarding to my Government the protest you refer to. The Order for your removal from the *Bellerophon* is imperative, and as an officer I am bound to obey it; but it is a document that must remain in my posession in common with all other orders.

I have Captain Maitland's letter before me, by which it appears that nothing like a promise or what could be construed into a promise was made on his part, but on the contrary a simple offer of good treatment and being carried to England; and I am happy in thinking that both these objects have been fulfilled with all possible kindness and attention.

The orders concerning your property are addressed to Rear-Admiral Sir George Cockburn, and as they appear reasonable, and are only calcu-

---

[6] According to Midshipman Home 'his clothes were ill put on, his beard unshaved, and his countenance pale and haggard.' Some historians relate that the Emperor said: 'Posterity will not be able to blame you for what has happened. You have been deceived as much as I have.' He may well have made such a remark.

[7] Three rolls of the drums, not royal honours, as has sometimes been said.

[8] Cockburn, who was waiting for the Emperor to appear, grew impatient at the delay. 'Pooh,' said Keith. 'Much greater men than either you or I have waited longer for him before now. Let him take his time.'

lated to prevent an improper use of an excessive sum, I am sure they will be executed with all possible delicacy. Of the laws I am not able to judge. My habits are of a different nature, but my study has always been to obey them in all the different countries that I have visited. It is true that I have said in the interviews that I have had the honour to hold with you, that it was a painful duty to communicate anything of a disagreeable nature to anyone, and I hope you will do me the justice to believe it is true; but still I am to perform the duties of my situation.

He expressed his relief at 'Boney's' departure in a rather less stiff style to Lady Keith:

I am this moment returned and the gentleman is off in good spirits. Bertrand, Las Cases, Gourgaud, Monthaleran (Montholon), the two ladies, four *enfants*, twelve domestics. His doctor would not go; I sent that of the *Bellerophon*, who speaks Italian.

One boat ran down another, some were drowned, in like manner as happened here; Anne Elphinstone and twenty of her friends were alongside, although we were twenty miles off and the weather indifferent.

XIII

ON BOARD THE *NORTHUMBERLAND*

✠✠✠

Farewells among the French – Conversation with
Lyttelton – The *Northumberland* sets sail for St. Helena.

✠✠✠

A scrupulous witness, William Lyttelton,[1] a relation of Admiral Sir
George Cockburn's and a member of Parliament, came on board the
Northumberland out of curiosity, and has left us a lively report of
this melancholy scene: the removal of the Emperor from the ship
he had boarded as England's guest, to that which was to become his
first prison.

He saw the barge approaching, with Napoleon sitting on Lord
Keith's left; then Bertrand slowly climbed the *Northumberland*'s
side, stood with his hat off and announced his master as calmly as at
the Tuileries. Bonaparte arrived on deck completely at his ease and
even smiling, and said to Cockburn who had advanced to meet him
'I am at your service, Monsieur.'

The Admiral introduced Captain Ross,[2] Colonel Sir George
Bingham,[3] Lord Lowther, M.P. for Westmorland, who had come
with Lyttelton, and Edmund Byng of the Colonial Audit Office, who
had presided over the inspection of baggage.

Napoleon had a pleasant word for everyone, including the ship's
officers, and surprised the company by saying graciously to an
artillery officer to whom he was presented, 'I belonged to that corps
myself.'

---

[1] Lyttelton, the Hon. William Henry (1782–1837) a relative of Lord Spencer and
M.P. for Worcestershire, was a zealous Whig and a distinguished Hellenist. He was noted
in Parliament for his violent attacks on the Regent and his favourites, and his inspired
speeches in defence of liberty and against using little boys to climb and sweep chimneys.
[2] Commanding officer of the *Northumberland*. His wife was Lady Cockburn's sister-
in-law.
[3] Appointed to command the garrison at St. Helena.

He had hardly been installed when those of the Frenchmen who were to stay in England came to say goodbye, headed by Savary and Lallemand. It was a painful moment, for even if the younger officers took the separation lightly, there were others who were reduced to tears. The Pole, Piontkowski, again begged to be allowed to go with his master, even as a servant.

'I renounce my rank,' he kept repeating to anyone who would listen.

Maitland put an end to the conversation by coming to find those who were to remain as his prisoners, to take them back to the *Bellerophon*. Napoleon embraced both Savary and Lallemand.

'Be happy, my friends. We shall never see each other again, but my thoughts will always be with you, with you and all those who have served me. Tell France that I wish her well.'

He kept his composure, and when his companions in misfortune had gone, he appeared on deck with a serene expression. Lyttelton watched him closely, and thought his countenance 'rather subtle than noble. His eyes had something of a haggard look' and 'were somewhat dimmed.' The group suddenly disappeared from view, as the Admiral did the honours of his ship and led 'Boney' aft.

❖   ❖   ❖

Lord Melville had expressed slight disapproval when he heard that Bonaparte had been received as a sovereign, both on the *Bellerophon* and the *Superb*. Cockburn therefore took all possible steps to prevent his passenger regarding himself as more than a general officer, 'not a commander-in-chief', travelling on one of His Britannic Majesty's ships.

The after-cabin consisted in a dining-room, a drawing-room and two cabins, normally occupied by the admiral and his flag-captain: Napoleon was to have one, Cockburn the other, and the two other rooms were to be open for the use of all the officers and gentlemen on board. To emphasise that the saloon was for general use, the Admiral unceremoniously pushed Lyttelton (who had slipped in), Lord Lowther and Sir George Bingham towards a sofa, and asked them to sit opposite the 'General'. Etiquette was at an end and there was no longer any need to stand up in 'Boney's' presence! But when the Admiral left the room to finish dealing with his dispatches, the three embarrassed Englishmen remained silent, awkwardly contemplating the pale thickset figure, and finding it hard to realise that he had once been the master of Europe.

'Who are you?' asked Napoleon suddenly.

'My name is Lyttleton, Monsieur le Général, I am a relation and friend of the Admiral's.'

'Are you on board this ship?'

'No, I am not a sailor.'

'So you have come here out of curiosity?'

'Yes, Monsieur le Général, I know of no object more worthy of exciting curiosity than that which has brought me here.'

'What county do you come from?'

'From Worcestershire.'

'Where is that? Is it far away?'

'Yes, Monsieur le Général, it is in the middle of the kingdom. I hope we are not inconveniencing you, Monsieur le Général.'

Napoleon made no reply, and asked Colonel Bingham some questions about the conditions and strength of the army and his service in Spain. But Bingham, who understood very little French, stammered and grew confused and gave way to Lyttelton.

'You speak French very well,' said Napoleon.

'I have had some practice, as I have travelled a great deal.'

'Have you travelled in France?'

'Very little, Monsieur le Général; as you know, no Englishman has been allowed to travel through France for many years; we were banned there.'

Just then, the Grand Marshal came in, surveyed the visitors suspiciously, and went out again with a haughty expression as if to show his disapproval of such informal behaviour. Bingham, who was extremely uncomfortable, whispered to Lyttelton:

'For God's sake say something to him, if it be about a dog or a cat.'

'Do you remember Lord Ebrington?' Lyttelton asked the Emperor amiably.[4]

'Yes. He is an excellent man.'

'Lyttelton is a member of Parliament,' put in Lowther.

'Do you belong to the Opposition?' Napoleon asked sharply

'My conscience often obliges me to vote against the King's ministers;

---

[4] Lord Ebrington had visited Napoleon at Elba.

we are a free people, and one must act according to what one believes to be the country's interests.'

'Have you spoken in Parliament?'

'A few unimportant harangues.'

'Monsieur Whitbread is dead, is he not?'

'Yes, Monsieur le Général.'

'What did he die of?'

'By his own hand.'

'How was that?'

'I mean that he killed himself; he was deranged.'

'His mind was deranged?'

'Yes.'

'Was it what you call the spleen?'

'No, Monsieur Whitbread was so mad that he believed everyone was plotting against him.'

'How did he kill himself?'

'He cut his throat with a razor.'

'Who will succeed him in Parliament? Ponsonby?'[5]

'No, Monsieur le Général; Mr. Ponsonby is a distinguished man but I do not think him qualified to succeed Mr. Whitbread. It is not so easy to replace great men, you know, Monsieur le Général!'

After half an hour's conversation, Lyttelton and his parliamentary colleague left the cabin for a quick luncheon before going ashore, taking Cockburn's final reports, which he had decided to entrust to them. However, when the Emperor passed through the dining-room on his way to take a walk on the deck, the young men's appetite gave way to curiosity and they soon followed him.

'This ship seems to have been fitted out in haste,' complained Napoleon.

'That's true, Monsieur le Général; on the other hand it is one of our best ships, and sails particularly well.'

'They might have sent a ship in better condition; there was the *Chatham*, for instance, at Plymouth, and also the *Tonnant*.'

When Lyttelton tried to convince him that all on board, particularly the Admiral, were eager to make his voyage to St. Helena as endurable as possible, Napoleon suddenly lost patience.

'You have tarnished the flag and your national honour by making me a prisoner like this.'

[5] George Ponsonby (1755–1817). Barrister and M.P. Lord Chancellor of Ireland under Fox in 1806. Leader of the Opposition in the House of Commons.

'No agreement with you has been broken, and it is vital to the country's interests that you should not be in a position to return to France.'

'You are behaving like a small aristocratic state, not like a great free nation! I came to take refuge on your soil, and only wanted to live in England as an ordinary citizen.'

'Your party in France is still too powerful; affairs might take such a turn that you would be recalled to the throne.'

'No, no, my career is ended.'

'You used the same words a year ago, in Elba.'

'Then I was a sovereign, I had the right to make war; the King of France did not keep his word to me. I made war on him with six hundred men!'

He laughed as he remembered Louis XVIII's misfortunes, and the Englishmen were infected by his good humour.

'I was pretty well received in France, wasn't I?'

'You are popular there, even among the peasants, in spite of conscription.'

Returning to his charges against the English Government he said gloomily:

'I should have done better to surrender to the Emperor of Russia or the Emperor of Austria.'

'The Emperor of Austria perhaps, but you must permit me to be doubtful about the project of surrendering to the Emperor of Russia.'

'The Emperor Alexander loves France. And I could have joined the army of the Loire, and should have been at the head of a hundred thousand men today.'

He could not get used to the idea of this final departure, and the cynicism of the Cabinet in condemning him without a hearing.

'You do not understand my character; you ought to have trusted my word of honour.'

'Will you permit me to tell you the truth?'

'Tell me.'

'From the moment that you invaded Spain there was hardly an individual in England who trusted your word.'

'I was summoned to Spain by Charles IV, to help him against his son.'

'But not, I believe, to put King Joseph on the throne.'

'I had a great political system; it was necessary to counterbalance your enormous sea power, and besides it was only what the Bourbons had done.'

'But one must admit, Monsieur le Général, that under your rule France was much more to be feared than under the last years of Louis XIV's reign; besides she had grown larger.'

'And England had also become more powerful; there were the Indian colonies!'

'Many well-informed people believe that England has lost more than she gained from those vast and remote possessions.'

Then, realising the futility of discussing European politics with this young member of parliament, Napoleon returned to his chief preoccupation.

'Well, I made a mistake; send me back to Rochefort. I wanted to give the Prince Regent the chance of the most glorious episode in his reign. If you merely wanted to be guided by the rules of prudence, why did you not kill me? That would have been the safest way. You have tarnished your flag.'

The obstinate Englishman was determined to pursue the conversation, and he changed the subject to Russia, Pitt, Fox and the continental system.

'I do not say,' Napoleon said shaking his head and swaggering a little, 'that it never entered my head to plan to destroy England. Why yes! during twenty years of war. Or rather not to destroy you, but to humble you; I wanted to force you to be just, or at least less unjust. . . .'

'We owe our progress in the art of war to you, Monsieur le Général.'

'Well, one cannot make war without becoming a soldier; the history of every country proves that fact.'

He spoke calmly, gesticulating very little; he was as exact about small details as about the problems of his imperial policy. The two young men were delighted. 'I imagine it impossible,' wrote Lyttelton, 'not to admire his quickness, adroitness and originality, and the excellent command of temper that accompanied these spirited and agreeable qualities.' The conversation lasted two hours, and Lyttelton made haste to record his impressions; until late that night he sat covering sheets of paper with his writing by the light of a candle, describing – with his companion's help – the extraordinary man they had had the good fortune to meet.[6]

Shortly before the ship hoisted sail for departure, and while waiting for the other vessels that were to make up the convoy for St. Helena, dinner was announced.

[6] Fifty-two copies of this account were published in 1836.

Once more the English were surprised: Napoleon ate with a good appetite, and drank with pleasure some Bordeaux and water. Bertrand and his wife, Montholon and the Countess, Gourgaud and Las Cases had been invited by the Admiral, and there was plenty of cheerful conversation; Napoleon described Moscow, the steppes and the murderous Russian winter.

After dinner Cockburn retired to his cabin; Napoleon walked on deck for a while with Colonel Bingham; the English soldiers stood up and saluted as they passed.

'That's because I was an artilleryman,' said Napoleon, mischievously.

'Yes, you were in the La Fère regiment,' retorted the Englishman quickly.

Napoleon smiled and pinched his ear. During the game of vingt-et-un that occupied the rest of the evening he lost a few gold pieces bearing his effigy.

✤   ✤   ✤

During August 8 the sea was rough, and the *Northumberland* pitched and rolled heavily off Start Point: Napoleon remained out of sight. When the rest of the squadron, escort ships and transports, had assembled, Admiral Sir George Cockburn hoisted the signal, and all the ships left the cape to the westward and prepared to leave the Channel.

Driven by those same winds that had so often opposed his undertakings, the Emperor was leaving behind the continent he had so often dreamed of making into one immense Western Empire, and quitting the world of politics, to enter – while still alive – that of legend.

What one nation had found over life-size and inhuman in his character fascinated others. By exiling him in the middle of the ocean, England presented him with a fresh conquest. Held prisoner on a rock for six years, contemplating the world, his career and his dreams with a philosopher's gaze, he succeeded in giving meaning to the hurricane he had let loose upon the old world, he transformed his thirst for adventure and conquest into a crusade for liberty, and his boundless arrogance into a European nationalism carrying all before it.

St. Helena, 1967–1968

APPENDIX 1

Paris, July 13, 1815.

Napoleon Bonaparte, who is on board the frigate under your command, is there merely as a prisoner, whom all the sovereigns of Europe can lay claim to. The King is not alone in claiming him. Nor would it even be possible today to allow his natural generosity of heart to prevail. The King of France is not acting alone and for his private cause in pursuing Napoleon Bonaparte. His cause is Europe's, just as the cause of Europe – in arms against Napoleon – is his own. All forces attacking Napoleon Bonaparte will be acting in the King's name. Consequently, all Frenchmen who do not wish to be regarded as rebels against their King and country, must treat as allies and friends the commanding officers of land and sea forces, who, if circumstances demand it, will fight to capture Napoleon. I therefore notify you, that the Captain of the English squadron blockading the Rochefort roads is authorised to ask the captain of the frigate, on which Napoleon is, to hand him over immediately. This demand will not be made in the name of his Britannic Majesty alone; but also in the name of the King, your legitimate sovereign.

You should not, therefore, consider the officer commanding the English naval forces who will bring you the present order as an English officer. He is an officer of all the sovereigns allied to His Majesty. He is an officer of the King of France. I therefore direct that you hand over Napoleon Bonaparte to the English captain who brings you this order, as soon as he asks you. If you should be so guilty or blind as to resist this order, it would be an act of open rebellion, and you would be responsible for the consequent bloodshed and the destruction of your ship.

APPENDIX 2

Letter from Lord Melville to Lord Keith.

Admiralty,
July 18, 1815.

My dear Lord,

I enclose for your Lordship's information a copy of a letter which Mr. Croker has addressed to Sir Henry Hotham or the Senior Officer of H.M. ships at Basque Roads by desire of Lord Castlereagh.

I do not feel myself at liberty to submit this document to the board of Admiralty for their formal sanction, because though the zeal and ability with which Mr. Croker discharges his duty are well known to us all and though the letter itself (subject to one remark which I shall have to make upon it) is perfectly proper, there can be no question that his functions can be exercised only in the presence of the immediate authority of the Board, and that if it had been signed by Lord Castlereagh, or the Duke of Wellington or Sir Charles Stuart, the British Minister accredited to Louis XVIII, the proceeding would have been more regular and conformable to the usual course. I am persuaded that any communication from either of those three persons would, under all the circumstances of the case, have been received by Sir Henry with the respect and attention which would justly have belonged to it, and I trust that in the present instance he will consider it as favourably as if it had proceeded from Lord Castlereagh.

The only remark which I feel it necessary to make upon the letter is with regard to the part which desires *the officer who may be fortunate enough to secure Bonaparte on board his ship, not to proceed with him to England immediately, but to retain him on the French coast till the officer receives a further communication from Lord Castlereagh.*[1] I have no objection to that deviation from the former instructions, with the understanding, however, which I have no doubt Lord Castlereagh meant to convey, that such British ship with Bonaparte on board should not remain in Aix Roads, or in any French port where she would be under the guns of their batteries; but that she should anchor in Basque Roads, or in some other safe anchorage, from whence she could proceed to England at any time without hindrance, and without the French authorities in the neighbourhood being able to prevent it if they should be so inclined. I take it for granted also

---

[1] Present author's italics.

that Lord Castlereagh meant to confine this request to the seizing of Bonaparte under the mission of the Capitaine de Rigny, but that if he was captured at sea, or under other circumstances than those described in Mr. Croker's letter, the captain of the British ship would act of course in conformity to the instructions he had received from the Admiralty and your Lordship. I have etc.

Melville.

APPENDIX 3

Admiralty instructions concerning the reception of the Emperor on his arrival in England.

Whereas the Earl Bathurst, one of H.M. Principal Secretaries of State, hath by his letter of yesterday's date acquainted us that having had the honour to submit to H.R.H. the Prince Regent the substance of the communication which we had caused to be made to his Lordship respecting the surrender of Napoleon Bonaparte to Captain Maitland of H.M. ship *Bellerophon*, he has been commanded by H.R.H. to signify his pleasure to the following effect:

That we should give immediate orders that upon the arrival of the *Bellerophon* Napoleon Bonaparte should remain until the Prince Regent's further pleasure shall be signified, on board of that or such other ship as we may appoint, and shall not be permitted upon any account to come ashore or to hold communication with the shore or with other vessels personally or by writing. Not more than four or five persons of his suite (exclusive of menial servants) are to remain on board the same ship with himself. The remainder of his suite are to be kept under similar restraint on board of other vessels of war. Napoleon Bonaparte is to be considered and addressed as a General Officer.

With regard to General Gourgaud, Earl Bathurst hath further signified H.R.H.'s pleasure that we should give orders that the said General Gourgaud should be conveyed on board H.M. ship *Bellerophon* and be considered in the same light as the other French officers comprising Bonaparte's suite. General Gourgaud cannot be permitted to land in England with a view to delivering the letter with which he is charged: but (if he shall think proper) the said letter may be conveyed through the medium of the naval Commander-in-Chief at Plymouth; and any additional communications which he may be desirous to make to be transmitted through the same channel. We do hereby require and direct your Lordship to issue the strictest orders to the captains and commanders of H.M. ships and vessels under your command in compliance with the pleasure of H.R.H. the Prince Regent, as above set forth.

Given under our hands the 25 July, 1815.

Melville, Yorke, Paulet.

By command of their Lordships.

J. M. Barrow.

APPENDIX 4

Napoleon as seen by Sir Henry Bunbury, July 31, 1815.

He is stockily built. His neck is short, and the head appears the larger for it; his face is square, especially towards the jaw, and he has a pronounced double chin. He is bald about the temples and the hair on the upper part of his head is very thin, but long and ragged, looking as if it were seldom brushed. In his movements Napoleon lacks grace, but . . . the carriage of his head is very dignified. . . . Napoleon's eyes are very grey, the pupils large, his eyebrows thin, his hair brown, his complexion pallid, his flesh rather puffy. His nose is well-shaped, the lower lip short, a good mouth, but teeth bad and dirty; he shows them very little. His expression was serious and almost melancholy, and showed no sign of anger or strong emotion.

APPENDIX 5

Letter from Maitland to Bertrand.

H.M.S. *Bellerophon*
Start Bay
August 7, 1815.

Sir,

I beg to acquaint you that I have this day received orders from Lord Keith, Commander in Chief of the Channel Fleet, to remove General Bonaparte from the ship I command to his Majesty's ship *Northumberland*; and I have to request you will intimate the above to the General, that he may prepare for the removal.

I likewise enclose a copy of an order respecting the arms of General Bonaparte and the whole of his attendants, and request you will give directions for their being delivered to me, that they may be disposed of as the order directs.

I have the honour to be, etc., etc., etc.

Fred. L. Maitland.

APPENDIX 6

Report by Admiral Lord Keith respecting the events of June 24 and August 17, 1815.

Plymouth Dock
August 17, 1815.

Intelligence was no sooner received at Plymouth of the glorious result of the battle of Waterloo and of the disastrous condition to which that unparalleled victory had reduced the Emperor Napoleon and the French Army, than measures were adopted by Lord Keith for intercepting him in case he should attempt to quit France by sea and escape to America.

To accomplish this important object in the most effective manner His Lordship not only stationed men-of-war of different descriptions along the French coast from Ushant to Bayonne, but another line from Ushant to Cape Finisterre; and the strictest orders were given to allow no vessel to pass unexamined.

As soon as it was known that Bonaparte had abdicated, these orders were repeated by the Admiralty and an Instruction was issued containing directions how the captains of H.M. ships were to conduct themselves in the event of their being fortunate enough to fall in with him.

The battle of Waterloo was fought on the 18th June and positive intelligence thereof reached Plymouth on the 24th. By the 5th July not less than thirty vessels of war were on the stations assigned to them between Ushant and Cape Finisterre, to which several others were subsequently added; and as Rear-Admiral Sir Henry Hotham had been stationed in Quiberon Bay for the purpose of assisting the Royalists in that neighbourhood and on the coast of La Vendée, the vessels of war on that part of the coast of France were under his immediate orders, and he made so judicious a disposition of them, in addition to the other arrangements made by Lord Keith, that Bonaparte's escape soon became extremely difficult if not impossible.

Sir Henry Hotham appears to have received information about the 3rd July that Bonaparte had arrived at Rochefort, and Captain Maitland of the *Bellerophon*, who was stationed off the Chasseron lighthouse, to watch two French frigates at Ile d'Aix, had about the same time or within a day or two afterwards, as well as from his own observation of the movements of the French ships as from intelligence that he gained from a galliot from the Charente, such strong reason to believe that such was really the fact that he redoubled his vigilance and took up anchorage in Basque Roads whenever the wind was favourable for the frigates to sail.

On the 10th July all uncertainty was at an end, for on that day the Duc de Rovigo and Count de Las Cases came from the Ile d'Aix in a flag of truce and presented to Captain Maitland a letter from Count Bertrand notifying Bonaparte's intention of proceeding to the U.S.A. with the two French frigates. and requesting to know if it was his intention to prevent it. The official report of this communication was immediately sent to Sir Henry Hotham in Quiberon Bay and he dispatched the *Dwarf* with it to Plymouth, where it was received by Lord Keith on July 19.

On July 22 at 11 p.m. Captain Sartorius of the *Slaney* arrived with a despatch from Captain Maitland reporting the circumstances under which he had consented to receive Bonaparte and his suite on board the *Bellerophon* for conveyance to England; and although it did not contain an account of his being actually on board, Captain Sartorius was immediately dispatched therewith to the Admiralty.

On the following morning, the 23rd, the mail coach came in decorated with laurel and the newspapers announced the fact from the French papers that Bonaparte had actually embarked on the 14th or 15th. The *Express* schooner on the morning of the 23rd was despatched to Torbay to wait the arrival of the *Bellerophon* with instructions to Captain Maitland. The First Lieutenant of the *Bellerophon* arrived at noon on the 24th bringing dispatches from Captain Maitland reporting the *Bellerophon*'s arrival in Torbay that morning with Bonaparte and his suite on board, and another from Sir Henry Hotham.

On July 26 Lord Keith received from the Admiralty instructions stating that the *Bellerophon* was ordered from Torbay to Plymouth Sound with Bonaparte and his suite, and containing directions as to the manner in which he was to be treated. Orders were immediately issued for restraining all intercourse in conformity with the intentions of H.M. Government and communicated to the Admiralty. In the afternoon about half past four o'clock the *Bellerophon* and *Myrmidon* arrived in Plymouth Sound.

The following day his Lordship received a message from Bonaparte by Captain Maitland expressing an anxious wish to see him, and in consequence of his having expressed great dissatisfaction at the confident assertions made in the newspapers that he was to be sent to St. Helena, Captain Maitland was enjoined to increase his vigilance to prevent the possibility of his escape.

On the 28th in the forenoon his Lordship went on board the *Bellerophon* and saw Bonaparte. The object he evidently had in view was to ascertain what were the intentions of the Government respecting him, and to induce his Lordship to write to the Prince Regent in his favour, but in this he failed and the interview was consequently short. Such part of the suite as were on board the *Myrmidon* was this day removed to the *Liffey* for their better accommodation.

On the morning of the 30th Lord Keith received a communication from Lord Melville that Sir Henry Bunbury was on his way from town with dispatches containing the determination of Government with respect to the disposal of Bonaparte; and in the evening at six o'clock Sir Henry arrived, bringing the letter from Lord Melville.

At eleven o'clock in the morning of July 31 Lord Keith and Sir Henry Bunbury went on board the *Bellerophon*, where his Lordship communicated to Bonaparte the intentions of H.M. Government. An official report of this interview was made to Lord Melville and Sir Henry Bunbury has furnished a memorandum of the conversation that passed on this occasion. In the evening Bonaparte's observations were received upon the communication that had been made to him and they were forwarded to Lord Melville.

On the afternoon of August 1 Sir Henry Bunbury returned to London; and in consequence of the *Liffey* being ordered to the eastward such part of Bonaparte's suite as had been put on board of her for accommodation and security were removed to the *Eurotas*. From the period of the arrival of the *Bellerophon* in Plymouth Sound it was usual for Bonaparte to make his appearance on the quarter-deck between five and six o'clock, a short time before he dined, on which occasions he generally showed himself on the gangway, and a knowledge of this circumstance had, from motives of curiosity to see a man who had had so vast an influence on the affairs of Europe for upwards of twenty years, daily attracted such an immense number of boats that it had not only become exceedingly inconvenient but altogether impossible for the guard boats to prevent them from approaching closer to the ships than was either compatible with his safe custody or the strict orders of H.M. Government for preventing communication. It therefore became necessary to issue an order and to request the General Officer of the district, the General of Marines, the Port Admiral, the Commissioner of the Dockyard, the Officers of the Ordnance and the Magistrates of Plymouth and Dock, to forbid the officers and men under their immediate direction, as well as the boatmen, from approaching nearer the *Bellerophon* than three hundred yards; and the boats of the men-of-war were also directed to assemble alongside the *Eurotas* at four o'clock to be stationed under the direction of the captain of that ship for enforcing in the most effectual manner the orders which had been issued.

Letters from Savary and Lallemand received the preceding evening were forwarded to Lord Melville, remonstrating against the exceptions made to their accompanying Bonaparte.

The 2nd and 3rd August passed without anything particular occurring, Bonaparte not having shown himself in the usual manner, nor quitted the cabin for the last three days; but the boats going off to the Sound were as numerous as ever, and they were with much difficulty kept at a proper distance from the *Bellerophon*. On the 3rd an indistinct telegraphic message was received: '*Tonnant – Bellerophon* – frigate – sail – Start.' This message was communicated to his Lordship by the Port Admiral at nine o'clock, and orders were immediately given for the *Tonnant*, *Bellerophon* and *Eurotas* to be ready to put to sea at a moment's notice. Connecting the above message with a letter from the Secretary of the Admiralty and others from Lord Melville that were received by post on the morning of the 4th, Lord Keith resolved on proceeding forthwith to the Start. Captain Maitland was directed to acquaint Bonaparte that not the slightest alteration could be made in the arrangements already communicated to him. His Lordship had scarcely left his residence to embark on board the *Tonnant* when a person named Mackenrot enquired for him, having a summons to serve upon Bonaparte as a witness in the Court of the King's Bench in a cause for libel, in which Sir Alexander Cochrane was plaintiff and himself defendant. Mr. Meek (Keith's secretary) being on the point of going off to meet his Lordship on board the *Tonnant* lost no time in appraising him of the circumstance and his Lordship immediately removed to the *Eurotas*, and afterwards went on shore at Cawsand, then on board the *Prometheus* coming in from the westward, standing out in her to sea again, and ultimately returning to the *Tonnant* at 8 o'clock in the evening. By his Lordship's decision and promptitude the service of this process was evaded, and in all probability great inconvenience, both to the public and himself, thereby avoided.

Shortly after his Lordship's arrival on board the *Tonnant* an Admiralty messenger arrived with dispatches. At noon on the 5th H.M. ship *Norge* was fallen in with on her way to Spithead from Jamaica, at which time Captain Maitland brought on board a protest from Bonaparte against the measures pursued in disposing by force of his liberty and person. This protest was forwarded by the *Norge* to Lord Melville. In the afternoon the *Actaeon* joined from Plymouth bringing a letter from the person desirous of serving a summons on Bonaparte which his Lordship sent to Lord Melville, as well as other subsequently addressed by the same person to Sir John Duckworth, Sir George Cockburn and Captain Maitland.

At ten o'clock in the forenoon of the 6th Rear-Admiral Sir George Cockburn joined from the eastward in H.M. ship *Northumberland*, accompanied by the *Ceylon* and *Bucephalus* troopships, and it was judged advisable from the state of the weather to stand for Torbay. At half past three o'clock the squadron anchored under Berry Head – *Tonnant*, *Bellerophon*, *Northumberland*, *Eurotas*, *Nimble*, *Ceylon*, *Bucephalus* in company; the *Actaeon* having been left off the Start to direct ships coming from Plymouth; and a signal having been previously made to the *Bellerophon* directing Captain Maitland to prepare to remove Bonaparte and his suite. Lord Keith's Flag Lieutenant and Sir George Cockburn's Secretary were sent by land to Plymouth with orders for the vessels preparing there to join the Rear-Admiral off the Start with all expedition. Upon Captain Maitland's coming on board he stated that Bonaparte was very anxious to see Lord Keith and that Count Bertrand was desirous of having a previous interview. With these requests it was thought proper to comply, and upon Bertrand's being brought on board the *Tonnant* after a short conversation he delivered a list of persons whom Bonaparte was desirous of accompanying him to St. Helena. Sir George Cockburn also delivered to him for the information of Bonaparte, an extract of such parts of his Instructions as he considered it right to be communicated to him; and it was arranged that the proposed interview should take place in the evening, at which time an introduction to Sir George Cockburn might likewise take place.

At half past eight in the evening Lord Keith, Sir George Cockburn and Mr. Meek went on board the *Bellerophon* and were received by Bonaparte in the after cabin. The particulars of what occurred at this interview will be found in a dispatch to Lord Melville.

On the morning of August 7 at eight o'clock, at the request of Bonaparte, his Lordship gave an audience to Count de Las Cases, who presented a demand from Bonaparte of certain official documents to enable him to obtain a judicial redress hereafter for the present proceedings against him. To this demand Lord Keith returned a written answer. At half past nine Sir George Cockburn went on board the *Bellerophon* for the purpose of taking an inventory of Bonaparte's effects and at seven, Sir George having sent a message to say that he was nearly ready, Lord Keith went on board to remove him. At half past one the removal took place, his Lordship in the *Tonnant*'s barge conveying General Bonaparte, General Bertrand and his wife, General Montholon and his wife, General Gouraud and Count de Las Cases to the *Northumberland*, and after delivering them into the charge of Sir George Cockburn he returned to the *Tonnant*.

At half past six in the evening weighed and made sail for Plymouth Sound, where the *Tonnant* anchored on the following morning at ten o'clock with the *Bellerophon*, *Eurotas*, *Myrmidon*, *Dwarf*, *Express*, having left Sir George Cockburn off the Start with the *Northumberland* and the other ships waiting for those directed to join him from Plymouth.

A circumstantial detail of the interview with Bonaparte, and other occurrences attending to his removal and that of his suite from the *Bellerophon* to the *Northumberland* for conveyance to St. Helena will be found in the dispatch to Lord Melville. Count Las Cases having in his interview with Lord Keith on the morning of the 7th made certain unfounded assertions a letter was written to Captain Maitland on the subject. His reply was transmitted to Lord Melville, and another letter upon the same subject was also forwarded to his Lordship upon the return of the *Slaney* from sea, Captain Sartorius of that ship having been present at all the conversations that took place between Captain Maitland and the Count de Las Cases.

On August 16 Lord Keith received from the Admiralty instructions directing how the remainder of Bonaparte's suite were to be disposed of, and orders were immediately given in conformity thereto, the *Eurotas* being directed to convey to Malta Lieut.-General Savary, Lieut.-General Lallemand, Lieut.-Colonels Planat, Resigni and Schultz, and the *Bellerophon* to proceed to Spithead with the remainder, except Captain Piontowski, a Pole, who was ordered to be sent on board the flagship at Plymouth to wait for a passage to St. Helena, it being his anxious desire to follow the fortunes of Bonaparte, as expressed in a letter which was forwarded to Lord Melville on the 9th inst. His Lordship at the same time received from Lord Melville a letter expressing the entire approbation of H.M. Ministers of all his proceedings, and of the zeal and judgement that he had evinced throughout the whole affair.

On August 17 a further instruction was received from the Admiralty directing Captains Autric and Mesurier, Lieut. Rivière, and Sub-Lieut. St. Catherine to be sent to Malta in the *Eurotas* with the others; and orders were given accordingly, except for St. Catherine, a nephew of the late Empress Josephine, who in consequence of his being a youth under sixteen years of age and having lived only a short time in France, as well as of a request preferred by Lieut.-Colonel Planat that he might be returned to his parents at Martinique, Lord Keith considered it right to detail him on board the *Bellerophon* for further orders.

The private letters from Lord Melville to Lord Keith contain some further particulars, and are therefore attached, as they may in some degree serve to elucidate parts of this interesting and important transaction that may not have been noticed in the official papers.

(*Unsigned. Probably by James Meek*).

APPENDIX 7

After the departure of Napoleon.

Once the *Northumberland* and Bonaparte had vanished over the horizon the London Cabinet could breathe again; Lord Keith merely had to set the stage in order and discharge the actors of minor parts. He began by closely examining Maitland's report – a document which soothed the anxieties that had been tormenting him for several days.

His recent adventure had made Maitland very circumspect, and he weighed every word; he felt the awkwardness of an ordinary officer who is involved in affairs of State. It was therefore a justification *pro domo* rather than a military report that he sent his chief, and its weaknesses are only apparent by comparing it with the statements of Las Cases and Savary. But alas! the Emperor was already dead by the time Maitland's account was printed.

H.M.S. *Bellerophon*,
Plymouth Sound,
August 8, 1815.

My Lord,
 I have to acknowledge the receipt of your Lordship's letter, informing me that Count Las Cases had stated to you that he had understood from me when he was on board the *Bellerophon* in Basque Roads, on a mission from General Bonaparte, that I was authorised to receive the General and his suite on board the ship I command for a conveyance to England, and that I assured him at the same time that both the General and his suite would be well received there; and directing me to report for your Lordship's information such observations as I may consider it necessary to make upon these assertions.
 I shall, in consequence, state to the best of my recollection the whole of the transaction that took place between Count Las Cases and me on the 14th of July, respecting the embarkation of Napoleon Bonaparte, for the veracity of which I beg to refer your Lordship to Captain Sartorius as to what was said in the morning, and to that officer and Captain Gambier (the *Myrmidon* having joined me in the afternoon) as to what passed in the evening.

Your Lordship being informed already of the flag of truce that came out to me on the 10th of July, as well as of everything that occurred on that occasion, I shall confine myself to the transactions of the 14th of the same month.

Early in the morning of that day, the officer of the watch informed me a schooner, bearing a flag of truce, was approaching; on her joining the ship about seven a.m. the Count Las Cases and General Lallemand came on board, when, on being shown into the cabin, Las Cases asked me if any answer had been returned to the letter sent by me to Sir Henry Hotham respecting Napoleon Bonaparte being allowed to pass for America, either in the frigates or in a neutral vessel. I informed him no answer had been returned, though I hourly expected, in consequences of those dispatches, Sir Henry Hotham would arrive; and as I had told Monsieur Las Cases when last on board that I should send my boat in when the answer came, it was quite unnecessary to have sent out a flag of truce on that account – there for the time the conversation terminated. On their coming on board I had made a signal for the Captain of the *Slaney*, being desirous of having a witness to all that might pass.

After breakfast (during which Captain Sartorius came on board) we retired to the after-cabin, when Monsieur Las Cases began on the same subject, and said:

'The Emperor was so anxious to stop the further effusion of blood, that he would go to America in any way the English Government would sanction, either in a neutral, a disarmed frigate, or an English ship of war.'

To which I replied, 'I have no authority to permit any of these measures; but if he chooses to come on board the ship I command, I think, under the orders I am acting with, I may venture to receive him and carry him to England; but if I do so, I can in no way be answerable for the reception he may meet with' (this I repeated several times); when Las Cases said:

'I have little doubt, under those circumstances, that you will see the Emperor on board the *Bellerophon*.'

After some more general conversation, and the above being frequently repeated, Monsieur Las Cases and General Lallemand took their leave: and I assure your Lordship that I never, in any way, entered into conditions with respect to the reception General Bonaparte was to meet with; nor was it, at that time, finally arranged that he was to come on board the *Bellerophon*. In the course of conversation, Las Cases asked me whether I thought Bonaparte would be well received in England; to which I gave the only answer I could do in my situation – 'That I did not at all know what was the intention of the British Government; but I had no reason to suppose that he would not be well received.'

It is here worthy of remark that when Las Cases came on board, he assured me that Bonaparte was then at Rochefort, and that it would be necessary for him to go there to report the conversation that had passed between us (this I can prove by the testimony of Captain Sartorius, and the first Lieutenant of this ship, to whom I spoke of it at the time), which statement was not fact, Bonaparte never having quitted Ile d'Aix, or the frigates, after the 3rd.

I was therefore much surprised at seeing Monsieur Las Cases on board again before seven o'clock the same evening; and one of the first questions I put to him was, whether he had been at Rochefort. He answered that on returning to Ile d'Aix he found that Bonaparte had arrived there.

Monsieur Las Cases then presented to me the letter Count Bertrand wrote concerning Bonaparte's intention to come on board the ship (a copy of which has been transmitted to your Lordship by Sir Henry Hotham); and it was not till then agreed upon that I should receive him; when either Monsieur Las Cases or General Gourgaud (I am not positive which, as I was employed writing my own dispatches), wrote to Bertrand to inform him of it. While paper was preparing to write the letter, I said again to Monsieur Las Cases, 'You will recollect I have no authority for making conditions of any sort.' Nor has Monsieur Las Cases ever started such an idea till the day before yesterday. That it was not the feeling of Bonaparte or the rest of his people, I will give strong proof, drawn from the conversations they have held with me. . . .

The night that the squadron anchored at the back of Berry Head, Bonaparte sent for me about ten p.m. and said he was informed by Bertrand that I had received orders to remove him to the *Northumberland*, and wished to know if that was the case; on being told that it was, he requested I would write a letter to Bertrand, stating I had such orders, that it might not appear that he went of his own accord, but that he had been forced to do so. I told him I could have no objection, and wrote a letter to that effect (a copy of which is here annexed,[1]) which your Lordship afterwards sanctioned, and desired me, if he required it, to give him a copy of the order.

After having arranged that matter I was going to withdraw, when he requested me to remain, as he had something more to say: he then began complaining of his treatment in being forced to go to St. Helena: among other things he observed: 'They say I made no conditions; certainly I made no conditions: how could a private man make conditions with a nation? I wanted nothing from them but hospitality. . . . My only wish was to purchase a small estate and end my life in tranquillity.'

On the morning we removed from the *Bellerophon* to the *Northumberland* he sent for me again, and said, 'I have sent for you to express my gratitude for your conduct to me, while I have been on board the ship you

[1] See Appendix 5.

command. My reception in England has been very different from what I expected; but you throughout have behaved like a man of honour; and I request that you will accept my thanks, as well as convey them to the officers and ship's company of the *Bellerophon*.'

Soon afterwards Montholon came to me from Bonaparte; but to understand what passed between him and me, I must revert to a conversation I had with Madame Bertrand on the passage from Rochefort. . . . She informed me that it was Bonaparte's intention to present me with a box containing his picture set with diamonds. I answered:

'I hope not, for I cannot receive it.' . . .

There the matter dropt, and I heard no more of it till about half an hour before Bonaparte quitted the *Bellerophon*, when Montholon came to me and said he was desired by Bonaparte to express the high sense he entertained of my conduct throughout the whole of the transaction: that it had been his intention to present me with a box containing his portrait, but that he understood I was determined not to accept it. I said,

'Placed as I was, I felt it impossible to receive a present from him, though I was highly flattered at the testimony he had borne to the uprightness of my conduct throughout.'

Montholon then added, 'One of the greatest causes of chagrin he feels in not being admitted to an interview with the Prince Regent, is that he had determined to ask as a favour your being promoted to the rank of Rear-Admiral.'

To which I replied, 'That would have been quite impossible, but I do not the less feel the kindness of the intention.' I then said, 'I am hurt that Las Cases should say I held forth any assurances as to the reception Bonaparte was to meet with in England.'

'Oh!' said he, 'Las Cases is disappointed in his expectations; and as he negotiated the affair, he attributes the Emperor's situation to himself: but I can assure you that he (Bonaparte) feels convinced you have acted like a man of honour throughout.' . . .

It is extremely unpleasant for me to be under the necessity of entering into a detail of this sort; but the unhandsome representation Monsieur Las Cases has made to your Lordship on my conduct, has obliged me to produce proofs of the light in which the transaction was viewed by Bonaparte as well as his attendants.

Maitland made it clear that this report only covered the conversation of July 14, and was careful not to mention his suggestion of the 10th, recorded by Las Cases and Savary: '*Why not seek asylum in England?*', any more than he had done in his dispatch to Sir Henry Hotham of the same day. This one small phrase was a weighty indictment: when he was in possession of orders, leaving no doubt at all as to the stern treatment awaiting the ex-Emperor, how did he dare use a word so full of meaning as 'asylum'? The Emperor's departure gave him the chance to glide over this weakness on his part, and leave in his report only the harmless: '*I had no reason to suppose he would not be well received.*'

Had he in fact allowed a doubt of this sort to appear, Napoleon would have given up the idea of coming on board the *Bellerophon*; it was undoubtedly Maitland's amiable insistence, and the word 'asylum' that drove him to this dramatic and dangerous gesture.

Efforts to carry the struggle into the domain of the law ended insignificantly. Lord Melville returned Mackenrot's letter to Keith, with the scornful comment: 'His menace is silly and impudent and empty; it is not worth any answer. Sir A. Cochrane is prosecuting him for a scurrilous libel, and the most charitable opinion which can be formed respecting him is that his intellects are not altogether sound.'

The Commander-in-Chief of the Channel Fleet was, however, congratulated for his services: 'I am very glad', Melville wrote, '. . . that the removal of Bonaparte and his attendants took place so quietly. I hope they are proceeding on their voyage.'

✽ ✽ ✽

Lord Liverpool's government, haunted by the fear of having acted illegally, were preoccupied with the idea of an Act of Indemnity which would whitewash ministers and high officials, and put an end to embarrassing questions. Especially as Lord Eldon, the Lord Chancellor, a bluff, forthright man, was not afraid to admit in a letter to his brother that he had 'not so far found a satisfactory answer to the problems of Bonaparte's case', and did not feel 'able as yet to affix his seal to the Convention between the Allies, signed at Paris'; he 'believed that they must have an Act of Indemnity'.

And on October 1, when the Emperor was nearing his prison, Lord Liverpool himself confided to the Chancellor:

'I have read and considered your argument respecting the situation of Bonaparte, and think there is great weight in it. I own that I was inclined to think the Master of the Rolls' view of the question correct, that you had your choice of considering him either as a French subject, or as a captain of freebooters or bandits, and consequently out of the pale of the protection of nations. Before he quitted Elba, he enjoyed only limited and conditional sovereignty, which ceased when the condition on which he held it was violated. In every character then, did he make war on the King of France, our ally? Not as an independent sovereign, for he had no such character, not as a pretender to the crown of France in any admissible sense, for he had absolutely and entirely renounced all claim to this description. He must then revert to his original character, of a French subject, or he has no character at all and headed his expedition as an outlaw and outcast; *hostis humanis generis*. I am quite clear that in whatever way the subject is viewed, it will be desirable to have an Act of Parliament to settle any doubts which may arise on such a question; but I trust we have one good ground to found it upon, if not two.'

So it was, and the Bill was passed, but not without a generous voice being raised at Westminster. Lord Holland entreated the Lords to ask the opinion of the country's legal experts before deciding such a burning question, in which the country's honour was engaged. He advised that the following questions should be set out before the lawyers:

What is meant in law by 'enemy alien'?

Can any person who is not an 'enemy alien' be detained as a prisoner of war?

Has an 'enemy alien', taken prisoner in wartime and held prisoner for the duration of hostilities, any right to a writ of Habeas Corpus from the moment a peace treaty is signed with the country of which he is a national, even if the peace treaty says nothing about the exchange or release of prisoners?

In law, again, can anyone be detained and treated as an 'enemy alien' if he is not the subject or ruler of any country?

Is it legal to treat anyone as an 'enemy alien' if the King of England is not at war with another country?

Can a prisoner of war conduct an action in the English courts against a British subject? If not, is this because he is a prisoner of war, or because he is the subject of a state with which the King of England is at war?

Lord Holland was muzzled by the Lord Chancellor. As a strategist, Lord Castlereagh knew that the outcome of a battle was decided in a moment. He was brutal and exact, and went straight to the point:

'There are those who are doubtful of the Crown's right to hold Napoleon prisoner after hostilities had ceased. For my part, I hold no such doubts, and in any case the present Bill is designed to put an end to them. That this policy is best, is not contested, while from a legal standpoint I feel it is entirely justified. The intention is to keep under strict guard the ex-sovereign of Elba, who was guilty of bad faith in making his escape. In general, it is of vital importance to ensure the public safety and the peace of the world.'

The vote was about to be taken. Lord Holland stood up and declared emphatically:

'I shall not vote for the present Bill of Indemnity. To consign to distant exile and imprisonment a foreign and captive chief, who, after the abdication of his authority, relying on British generosity, had surrendered himself to us instead of his other enemies, is unworthy of the magnanimity of a great country.'

British sense of honour had found its champion.

BIBLIOGRAPHY

MANUSCRIPT SOURCES

Aix, Ile d'   Musée Gourgaud.
Paris   Bibliothèque Nationale.
               Archives du Ministère des Affaires étrangères.
London   British Museum.
               Public Record Office.
St. Helena   Archives of the colonial government.

The documents contained in the Keith Papers are published with the permission of the council of the Navy Records Society, the Royal Naval College and Lord Lansdowne, to whom I wish to express my lively gratitude for having directed and helped my research.

The facsimile of the letter from Napoleon to the Prince Regent is reproduced with the gracious permission of Her Majesty Queen Elizabeth, and that of the letter to Lord Keith of August 4, 1815, with the permission of the Trustees of the British Museum.

PRINTED WORKS

Ali, *Souvenirs*. Payot, Paris, 1926.

Allardyce (Alexander), *Admiral Lord Keith*. W. Blackwood & Sons, London, 1882.

Arthur-Lévy, *Les Dissentiments de la Famille impériale*. Calmann-Lévy, Paris, 1932.

Aubry (Octave), *Sainte-Hélène*. Flammarion, Paris, 1935.

Augustin-Thierry (A.), *Madame Mère*. Albin Michel, Paris, 1939.

Bertaut (Jules), *Le Roi Jérôme*. Flammarion, Paris, 1954.

Bonaparte (Joseph), *Lettres d'exil*. Charpentier, Paris, 1912.

Brooke (T. H.), *A History of the Island of St. Helena*, London, 1808.

Brookes (Dame Mabel), *St. Helena Story*. Heinemann, London, 1960.

Broughton (Lord), *Recollections of a Long Life*. John Murray, London.

Bryant (Arthur), *The Age of Elegance*. W. Collins, Sons & Co., London, 1950.

Caulaincourt (Général de), *Mémoires*. Plon, Paris, 1933.

Chaplin (Dr. A.), *A St. Helena Who's Who*. A. Humphreys, London, 1919.

Chateaubriand (A. de), *Mémoires d'outre-tombe*.

Couchoud (P.-L.), *Voix de Napoléon*. Milieu du Monde, Genève, 1949.

Fabre (M.-A.), *Jérôme Bonaparte*. Hachette, Paris, 1952.

Fain (Baron), *Manuscrit de 1815*. Bossange, Paris, 1825.

Fleury de Chaboulon, *Mémoires*. Rouveyre, Paris, 1901.

Forsyth (William), *History of the Captivity of Napoleon at St. Helena*. John Murray, London, 1853.

Fulford (R.), *George the Fourth*. Duckworth, 1935.

Glover (John R.), *Napoleon's Last Voyages*. T. Fisher Unwin, London, 1895.

Goldsmith (Lewis), *Procès de Buonaparte*. J. Moronval, Paris, 1815.

Gourgaud (Général), *Journal de Sainte-Hélène*. Flammarion, Paris, 1947.

Hauterive (E. d'), *Sainte-Hélène au temps de Napoléon et aujourd'hui*. Calmann-Lévy, Paris, 1903.

Hegemann (W.), *Napoleon or Prostration before the Hero*. Constable & Co., London, 1931.

Heine (Heinrich), *Poésies*. Mercure de France, Paris, 1924.

Holland Rose (J.), *Napoleonic Studies*. G. Bell and Sons, London, 1904.

—— *Life of Napoleon I*. G. Bell and Sons, London, 1929.

Hortense (Reine), *Mémoires*. Plon, Paris, 1927.

Houssaye (Henry), *1815*. Librairie Académique Perrin et Cie., Paris, 1906.

Home (George), *Memoirs of an Aristocrat*.

L'Ile d'Aix et ses musées. Édité par la Société des Amis de l'ile d'Aix.

Itineraire de Buonaparte de l'ile d'Elbe à Sainte-Hélène. Paris, 1817.

Jackson (E. L.), *St. Helena*. Ward, Lock & Co., London, 1903.

Keith Papers, published by Christopher Lloyd. Navy Records Society, 1955.

Kemble (James), *Napoleon Immortal*. John Murray, London, 1959.

Kerry (Earl), *The First Napoleon*. Constable & Co., 1925.

Las Cases (Comte de), *Mémorial de Sainte-Hélène*.

Las Cases (Emmanuel de), *Notice*. Remquet, Paris, 1854.

Madelin (Louis), *Histoire du Consulat et de l'Empire*. Hachette, Paris.

Maitland (Captain F.), *Narrative of the surrender of Bonaparte*. Henry Goulburn, London, 1826.

Manceron (C.), *Le Dernier Choix de Napoléon*. Robert Laffont, Paris, 1960.

Marchand (Louis), *Mémoires*. Plon, Paris, 1955.

Masson (F), *Une Journée de Napoléon*. Flammarion, Paris, 1934.

—— *Napoléon a Sainte-Hélène*. Albin Michel, Paris.

Melchior-Bonnet (C.), *Dictionnaire de la Révolution et de l'Empire*. Larousse, Paris, 1965.

Misciatelli (P.), *Lettere di Leitizia Buonaparte*. U. Hoepli, Milano, 1936.

Montholon (Général de), *Récits de la captivité de l'Empereur Napoléon*. Paulin, Paris, 1847.

Nabonne (B.), *Joseph Bonaparte*. Hachette, Paris, 1949.

Napoleon I, *Correspondance*. Librairie Impériale, 1859.

Napoleon (Prince), et J. Hanoteau, *Lettres personnelles des souverains à l'Empereur Napoléon*. Plon, Paris, 1939.

O'Meara (Dr. B.), *Napoleon in exile, or a Voice from St. Helena*. London, 1822.

Pardee (M. A.), *Sainte-Hélène*. 1933.

Pesme (Gerard), *Les Dernieres Heures de Napoléon à l'ile d'Aix*. Corignan et Lachenaud, 1954.

Rémusat (Madame de), *Mémoires*. Calmann-Lévy, Paris, 1881.

Plumb (J. H.), *England in the Eighteenth Century*.

Rosebery (Lord), *Napoleon, the last phase*. A. Humphreys, London, 1900.

Runciman (Sir W.), *The Tragedy of St. Helena*. T. Fisher Unwin. London, 1911.

Shorter (C.), *Napoleon and his Fellow Travellers*. Cassel & Co., London, 1908.

Stendhal, *Napoléon*.

Thompson (J. M.), *Napoleon Bonaparte, his rise and fall*. Blackwell, Oxford, 1958.

Tschudi (C. de), *La Mère de Napoléon*. Fontemoing, Paris, 1910.

Vaulabelle (A. de), *Histoire des deux Restaurations*. Perrotin, Paris, 1855.

Wolseley (Viscount), *Le Déclin et la Chute de Napoléon*. Ollendorff, Paris, 1894.

INDEX